THE
FALLEN ANGELS
AND THE
HEROES
OF
MYTHOLOGY

ORIGINALLY PUBLISHED BY HODGES, FOSTER & FIGGIS
TO THE UNIVERSTIY OF DUBLIN, 1879

THE
FALLEN ANGELS
AND THE
HEROES
OF
MYTHOLOGY

TIMELESS CLASSICS

THE SAME WITH,
"THE SONS OF GOD" & "THE MIGHTY MEN"
OF THE SIXTH CHAPTER OF THE
FIRST BOOK OF MOSES

Rev. John Fleming, A.B.

Incumbent of Ventry and Kildrum, Diocese of Ardfert;
Rural Dean; and Irish Society's Missionary

DEFENDER
CRANE, MO 65633

THE FALLEN ANGELS AND THE HEROES OF MYTHOLOGY
The Same with, "The Sons of God" and "The Mighty Men" of the Sixth Chapter of the First Book of Moses
Rev. John Fleming, A.B.
Incumbent of Ventry and Kildrum, Diocese of Ardfert; Rural Dean; and Irish Society's Missionary

Originally published by Hodges, Foster, and Figgis, Publishers to the University in Dublin, 1879; reproduced by Defender Publishing, Crane: MO, 2017.

CONTENTS

Preface v

Introduction 1

Chapter 1—
The Filii-Magnatum, or Jewish Interpretation 11

Chapter 2—
The Sethite Interpretation 23

Chapter 3—
The Angel-Interpretation 57

Chapter 4—
The Angel-Interpretation (Continued) 85

Notes 127

Footnotes 157

PREFACE

The passage of Holy Scripture which the writer of the following pages endeavours to elucidate, is one on which a large amount of labour has been expended, and no inconsiderable share of learning and ingenuity employed, by Biblical interpreters, in ancient, mediaeval, and modern times, in order to ascertain and exhibit its meaning. From the commencement of our era, at least, no century has elapsed, in which it has not, in some shape, been explained or commented on. Jewish and Christian theologians, in the east and in the west, have offered, in the form of commentary, or paraphrase, or translation, interpretations of the passage, according to their respective views: while writers of history, in the middle ages, have embodied, in their works, a widely-received version of the brief narrative which it contains. The opinions which have been propounded on the subject, are, as might be expected, various: and the languages in which these have been expressed, are many—Hebrew, Chaldee, Syriac, Ethiopic, Arabic, Greek, Latin, German, French, and English, being included in the number.

The view which the present writer adopts, from a full conviction that it is the only admissible one, has been deemed not merely absurd, but impious and heretical, and is still regarded by many as, at the least, fanciful, and by some, it is to be believed, with a feeling of aversion so strong, that they avoid even an allusion to it, no doubt, lest they should appear to give it even a small measure of countenance.

The opinions entertained, respecting the meaning of the passage, by Jewish and

Christian writers, in ancient and mediaeval times, as well as by the principal modern commentators, are noticed in the following pages. The ablest treatise on the subject, and the most exhaustive of it, with which the writer is acquainted, is that by John Henry Kurtz, D.D., Professor of Theology at Dorpat, entitled, "Die Ehen der Söhne Gottes mit den Töchtern der Menschen;" Berlin, 1857, 8vo., pp. 100—and advocating, for the most part, views similar to those here advanced. Dr. Kurtz's book was written in reply to an essay by Professor Dr. G. F. Keil, bearing a somewhat similar title,[1] but assailing the opinions already propounded on the subject by the former, in his History of the Old Covenant, and contending for a different interpretation of the passage. Dr. Keil's treatise appeared in the "Zeitschrift für die lutherische Theologie und Kirche," 1855, pp. 220–56: and of its author, Dr. Kurtz says that, "Of all the supporters of his (Keil's) view, there is not one who has treated the subject so thoroughly and comprehensively—has brought to the investigation of it so much diligence, acuteness, and learning—has so carefully arranged and exhibited the arguments which may be advanced in its favour, and has endeavoured with so much earnestness, and so much appearance of success, to overthrow those which are brought forward on the opposite side."

These two divines may be regarded as able representatives of the holders of their respective views: and, indeed, had an English translation of Professor Kurtz's book appeared, there would be little pretext for the present publication, although differing considerably from it, as well in point of matter, as in the arrangement and treatment of the several parts of the subject. Dr. Keil has, besides, devoted to the examination of the passage a section of twelve pages (137–139) in his Commentary on the Pentateuch, a work which has been translated into English, and forms three volumes of that valuable and important series, the Foreign Theological Library of Messrs. T. & T. Clark.

Of the works mentioned, and especially of Kurtz's "Die Ehen," &c., much use has been made, as well as, of Maitland's Essay on "False Worship," (Lond. 1856.) and that on "The Fallen Angels" in the collection entitled *Eruvin.* (Lond. 1831.) To the "Daily Bible Illustrations" of Dr. Kitto the writer is also under obligation: other writers are named below, and throughout the essay.

Should any regard the subject of this book as one of no practical value, and be disposed to ask, What profit is to be derived from its discussion? It might be sufficient perhaps to quote, in reply, the following words of a writer already named, who has anticipated and answered the question—

Some reader, [says Dr. Maitland,] may say (for I often hear such language, and never without pain and pity), 'What does it matter to us which opinion is right? Of what use would it be to us to know when, and why, and how, the angels fell? Is it not a curious, speculative question, and will not one opinion do quite as well as another?' Such persons I am not anxious to answer in detail: being persuaded in my own mind, that it is an important duty to get rid of error, as much as we can, on all subjects, and especially of all error which has fastened on the Word of God: and that he who attempts to explain *any* verse of the Bible, which has been misunderstood, or to illustrate any fact of revelation, which has been misconceived, is well and usefully employed. The objector would, perhaps, see the nature of his objection in its real light, if he were to say distinctly (as he does impliedly), 'What was the use of revealing this or that? We could have done well enough without knowing it. In fact, we are so well without that knowledge, that when it is offered to us, we do not see it worthwhile to trouble ourselves about it.'

It may be added to this, that if the occurrence related in this passage of Scripture were, as all are agreed, the cause which ultimately led to the most tremendous judgment with which this world has been visited, little argument is needed to show the propriety of inquiring into the real nature of such an occurrence. To this point the reader's attention will be directed. And if, while thus occupying no unimportant place in the Bible history, this passage of Scripture further serves, when rightly interpreted, and viewed in connexion with other Scriptures, to throw light upon the relations, and yet wide distinction, which subsist between the angelic and human worlds—if it helps to explain a portion of the pagan mythology—if it contains a solemn warning against sins of the flesh, and reminds the reader of the awful punishment with which, more than once, such sins have been visited—and finally, if it tends to impress the members of one sex with a sense of the duty inculcated in Prov. vi. 25, and Matt. v. 28—to remind those of another sex of the importance of attending to the apostolic admonition, i Tim. ii. 9; and that, to use the words of the ablest writer on the subject, not only in the presence of men, but even where no man's eye may penetrate—and to enforce, in the case of both, the lessons which may be learned from such portions of Holy Writ, as Genesis xxxix, 2 Samuel xi., and, it may be added, Mark vi. 17–38—then, it is not easy to see, how an inquiry into the true meaning of the passage can be a profitless one, or how the general description of the Sacred writings given by St. Paul can be inapplicable to it, "All Scripture is given by inspiration of God, and is profitable for doctrine, for reproof, for correction, for instruction in righteousness."

It is proper to note here that the following works are generally referred to by the names of their respective authors, with page or section, viz.:—F. Delitzsch, *Commentar über Die Genesis*, Leipzig, 1872; Dr. M. Drechsler, *Die Einheit und Aechtheit der Genesis*, Hamburg, 1838; C. W. E. Nägelsbach, Der Gottmensch, I Band—*Der Mensch der Natur*. Nürnberg, 1853; Dr. John Richers, *Die Schöpfungs- Para- dieses- und Sündfluthgeschichte*, Leipzig, 1854; J. C. K. Hofmann, *Weissagung und Erfüllung im alten und im Neuen Testamente*, Nördlingen, 1841; Hävernick, *Introduction to the Old Testament* (transl. Clarks' Foreign Theological Library), 1852; Subrector E. H. Engelhardt, *Die Ehen der Kinder Gottes mit den Töchtern der Menschen*, Gen. vi. 1–4, in the *Zeitschrift für lutherische Theologie*, &c., 1856, pp. 401–412; also the treatises, *Die Ehen*, &c., by Professors Kurtz and Keil, above referred to. References to Dr. Keil's Commentary on the Pentateuch (*Keil. Pent.*) are to Vol I. only.

Introduction

**The Greek Mythology—Gen. vi. 1–4—
Demigods and Heroes**

The scientific study of mythology has engaged the attention of learned men in ancient and modern times, and, as the question of the origin of its various legends affords room for speculation, more than one theory has been advanced, and more than one method of mythical interpretation introduced, with a view to supplying a solution of it. Some distinguished scholars, in modern times, have been disposed to refer the heathen mythology to a corruption of Old Testament history and doctrine, and to find in the patriarchs the first gods of the Pagan world.

Mythologists of this class, amongst whom may be named, as occupying a prominent place, Bochart (*Phaleg* and *Canaan*), Huetius (*Demonsiratio Evangelica*), Gerard John Voss (*De Orig. ac Progr. Idol. Lib. I.*), and, of English writers, the learned Jacob Bryant and G. S. Faber, have sought to connect the sacred persons and legends of the heathen with persons, events, and institutions belonging to the early ages of the world—the knowledge of these having been derived by the Gentile nations, either from intercourse with the Israelites, or from access which they may have had to the Old Testament Scriptures, or, perhaps in very many instances, from traditions, variously corrupted and obscured, preserved from the first amongst the nations—the true history of these persons and events having been committed to writing at a period comparatively late, and being now contained in the earlier portion of the Sacred Volume.

Idolatry, [says Mr. Faber,] was a gradual corruption of Patriarchism: whence it seems necessarily to follow, that, with due allowance for apostatic perversions, the great outlines of the latter were really the great outlines of the former. Such being the case, Pagan idolatry will be Noëtic Patriarchism in grotesque masquerade; and from the distorted features of the one, we may collect, with tolerable accuracy, the genuine features of the other. In prosecuting this inquiry, Scripture will be of prime importance to us: for there only have we any authentic information respecting the nature of uncorrupted Patriarchism.

To the same effect, Mr. Bryant writes in the preface to his elaborate and learned *Analysis of Ancient Mythology*:—

In the prosecution of my system, [he says,] I shall endeavour particularly to compare sacred history with profane, and prove the general assent of mankind to the wonderful events recorded. My purpose is…to divest mythology of every foreign and unmeaning ornament, and to display the truth in its native simplicity; to show that all the rites and mysteries of the Gentiles were only so many memorials of their principal ancestors, and of the great occurrences to which they had been witnesses. Among these memorials, the chief were the ruin of mankind by a flood, and the renewal of the world in one family. They had symbolical representations by which these occurrences were commemorated, and the ancient hymns in their temples were to the same purpose. They all related to the history of the first ages, and to the same events which are recorded by Moses.

The patriarch Noah is the principal personage in the mythological system of Bryant.

The history of Noah, [he writes,] has been recorded by the ancients through their whole theology, but has been obscured by the many names and characters given him. He is Thoth, Hermes, Menes, Osiris, Atlas, Prometheus: his history is found in the mythology of Janus, Saturn, Poseidon. All the mysteries of the Gentile world seem to have been memorials of the Deluge, and of the events which immediately succeeded.[2]

The same writer adds that, although the Deluge was the grand epocha to which the nations referred—the highest point to which they were able to ascend—yet that, in the rites and mysteries of the Gentiles, traces may be discerned of the antediluvian system, although these are obscure and few. Accordingly, these, mythologists recognise, in the deities of the Greek or other mythologies, some of those remarkable persons who appear in the Mosaic and some other sacred writings. In Adam, and again in Noah, they see Saturn; in Jubal, Apollo; in Tubal-Cain, Vulcan; and in his sister, Naamah, Venus or Minerva. Ham is identified with Jupiter Ammon;

Nimrod with Mars; Moses with Osiris and Bacchus; Joshua and Samson with Hercules. The visit of Jupiter, Neptune, and Mercury to Hyrieus, reminds them of the visit of Jehovah and two angels to Abraham; and that of Jupiter and Mercury to Philemon and Baucis, of the coming of the angels to Lot. They further discern, in the Hindu *avatárs*, or descents of the Deity, the manifestations of Jehovah in human form: while the sacred grove and the pillar-stone of the heathen bring to their recollection the patriarchal grove of Gen. xxi. 33, and the anointed stone of xxviii. 18. In the Sacred Ark of the Pagan mysteries; in the representations of Dagon and Vishnu, under the mixed figure of man and fish: in the ox or bull of Egyptian mythology: and in the figure of the Minotaur, man and bull, they find memorials of the Ark of Noah, and of the patriarch himself, not only as saved from the waters of the Deluge, but also in his subsequent character of husbandman.

The Greek tradition of the division of the universe between the three sons of Saturn, evidently points to the division of the earth between the three sons of Noah: and, to mention only one other instance, it is in the highest degree probable, as supposed by Mr. Faber, that the several theologies, Hindu, Chinese, Pythagorean, Orphic, and Platonic, respecting a Divine Triad, presided over by a Monad, have relation to Adam, the father of the human race, and his triple offspring, transmigrating into, and reappearing in, Noah, the second father, and his, in like manner, triple offspring.[3]

That the whole of the pagan, or even of the Greek, mythology may be explained in accordance with this method of interpretation, is an opinion which can hardly be maintained, as it appears to be certain that mythological systems arose not from any one source, but from several.[4] At the same time, it is very evident that, in many of the legends, not only of the Greek, but of the Hindu and other mythologies, the Gentile nations have embodied their remembrances of events, the true record of which is found in the Mosaic Scriptures. We are thus enabled to throw light on the origin of some traditions of the heathen, for which it might otherwise be impossible to account. Comparison of the various traditions which have existed, both in East and West, with reference to the Golden Age or Paradisiacal state, the Temptation, the Serpent, the Fall, the Flood, or the building of Babel, with the Biblical record of these, must carry with it a conviction of the truth of our remark—these traditions being evidently nothing else than distorted versions of the Mosaic accounts, the main circumstances in each case, as related by Moses, being readily recognizable in them.

An attentive consideration of the subject with which the following pages are occupied, must produce, we think, a like conviction in the minds of those who are acquainted with the Grecian mythology; for, although the object which we propose to ourselves in this treatise is, not to explain the origin of sacred legends of the heathen, but to give an exposition of a remarkable passage of Scripture, yet the exposition which we hope to present to the reader—the only one, as it appears to us, which meets the requirements of the case, and which it is possible to defend on exegetical grounds—can hardly fail to impress him with the belief that at least one distinguished legend of the mythology of Greece must have had for its foundation a singular occurrence recorded in the Inspired Book—an extraordinary event, of which those who survived the Deluge had personal knowledge, and with reference to which their descendants carried with them traditions when they began to migrate westward after the Dispersion. These traditions, preserved amongst some of the families of Noah's descendants for a thousand years or more—subject, of course, to the various influences which more or less affect all tradition—at length assumed the forms in which they appear in some of the earliest Grecian poetry, relating the birth of the Titans and giants, and their wars with the gods, and in which the real facts which constituted the basis of these traditions are not only, in great measure, disguised and altered, but also very highly embellished.

In the Grecian mythology an important place is occupied by certain powerful beings, described as being of mingled heavenly and earthly, or divine and human origin, and variously designated by the names of *giants, Titans, demigods, heroes.* (See Note A.) With the history of these classical scholars are familiar; but of the many who, in youth or after-life, may have become acquainted with the giants and heroes of mythology, only a few, perhaps, have regarded them otherwise than as imaginary beings, or the legends respecting them as aught else than poetic fictions, intended either to amuse, or, at best, to rep-

resent certain changes and appearances of external nature. Few, comparatively, have believed that in these legends were preserved the memorials of a real race—a race of beings of superhuman origin—who, by whatever names they may have been called in after times, or however extraordinary the sources to which heathen tradition ascribed their origin, or however monstrous the forms or extravagant the exploits which have been attributed to them, were living in the world at a remote period of its history—a period, "When the earth Saw men and spirits walking side by side"—and have left behind them a name which has endured for four thousand years. There are those, however, who believe that the pagan traditions were not pure inventions—not wholly without foundation—and who are able to see in those famous legends of the Greeks which tell of the more than earthly origin of the giants and Titans, of their wars with Saturn and Jupiter, and of the marvellous feats which they performed, an unmistakable reference to real events, the brief narrative of which forms a portion of the Old Testament Scripture, and may be read, in the words of the Authorized English Version, in the sixth chapter of the Book of Genesis, verses 1–4, as follows:—

And it came to pass, when men began to multiply on the face of the earth, and daughters were born unto them, that the sons of God saw the daughters of men, that they were fair: and they took them wives of all which they chose. And the Lord said, My spirit shall not always strive with man, for that he also is flesh: yet his days shall be an hundred and twenty years. There were giants in the earth in those days: and also after that, when the sons of God came in unto the daughters of men, and they bare children to them, the same became mighty men which were of old, men of renown.[5]

What were the two classes whose union produced the powerful and mighty race which acquired such bad eminence in the primeval world? Such is the question which naturally presents itself to the mind of the reader of this passage of Holy Scripture.

Dr. Kitto, in whose words we have stated it, says in reply, "The first impression of many readers will, perhaps, be that the 'sons of God' were angels, and the 'daughters of men' human females;" and he adds—although not coinciding in opinion with those who adopt it—that this view of the subject has been entertained by many, both in ancient and modern times.[6]

We are not sure that, to a person reading the passage for the first time, and unacquainted with any of the interpretations which have been assigned to it, the idea would at once suggest itself that the "sons of God," whom it represents as having taken to themselves wives from amongst the daughters of men, were angels, so very remote is such an occurrence from the ordinary range of our conceptions. Not more likely, however, would he be to conceive of them as descendants of the patriarch Seth.

Calling to mind, were he acquainted with it, the usus loquendi of the New Testament, he might probably suppose that these "sons of God" were certain pious men—men regenerated by the Spirit of God; but observing the very intimate connection evidently implied in the narrative as having subsisted between the marriages of the sons of God with the daughters of men and the judgment of the Deluge—for why, otherwise, has any mention of these alliances been made—he would naturally be at a loss to conceive in what way the marriages of godly men could have contributed to the bringing about of a catastrophe so terrible.

But, were this person to be informed that the original expression, translated in our version "sons of God," is universally admitted to designate *angels* in the only other places in the Hebrew Scriptures in which it occurs, he would feel himself called upon to take it in the same signification in Genesis vi.; and not only so, but in the fact of a union of this nature—the confounding of two distinct orders of creatures—and the consequent production of a mixed race, partly angelic, partly human—in this derangement of the divine plan he would probably discern a solution of the difficulty which had presented itself to his mind—a sufficient explanation of the cause which necessitated the almost total extermination of those who were then upon the earth. Were he further to be informed, that no other view of the subject was prevalent generally—at least, amongst Christian theologians—until some three or four centuries had elapsed from the commencement of the Christian era, when it was exchanged for one which seemed to be more in harmony with certain erroneous practices and opinions then beginning widely to spread themselves in Christendom, he would have little doubt that "the sons of God" of Gen. vi. were inhabitants originally of another world than this, beings of a nature diverse from that of mankind.

But, in the minds of very many, even of those who receive, with humble and unhesitating faith, whatever information they believe to be set before them in the Bible, and who have no desire to explain away the supernatural or extraordinary occurrences which it relates, or to interpret the mention of an angelic visit to mankind as a figurative mode of speaking—in the minds of many such there exists a strong prejudice against the idea of such intercourse between the visible and invisible worlds as that which the old interpretation of our passage implies—a prejudice so decided, that they are ready, as has been remarked by a writer on the subject, to swallow almost any absurdity, or catch at anything, however ridiculous, provided they can thus get rid of whatever might seem to give countenance to such a notion.

It will be our aim, in the following pages, to prove that the fact of such unnatural connection between beings of two orders widely different from each other is asserted in our passage, however inconceivable or inexplicable by us such a fact may be, or however deeply the minds of the many may be prejudiced against the reception of it. We will endeavour to show that the only admissible interpretation of Gen. vi. 1—4 is that in which the expression *Bne-ha-Elohim* (*sons of God*) is regarded as designating *angels*, and the term *Nephilim* (*giants*) the superhuman progeny to which the lawless desires of these angels gave birth—an interpretation which, as it appears to have been the earliest, was also that most generally received in the ancient synagogue and early Christian Church—one which is neither at variance with the usage of the Hebrew language, nor supported by arbitrary and irrational assumptions, but which meets at once the requirements of the language and the necessities of the case, and which, while it brings before us things that are mysterious and beyond our power to explain, does not, nevertheless, present anything that can be pronounced to be contrary to the dictates of reason.

Our exposition of the passage will set before the reader those facts which, we feel assured, it was the intention of the sacred writer to record. It will show that the occurrence which he relates involved the renouncing by a portion of God's creatures of their original divinely-appointed station and destination—their voluntary descent to a lower sphere, for the purpose of forming with beings inferior to themselves alliances unbefitting their own higher nature, and inconsistent with the ordination of God—and, as the result of this, the forcing into the creation of a new and monstrous race, whose existence had not been intended by the Creator. In thus ascertaining the fact which the Holy Spirit has in this place recorded—the unlawful commingling of different classes of creatures—the adulteration, as we may term it, of the race on earth, which was now no longer purely Adam's—the disturbance of the order of creation, and displacing of limits which God had assigned—our interpretation furnishes an answer to the question. Whence the necessity for a judgment so fearful, and so universally destructive, as that of the Deluge?—a question to which no satisfactory answer is afforded by any of those other interpretations of the passage which have been proposed.

Interpretations of the terms Bne-Elohim and Bnoth-Adam

There are, in our passage, four principal terms, viz., בביהאלהים (Bne-Ha-Elohim), rendered "sons of God"—and בבוח האדם (Bnoth-Ha-Adam), "daughters of men"—in verse 2: and הכפילים (Han-Nephilim), the "giants," and הכברים (Hag-Gibborim) the "mighty men"—in verse 4. On the right interpretation, especially of the first, of these terms, the true exposition of the passage depends. The terms in verse 4 will hereafter come under notice: of the other two the following interpretations have been proposed:—

1. BNE-HA-ELOHIM = *filii magnatum*, or *magnates*, sons of princes, judges, rulers—men of authority and rank—who married Bnoth-ha-Adam = women of inferior station. "*Filii judicum vel potentum filias hominum*, i.e: *plebeiorum, uxores duxerunt*"—Poli Synopsis, *in loc*. From the time, at least, of the publication of the Targum of Onkelos, this was the favourite explanation of these

terms by Jewish writers, a few of the later excepted. (See Chapter I.)

2. BNE-HA-ELOHIM = *Pious Men*, descendants of Seth, who styled themselves, or were styled, on account of their godly and virtuous character, *Sons of God*, and who chose for wives Bnoth-Ha-Adam= women of profligate or godless life belonging to the race of Cain, or other branches of the human family outside their own. This view was maintained by all Christian writers from the fourth to the close of the eighteenth century, and by many from that to the present time. (See Chapter II.)

3. BNE-HA-ELOHIM = *Angels*, till then unfallen, as Lactantius, in ancient time, and Maitland, Kurtz, and others, in our day, believe; or, *angels* already fallen with Satan—the *dæmones incubi* of the middle ages. The latter is stated to have been the view of the Cabbalistic Jews, as well as of some Christian writers, named by Drs. Kurtz and Keil. From the intercourse of the angels with *women*, = Bnoth-Ha-Adam, sprang the *Nephilim*, called in the English version, *giants* and *mighty men*, a superhuman race. The oldest explanation of the passage. (See Chapters III. and IV.)

4. BNE-HA-ELOHIM = *the earlier descendants* of Adam and Eve, as distinguished from *the later*, with whose daughters, = Bnoth-Ha-Adam, they intermarried; the men of the former race excelling those of the latter in physical and intellectual qualities, as well as in moral and

religious character, were thence styled *Sons of God.*—Mendelssohn's view.

5. BNE-HA-ELOHIM = *the Patriarchs named in Gen.* v., supposed to have been so called on account of the vast duration of their lives, in virtue of which they might be regarded as resembling, in some degree, the real *Sons of God,* the angels. R. Isaac Abarbanel (a Spanish Jew of the 16th century), in a Dissertation on the Longevity of these Patriarchs (translated into Latin by the younger Buxtorf—Basil, 1662), refers, page 417, to *Bereschith Rabba,* a rabbinical commentary on Genesis, to show that this opinion was propounded by certain rabbins who are there named.

6. BNE-HA-ELOHIM = *Giants*—persons or things distinguished by their greatness, power, strength, or other remarkable qualities, being sometimes designated, in Hebrew, by the addition of *Elohim* to their names hence, *filii Dei-homines proceri,* or *magni.* These gigantic men are supposed to have chosen wives of like physical proportions with themselves, מוב, being taken to mean *tall* or *large,* rather than *fair*—a signification thought to be warranted by its use in i Sam. ix. 2. From these unions sprang the powerful race mentioned in verse 4. This is the view of Oleaster (Jerome Olivier, or De Oleastro) a learned Portuguese Dominican monk, author of a comment on the Pentateuch (Lisbon, 1556)—and, although we may not adopt it, is at least a

more rational one than either the first or second above mentioned.—Poole's *Synopsis,* Gen. vi. 2.

The following, in addition to the three principal interpretations of *magnates, pious Sethites,* and *angels,* are noticed in Dr. Smith's *Dictionary of the Bible,* Article *Giants.*

7. BNE-HA-ELOHIM = *men,* with great gifts, "in the image of God"—(Ritter, Schumann).

8. BNE-HA-ELOHIM = *Cainites* arrogantly assuming the title of sons of God. (Paulus.) Gesenius (Thes.) refers to this interpretation. Some of the moderns, he says, as Ilgen, understand by this term the posterity of Cain, who prided themselves on their inventions and skill in arts.

9. BNE-HA-ELOHIM = *worshippers of false gods*—Aqu., making *Bne* = "servants." (Comp. Deut. xiv. I; Prov. xiv. 26; Ex. xxxii. I; Deut. iv. 28, *etc.*) This view, the writer in *Smith* says, is ably supported in "*Genesis of Earth and Man*" pp. 39, *sq.* Dr. E. Harold Browne, Bishop of Ely (in the Speaker's Commentary), mentions this interpretation. He says:—

The author of '*The Genesis of the Earth and of Man*' suggests that '*the sons of the gods*' (so he would render it) may mean the worshippers of false gods. These he looks on as a pre-Adamite race, and would render, not 'daughters of men,'

8

but 'daughters of Adam.' The pre-Adamite worshippers of the false gods intermarried with the daughters of Adam.

We have not seen this book. The interpretation appears to be partly founded on the rendering of Aquila, (who, however, has υιοι των Θεων), but what that translator really understood by the expression in the original is uncertain.

CHAPTER ONE

THE FILII-MAGNATUM,
OR JEWISH INTERPRETATION

Bne-Elohim = Men of Rank.
Bnoth-Adam = Poor Women.
Improbabilities involved in this view.

Of the several interpretations enumerated in last section, only the first three appear to have met with any sort of general acceptance, and, of these, two at least are still maintained. The interpretation of the rabbins, which we have placed first in order, and which may be termed the *filii magnatum* interpretation, is summarily disposed of by some of the commentators. Professor Kurtz merely remarks (*Hist. Old Cov.* I., p. 96) that it is at present generally abandoned. Another, that it may be dismissed at once, as not warranted by the usages of the language, and as altogether unscriptural (Keil. *Pent,* 128); while a third (*Nagelsb,* 125) writes that, to translate Bne-Ha-Elohim, *sons of the great,* as does Onkelos, or *filii-illustrium,* with Saadias, is a proceeding utterly injudicious and arbitrary. This may be true, although, indeed, Delitzsch admits that, "having regard to Ps. lxxxii. 6, *sq.,* this interpretation of Bne-Ha-Elohim commends itself to us more than that which makes it mean children of God in the spiritual sense." At all events, an interpretation which has the sanction of such names as Aben-Ezra and Raschi, as well as of the Targums and several versions, deserves a somewhat more extended notice than modern writers have bestowed upon it.

It is maintained by the advocates of this interpretation that, by the expression *Bne-Ha-Elohim,* we should understand persons of greatest eminency for place and power—

princes, judges, rulers, chiefs, *magnates*, or *filii magnatum*—whether of the family of Cain or Seth: while, by *Bnoth-Ha-Adam*, Moses is supposed to have meant women of the humbler classes, belonging, as in the other case, to both families: and that, from the marriages of these, sprang the *gibborim*, the *mighty men* of ver. 4, who are supposed to be *giants*, in the common acceptation of the word.

Dr. Adam Clarke (*Holy Bible, with Commentary and Notes*, &c. London: 1836), in his observations on Gen. vi. I, having noticed the Sethite and Cainite explanation, and rejected that for which we contend, says,

> Dr. Wall supposes the first verses of this chapter should be paraphrased thus—'When men began to multiply on the earth, the *chief* men took wives of all the handsome *poor* women they chose. There were tyrants in the earth in those days: also, after the antediluvian days, powerful men had unlawful connexions with the inferior women, and the children which sprang from this illicit commerce, were the renowned heroes of antiquity, of whom the heathens made their gods.'

The Jewish interpreters, with whom this explanation of the passage appears to have originated, were evidently in no degree influenced by a regard, either to the improbabilities which it involves, or to the fact that it fails to discover any cause for the judgment of the deluge. They merely sought, it would seem, in the genius and idiom of the Hebrew language, an explanation of the expressions *Bne-Elohim* and *Bnoth-Adam*, and believed that they found it in this—that some things peculiarly distinguished or excellent in their kind, or things or persons of beautiful, august, or striking appearance, were regarded by the Hebrews as being in a special manner from God. This conception the Hebrew expressed by joining the name *Elohim* to the name of the distinguished object—פבלג אלהים *river of God, i.e.,* mighty river, Ps. lxv. 10, גשיא אלהים, *prince of God, i.e.,* mighty prince, Gen. xxiii. 6: כפתולי אלהים, *wrestlings of God, i.e.,* great wrestlings, Gen. xxx. 8—as in Greek, Τῷ Θεῴ is sometimes joined to adjectives, for a like purpose (Acts vii. 20). But, the ground on which, especially, the interpretation appears to have been founded, is, that Elohim in some places in the Old Testament, was supposed to denote *judges* or *princes*; and a like signification being affixed to it in our passage, it was concluded that the Bne-ha-Elohim were *sons of princes,* or of *judges,* or else these exalted personages themselves—"filii magnatum aut principum, vel magnates"—(Mercerus)—the expression *Bne-ha-Elohim* being regarded as analogous to that of *filii Israel = viri Israelitae,* or to that of *filii hominum = homines.* (Poole's *Synopsis*).

For the meaning which these interpreters attach to the other term, *Bnoth-ha-Adam*—poor women, or women of humble rank in life—sufficient authority is thought to be furnished in the occasional use of the word אדם to denote one whose station or condition in the world is lowly or poor.

The sole support for the Jewish view being thus derived from the use, in the significations alleged, of the terms אלהים and אדם, we need only inquire whether, and in what connexion, these terms are so used, and whether such usage may be deemed sufficient to warrant us in adopting this interpretation of the passage.

The word *Elohim* is, in the Hebrew Scriptures, applied for the most part to the One True God, the God of Israel. It is employed, though less frequently, to denote the gods of the heathen, and also the holy angels: while in a few instances (Ex. xxi. 6; xxii. 8, 9, 28; I Sam. ii. 25; Ps. lxxxii. I, 6): it is supposed to be applied to men who filled judicial offices in Israel. Of the passages just mentioned, two (Ex. xxii. 28; I Sam. ii. 25) may be dismissed from the account, as, in them, the word may mean either God or human judges, while in the remaining five, *Elohim*, undoubtedly appears to be applied to the latter. It is the opinion, indeed, of Bishop Horsley (*Biblical Criticism*, ed. 1844, vol. 1. p. 16) that "not a single unquestionable instance is to be found in the whole Bible, of the supposed application of the word to princes, rulers, magistrates, or judges;" and, in confirmation of this opinion, he refers to Parkhurst, who, in his *Heb. Lexicon*, has examined the passages referred to, and rejects the idea of the term *Elohim* being ever so applied. But reading Ex. xxi. 6, or xxii. 8, 9, it is impossible to avoid the conclusion that the word is applied directly to *men*—only, however, as they are representatives, by virtue of their office, of the true *Elohim*, whose vicegerents for the time they are, in whose name they act, and with whose authority they are in some degree intrusted. The sacred writer, while applying the name

to the human judge, evidently regarded the cause as really referred to the judgment of God, through the medium of His minister. This appears from such passages as Deut. 1. 16, 17: xix. 17: 2 Chr. xix. 6: and it may also be remarked that the LXX. have rendered *Elohim* in the passages in Exodus. Accordingly, this view appears to be taken by most commentators, by Onkelos, Raschi, Ainsworth, Whitby (John x. 34), Patrick, Stuart (*Comm. on Hebrews*), Bloomfield, Robinson (*Lexicon*), Delitzsch, Kurtz, Keil, Archdeacon Lee (*Inspiration*, p. 375) who also refers to Hengstenberg and Olshausen, and by Dr. Nägelsbach.

Admitting, then, that *Elohim* is applied in the Old Testament, though only in a few instances, to the Israelitish magistrates, as representatives, in their official capacity, of Jehovah, and accordingly, that it does thus sometimes designate distinguished persons, there is yet little to be gained from this admission in favour of the Jewish interpretation; inasmuch, as, firstly, there is no sort of resemblance between any of the passages in which it is so used, and our passage, which might afford ground for a like application of the term in the latter: and, secondly, because the title in Gen. vi. is not *Elohim*, but *Bne-ha-Elohim*, a very different expression. To take *Bne* in *Bne-ha-Elohim* as equivalent to *viri* is a purely arbitrary act, and one not authorised by such cases as *filii Israel = viri Israelitae, filii hominum = homines*. The term *Bne-ha-Elohim*, in the other passages of Scripture in which it occurs, is admitted to denote beings higher in the scale of creation, than the great ones of the earth: and had Moses, in Gen. vi. 2, intended to speak of the latter, he would, no doubt, have designated them, not by *Elohim*, or *Bne-ha-Elohim*, but by some such term as *shophetim* (judges), *sarim* (princes), or *haggedölim* (the great).

But we are further required, by the Jewish interpreters and those who adopt the *filii-magnatum* explanation, to believe, not only that the *Bne-ha-Elohim* were the great men of their day, but also that by *Bnoth-ha-Adam*, "daughters of men," are intended women of lowly station, in contradistinction to their supposed admirers. "Viderunt filii illustrium filias plebis pulchras."—*Arab. Saad.* "Those great persons" says Bp. Patrick, who, in his commentary, mentions this interpretation, although preferring another, "were taken with the beauty of the *daughters of men, i.e. of the meaner sort* (for so sometimes *men* signifies, Ps. xlix. 2, &c.) and *took*, by force and violence, as many as they pleased, being so potent, as to be able to do anything with impunity." It is certain that אדם is, in some places, used in this sense, as in the passage referred to, and in Ps. lxii. 10 בכי איש—בכי אדם "men of low degree—men of high degree." But this is not a proof that Bnoth-ha-Adam must mean *women of low degree*, as אדם appears to have this signification, only when in contrast with איש. When not in this connection, *Adam* and *Bne-Adam* denote, respectively, the man *Adam*, or *a man, any man*, (Gen. iv. I: Lev. 1. 2: Prov. xviii. 16) and *mankind, men* in general; (Ps. xxxi. 20. Heb. Eccl. ix. 12, &c.)—in both cases, without distinction of class or condition in life. The expression *Bnoth-ha-Adam*, does not, so far as we know, occur in the Old

Testament, except in our passage: hence, no argument can be founded on usage. It is an expression, however, analogous to בכותחת, Gen. xxvii. 46, and בכת ישראל, Deut. xxiii. 18: and as these denote the female members of the races of Heth, and of Israel, without reference to station, character, or circumstances in life, so does *Bnoth-ha-Adam* denote the female portion of Adam's race, the women, generally, then in the world, irrespective of quality or station.

The signification which the Jewish interpreters have assigned to *Bnoth-ha-Adam*, was, no doubt, chosen with a view to providing a suitable antithesis to the great men supposed to be meant by *Bne-ha-Elohim*. It will not be denied by any that אדם, in verses 1 and 3, and it may be added, in verse 5, designates the race of mankind, generally: and no reason can be shown, sufficient to warrant the limitation of its meaning, in verse 2, and make it denote a class or portion of the race, when the only term, איש, in connection with which it has a limited application, is wanting. Even though the rendering of Bne-ha-Elohim, *magnates*, or *sons of the great*, were the proper one, it would not follow that Bnoth-ha-Adam must mean *poor women*, for *Bne-ha-Elohim* and *Bne-Ish* are different expressions. Dr. J. C. K. Hofmann rightly says (I. 85), "The antithesis of Bne-Adam and Bne-Ish has nothing to do with that of Bnoth-ha-Adam and Bne-ha-Elohim"—and he adds the weighty remark, that "האדם, in Bnoth-ha-Adam, must designate the whole race, not less in verse 2, than in verses 1 and 3, especially as it is said in verse 1, that daughters were born *to them* (להם), that is, to men *generally.*" In short, women of high station, as well as of low, are Bnoth-ha-Adam, and the title can have no other signification than that, which any impartial and unprejudiced reader of the passage would attach to it—Adam's daughters—his female descendants—*womankind*—just as Bne-Adam, when not in contrast with Bne-Ish, means simply *mankind*, men in general, without distinction. (See Deut. xxxii. 8.) Nor will this be questioned, unless by those who are resolved, at all hazards, to uphold a favourite interpretation of a passage in the Bible.

It is somewhat difficult to understand how this explanation of the passage found favour and acceptance to the extent that it appears to have done. Even though we should grant that the terms Bne-ha-Elohim and Bnoth-ha-Adam, may have the significations assigned to them, who can fail to see the extreme improbability of such an occurrence as that which the interpreters suppose? How utterly unlikely it is, or rather, how absurd the supposition, that all the great men of the day, or even a large proportion of them—persons occupying high places in the antediluvian world—should, with one consent, as it were, and about the same time, have been led to form such alliances, although these might not be contrary to the Divine ordination, as those of Gen. vi. 2 undoubtedly were. How remarkable, too, the circumstance, that female beauty should then have appeared, only or chiefly, as is implied, in women of the lower ranks of life: and not less strange, that it should have possessed such strongly attractive power, in the case of *all* these Bne-Elohim.

But stranger still were the results which followed these alliances. How shall we explain the fact, that "when the sons of God—*judges and princes of the primeval age*—came in to the daughters of men—*women of low condition in life*—and they bare children to them, the same became *mighty men which were of old, men of renown*"—an heroic race, of gigantic size, celebrated for their exploits through all succeeding time?—a result, not less unaccountable then, than now: but, indeed, an impossible result, if these gigantic heroes were, as there is reason for believing, identical with the *Nephilim* (called *giants* in our authorized version) who, we have no doubt, were something more than human beings, and derived their origin, in part, from a superhuman source.

Interpreting the passage in accordance with the usage of the Hebrew language, we find that all such difficulties disappear. It seems hardly possible to believe that the "*filii illustrium,*" or the "υιοι των δυναστευοντων" of those times should, *generally*, have been so captivated by the beauty of the "*filiæ plebis,*" the women "of the meaner sort," as to "take them wives of all which they chose." But it does not appear to us so inconceivable, that beings of a high order in creation should admire the beauty, peculiar to them, of creatures of another order in the great family of God—

Creatures of other mould, earth-born
   perhaps,
Not spirits, yet to heavenly spirits bright
Little inferior—

creatures made originally "but a little lower" than themselves—capable, like them, of interchanging thought with other rational beings—and further, possessed of the attribute of fleshly corporeal beauty—an attribute not belonging to their own, although the higher nature. "The angels," says Nägelsbach, "saw corporeality display itself in beauty and fulness in humankind, and in loveliest form in woman, who represents pre-eminently the corporeal element in the dualism of the sexes."[7] They thus beheld a loveliness, which did not appertain to their own ethereal corporeality (see Note E): and that they should regard it with feelings of pleasure or admiration,[8] is not more wonderful, than that we should contemplate, with feelings of a like kind, the beauty, the gracefulness, or other excellence of creatures, between whom and ourselves the disparity is greater, than that which exists between human beings and angels.

"That the rational inhabitants of one world," says Dr. Dwight (System of Theology—Sermon 20), "should be interested in the concerns of another, and, if allowed by God thus to act, interfere in them, in a manner suited to their respective dispositions, is in a high degree probable. *We*, certainly, if we were able, and were permitted to visit the planetary worlds, should take such a part in the important concerns of their inhabitants as suited *our* dispositions. If we were governed by benevolent motives, we should save or relieve them, so far as was in our power, from dangers and sufferings: if by malevolent ones, we should promote their distress and ruin. We do, in reality, thus act in this world,

not in our own affairs only, but in those of others—in the affairs of strangers, as well as of our friends, and of those of distant nations and countries, as well as our own. But there is nothing more unnatural or improbable in our interference, if it were permitted, in the concerns of distant worlds, than in those of distant nations."

This view is quite reasonable, and not less so in the case of angelic, than of human beings. "What degree of communication might have existed between the human race, and the inhabitants of the other world, had our first parents kept the commands of the Creator, can only," to use the words of Sir W. Scott, "be subject of unavailing speculation." "We do not perhaps presume too much," he continues, "when we suppose with Milton, that one necessary consequence of eating the 'fruit of that forbidden tree' was, removing to a wider distance from celestial essences, the beings who, although originally but a little lower than the angels, had by their own crime forfeited the gift of immortality, and degraded themselves into an inferior rank of creation."—*Letters on Demonology*. London, 1830, p. 50. That communication between the inhabitants of the two worlds would have been of a more intimate character than it is, had mankind continued in their original state, cannot admit of a doubt. Angels and human beings are still, however, members of the great rational and morally-accountable family of God: and on this ground alone we claim with them a relationship not remote. That angels occupy the highest place in the scale of created intelligences, is reasonably inferred from the titles bestowed upon them in the Bible—Thrones, Dominions, Principalities, Powers—from the intimate communion with God (Matt. xviii. 10; Luke 1. 19; Rev. vii. 1 1) to which they are admitted—and from the circumstances of splendour and glory in which they have occasionally appeared in the world. Man occupies a station in the same series of rational and accountable[9] beings—a lower one, indeed, than that occupied by the lowest order of angels—for we prefer the view of those who think there are more than one—

but to that circle of spirits he unquestionably belongs. He is one of them, not as a proscribed and degraded race, to be cut off from all fellowship with the heavenly hosts, and with the bare claim of immortality to sanction his admission into their order; but he is offered the means of restoration to what he was in that golden age, when he conversed even with the Highest Intelligence, and was the companion of angels. This restoration will place him again in direct communion with those beings, to whom, by his immortality, he is legitimately connected.[10]

Angels and men are thus but different members of a family; and "as in the members of a family on earth, there is a family likeness apparent in the midst of peculiar and individualizing traits, of features, complexion, and form; so is there a family likeness existing among all the members of the family of God, both in heaven and on earth." The angel is an immaterial being, clothed, we believe, with a subtile, ethereal, corporeal form: man is, likewise, an immaterial being, clothed indeed, now, with a gross, earthly body, akin to that of the beast, but hereafter to be clothed with a spiritual, celestial one, akin to that of the angel—"half-beast, half-angel," the description we have somewhere met with, might thus, not altogether inappropriately, be applied to the human being. He forms, in fact, the connecting link between, perhaps, the lowest of the angelic orders and the order of terrestrial beings inferior to himself. And "as we have borne the image of the earthly, we shall also bear the image of the heavenly," for we shall be "as the angels which are in heaven." If there is thus, in the nature and constitution of man, the capability of becoming like unto the angels—if the body of flesh and blood can be so changed, as to become spiritual and incorruptible, while yet the identity of the glorified body with that which was entombed in corruption remains—then it may be thought, perhaps, that these classes of beings cannot, even now, be so completely dissimilar in their natures as some people evidently imagine. That affections and dispositions which belong to human nature do likewise exist in the angelic, must be evident to the reader of the Bible. Of the interest which holy angels feel in the well-being of mankind, as well as of the part which they take in promoting it, we have ample assurance; and not less clearly is there indicated there the disposition, alas, of wicked spirits towards our race. From the same infallible source we learn that, however unlike to ours the angelic constitution may be, it has not been a bar to intercourse with human beings, nor has it prevented them from acting upon, or in conjunction with, mankind in a variety of ways; and yet their capability of performing some of the acts attributed to them is as far beyond our power to explain, as is their capability of having the connexion with human beings, which the true interpretation of our passage implies.

Having regard to these considerations, and to the fact that, notwithstanding the Fall, visible intercourse still subsisted, to some extent, between the angelic world and ours, and that the general character of the antediluvian period was a strange and preternatural one—we cannot think it incredible, or even unlikely, that the regard of angels could be attracted by the beauty or the comeliness of creatures, different indeed from themselves, and inferior in the scale of creation, yet not so far inferior, or so wholly different, as to render impossible, or even incompatible with their own higher nature and properties, the existence of an intimate companionship. We cannot hold it to be an absurd supposition that "angels," to adopt the words of the ablest writer on this subject, "who, *in their state of holiness*, desire to look into the deepest mystery of *grace* on earth (i Pet. i. 12), should, *in their apostasy* from that holiness, have desired to look into the deepest mystery of *nature* on earth"—and, transgressing the limits of their nature and destination, not merely to look into that mystery, but also, if it were possible for them, to participate in it themselves.[11]

Supporters of this Interpretation

The Jewish interpretation of our passage appears for the first time, as Professor Kurtz thinks, in the first century of our era, in the Targum of Onkelos, in which Bne-ha-Elohim is rendered בכירברביא, "sons of the great." It is believed, indeed, by some, that the Targum called by the name of Onkelos cannot lay claim, at least in its present shape, to a higher antiquity than the end of the third, or beginning of the fourth, century, having been finally redacted about that time in the Babylonian schools. Dean Prideaux, on the contrary, supposes it to have been published before the birth of Christ; but Hävernick seems to agree with those who place its publication in the first century. He represents Onkelos, in accordance with the Jewish tradition, as having been the disciple of Gamaliel (Acts v. 34 and xxii. 3), St. Paul's teacher, who died eighteen years before the destruction of Jerusalem.

Rabbi Simeon Ben Jochai (2nd cent.), a disciple of Akibha, may be named as a supporter of this interpretation. Delitzsch says, on the authority of *Bereschith Rabba*, that he translated *Bne-ha-Elohim*, בכי דיכיא, the term, it may be remarked, which Onkelos employs, Deut xix. 17, as the rendering of the Hebrew *shophetim*, judges. About the same time flourished, also, the two Hellenistic Jews, Aquila and Symmachus, of whom at least the latter adopts *filii-magnatum* interpretation. Aquila, if we may judge from what remains of his version (published a.d. 128), adhered closely to the letter of the Hebrew, so much so, that he is sometimes unintelligible. (Häv. 307.)

Hence, it is impossible to determine what meaning he may have attached to *Bne-ha-Elohim*, or to the υιοι των Θεων, by which he has translated it. Delitzsch reckons him (on the insufficient ground of, as it appears, Jerome's remark, quoted below) amongst the supporters of the angel-explanation. Drs. Kurtz and Keil regard him, perhaps rightly, as a supporter of *filii-magnatum* view. "The υιοι των Θεων of Aquila," says the latter (Zeit. 222), "denotes not sons of gods, or angels, but sons of princes or judges of the earth, because we dare not impute to this strict Jew, that he entertained the pagan notion of sons of the gods," "although," he adds in a note, "Jerome has already understood it so—*Aquila plurali numero filios Deorum ausus est dicere, Deos intelligens angelos sive sanctos.*" Dr. Keil is wrong, however, in attributing to paganism exclusively the notion of "sons of gods," *i.e.,* of beings whose origin is partly human, partly superhuman, as this idea has been entertained by Jews and Christians: we are also, perhaps, hardly warranted in concluding that Aquila was quite uninfluenced by pagan opinions, inasmuch as he was originally a pagan: and having, from motives of a corrupt kind, professed Christianity, he was, after some time, excommunicated, on account of the practice of magical arts, whereupon he became a Jewish proselyte. (Prideaux, *Conn.*, Part II.—Townley's *Illustrations*, vol. i.) Of Symmachus, who flourished in the reigns of Severus and Caracalla, Dean Prideaux says that he sought to express the meaning of the writer without following his words too closely, thus making his work rather a paraphrase than a translation. He renders, accordingly, υιοι των δυνασευοντων, "sons of the rulers." (*Hexapla* of Origen, ed. C. F. Bahrdt, 1769.)

The Jewish interpretation is found in the Samaritan version—a translation of the Samaritan Pentateuch into the Samaritan dialect, made, like the Targums, for popular use, when the original language had ceased to be understood. Its age has not been determined: but Hävernick supposes it to have been mainly dependent on a Greek translation of the Samaritan Pentateuch, mentioned by some of the Fathers, and made probably not earlier than the second century. *Bne-ha-Elohim* is represented, in the Samaritan version, by a term equivalent to *filii Sultanorum*, or *Dominorum*: but the Latin of Morinus, which serves for both the Samaritan version and Samaritan Text, in the Paris Polyglot, is *filii Dei*.

Next in point of time may be mentioned the Targum on the Pentateuch, wrongly ascribed to Jonathan Ben Uzziel, which from "the mention in it of the Talmud, and the use which it makes of the latter—the expressions indicative of a later age—and the barbarous style, abounding in foreign words"—is believed to have originated in the second half of the seventh century. (Häv. 337.) The rendering here is the same as that of Onkelos—*Bne-Ravrevaya*, "sons of the great." It may be observed, however, that the author, like Raschi, as will appear hereafter, while assigning this meaning to Bne-ha-Elohim, evidently believed that the passage contained also a record of the abode on earth of fallen angels.

In some writings of a later date, a like

interpretation of Bne-ha-Elohim appears, as in the Arabic translation of the Pentateuch made by R. Saadias Gaon (10th cent.), President of the Jewish school at Sura in Babylonia: and in another, known to Biblical interpreters as *Arabs Erpenii*, from the name of its editor, Thomas Van Erpen (Latinized Erpenius), a native of Holland, and one of the earliest of European orientalists. The version of Saadias is printed in the London and Paris Polyglots. It is worth remarking that, while in v. 2 the author has "viderunt *filii iilustrium* filias *plebis* pulchras"—in v. 4 he renders "*filli Elohim* ingressi sunt ad filias *Cain*." (*Lat interp. Paris Polyglot.*) The Pentateuch, edited by Erpenius (Pentateuchus Mosis, Arabice, Lugduni Batavor. ex typographia Erpepiana linguarum orientalium. 1622. 4to,), was the work, according to Hävernick, of an African Jew of the 13th century: and is mentioned by Delitzsch as supporting the Jewish view.

In the period which intervened between the making of these Arabic versions, flourished the two celebrated rabbins, Solomon Ben Isaac (11th cent.) known as Raschi, and also, though erroneously, as Jarchi: and Aben Ezra (12th cent.) These rabbins make mention, in their commentaries, of other explanations of our passage, but give the preference to that of the *filii magnatum*. Raschi explains *Bne-ha-Elohim*, 6en. vi. 2—השרים והשופטים בכי , "sons of princes and judges:" Aben Ezra, בכיהשופטים,[12] "sons of the judges." Kimchi, also, is mentioned in the Speaker's *Commentary*, as supporting this interpretation.

Not unjustly, in view of its history, has Dr.

Keil said that this explanation of the passage may be regarded as the traditional one of the Jewish schools in Palestine and Babylon. He also observes that it has never found much favour with Christian expositors, while Kurtz adds that the Sethite-explanation has had few supporters amongst the Jews. Of Christian writers, who adopt the former, Keil names only three—Molina, Varenius, and Mercerus—the last-named (Jean Le Mercier) a Frenchman, author of a comment on Genesis, editor of the Hebrew Lexicon of Pagninus, and one of the greatest masters of that language in the 16th century. Selden and Vorstius, also, are mentioned in the Speaker's Commentary: but by far the greater number of Christian writers, who comment on this portion of Genesis, have preferred either the Sethite, or the angel-interpretation.

The occurrence related in our passage has been represented by Schiller, Herder, and Ph. Buttmann, in accordance with the Jewish interpretation. (Delitzsch.) The poet Moore, likewise, notwithstanding his treatment of the subject in his poem of "The Loves of the Angels," appears to have regarded this as the true explanation. He did not believe, as we learn from the short preface to the poem, that the subject of his story could properly be termed a Scriptural one: or, that any other origin could be assigned to the notion on which it is founded—that of the love of angels for women—than an erroneous translation (as he supposed it to be) by the LXX. of Gen. vi. 2. The reasons which may have induced the Seventy to adopt the rendering, αγγελοι του Θεου (if this be, indeed, the genuine reading), or the ample grounds on which it may be supported, the poet does not seem to have taken into consideration. He adds, that he has sought to communicate to the story a moral interest, using the subject as

an allegorical medium, through which might be shadowed out the fall of the soul from its original purity—the loss of light and happiness which it suffers, in the pursuit of this world's perishable pleasures—and the punishments, both from conscience and from Divine justice, with which impurity, pride, and presumptuous inquiry into the awful secrets of God, are sure to be visited.

Such an application of the subject may be made, with propriety and advantage. For ourselves, however, believing, as we do, that the notion, on which the poet founded his story, has a real foundation in Holy Scripture, "The Loves of the Angels," and Byron's grander piece of "Heaven and Earth," possess a charm, beyond what they could have, did we look upon them as nothing more than creations of poetic fancy. In the scenes which they present to our view—in the sentiments of love, of pity, or of terror, which they portray—in the words of endearment, or of regret, to which they give expression—in the "impassioned picture of the strong and devoted attachment inspired into the daughters of men by angel forms"—and in the representation of the human passions that "drew angels down to earth"—we feel that we have before us something not quite unlike to that, which, we are convinced, had real existence in the days preceding the Deluge.

We conclude this notice of the Jewish explanation of our passage, by observing, that previously to the time, about which it appears to have been first propounded, the correct view of the meaning of Bne-Elohim and of the passage, generally, had been taken by Jewish, and, not improbably, by some Christian writers also. Apart from the fact, that the Septuagint translators may, with much reason, be regarded as supporting our view, the angel-story was set forth, but with mythic embellishments, by the author of the Book of Enoch, as early, according to some, as 110 B.C., and, at all events, not later than some thirty years before the birth of Christ. Indeed, this appears to have been the view entertained by the ancient Jewish Synagogue, no other, perhaps, having been advanced, or at least having met with any general acceptance, until about the commencement of the Christian era. It is also possible that the opinions of the two Hellenistic Jews, Josephus and Philo, were made known to the world, previously to the completion of the Targum of Onkelos: as well as those of SS. Peter and Jude—assuming, for the present, that the passages in their epistles, hereafter to be noticed, refer to the sin of the Bne-ha-Elohim, and were so intended by these apostles. What may have been the motives which prompted Jewish writers to devise a new and very different explanation of immediately preceding: for if the fact of physical degeneracy be assumed, it follows that the immediate progeny of these elder generations would, according to the common analogies of life, be more powerful men than would arise from intermarriages between persons on both sides of the best generation.

"We have thus wrought out," he adds, "the view suggested in the extract we have given, because it appears in some respects to meet the difficulties which, on the one hand disincline us to suppose the 'sons of God' were merely men of the same generation; and which, on the other, make one afraid to say that they were angels."—*Daily Bib. Illustr. Antediluvians*, &c., pp. 138–140.

Against this explanation the same objections lie, as against all others which exclude the superhuman. It must be rejected as resting on assumptions and suppositions, for which there is no foundation in the Sacred Record. It is, for example, assuming what should be proved, when it is said that the first descendants of Adam and Eve were known as *sons of God*, and the remoter as *sons or children of men*: nor does there appear to be reason for supposing that the latter, in the antediluvian times, were inferior physically or intellectually to the former. We cannot but think, too, that an objection to this theory, more serious than Dr. Kitto seems to regard it, arises from the fact of the great disparity, in point of age, of the supposed parties. It is not probable that such alliances would have been contracted to so great an extent as that implied. Finally against this, and all other explanations of our passage, which regard the *Bne-Elohim* as human beings, one grand objection may be urged, namely, that they do not suggest any adequate cause for the enormous wickedness which, it is admitted by all interpreters resulted from the union of the sons of God with daughters of men, and that they fail to account for the necessity of a judgment so tremendous, and so universally destructive of the race, as was that of the Deluge.

CHAPTER TWO

THE SETHITE INTERPRETATION

General View—Supporters of the Interpretation—Causes of its Adoption

The explanation of the passage, Gen. vi. 1–4, now to come under consideration, is one which was universally received, both in the eastern and in the western Church, for some thirteen or fourteen centuries—in other words, from about the fourth century of our era, to almost our own times—and which, slightly modified by some recent writers, has probably, at this day the largest number of adherents, although having really as little foundation in the text, as the traditional one of the Jewish schools.

This exposition of our passage, which has been called *the Sethite*, of later origin than the *angel* and *filii magnatum* explanations, may be found, in form more or less complete, in the works of many theological and other writers, in ancient, mediæval, and modern times. It is given, in the words of several of our own commentators, by Maitland—himself a supporter of the true interpretation—and we cannot better present it to the reader, conveying to him, at the same time, an idea of the groundless suppositions and assertions, by which it is sustained, than by transcribing a passage from that writer's essay on The Fallen Angels.

Having quoted the words of Gen. vi. 1–4, he says,

With regard to what I have called the current explanation of this passage, I must say that it is not only in the highest degree *fanciful*, as being founded on mere imaginations; but also, that the fiction, when dressed up in its most plausible form, is grossly insulting to common sense. I will give it, as it stands, in three of the most commonly used recent expositions; only taking leave here and there to interpolate a question or remark between brackets, believing that to be the most concise way of commenting, and the best mode of indicating that progress of assumption, by which error is rendered plausible.

Mr. Scott says:—

The spiritual worshippers of God are His children: and this honourable title is sometimes conferred on all who profess the true religion. [Where?] These seem [how?] to have kept themselves for a long time distinct from such as were openly irreligious or idolatrous [if there were openly irreligious and idolatrous persons at that time]: the former uniting with Seth's descendants, the latter with Cain's. But at length, when the human race had greatly increased, and vast numbers of very beautiful women were observed amongst the irreligious or idolatrous party [of which party, and the 'vast numbers' of the beautiful women, we hear nothing in the Scriptures]: the worshippers of God were induced by unworthy motives, unreservedly to contract marriages with them, which made way for a rapid increase of wickedness, and an almost universal apostasy. These women are called the 'daughters of men,'

or rather of Adam [which, of course, could not distinguish them from the daughters of Seth or of anybody else]; as inheriting his fallen nature, and imitating his sin [though we do not hear of their sinning at all in the matter], but not his repentance.

The note in Mant and D'Oyly's *Commentary* (after a reference to the Jewish interpretation) is as follows:—

There are other ancient interpreters, and most of the later, who by 'the sons of God' understand the posterity of Seth, who were worshippers of the true God, Gen. iv. 26, and who now 'saw' or conversed with 'the daughters of men,' that is, the daughters of the ungodly race of Cain.— Bp. Patrick, Bp. Kidder.—Of all which they chose.] Whomsoever they liked, without regard to anything else but their beauty. It is supposed [supposed? what a foundation for such a long story of wonders], that the Cainites spent their time in feasting, music, dancing, and sports: this allured the children of Seth to come down from the mountainous country, which, under a solemn injunction from their godly forefathers, they inhabited [which mountainous country is supposed to have existed, in order that they may be supposed to have inhabited it, under a supposed injunction from their forefathers, who are supposed to have been godly], and marry with the descendants of Cain. The consequence was all manner of impurity, impiety, idolatry, rapine, and violence. For 'evil communications' naturally 'corrupt good manners,' and so the example of the wicked prevailed, and by degrees consumed, with few exceptions, all remains of religion in the posterity of Seth, &c.—Stackhouse.

The following notes from the Douay Bible may be interesting to some: the orthography of the edition of 1635 is preserved:—

Genesis vi. 2.—The sonnes of God seeing the daughters of men that they were faire, tooke to themselves wives out of al which they had chosen.

The progenie of Seth, possessing true faith and religion, were called the sonnes of God: and those of Cain's issue and congregation, following erroneous and wicked opinions, were called the sonnes of men. Which were then the distinctive termes of true and false religion, as afterwards were the termes of Jewes and Gentiles; after Christ, Christians and Pagans: and lastly, true and false Christians are distinguished by the names of Catholikes and Heretikes, as S. Augustin teacheth in his questions upon Genesis, and other places. Which is confirmed by the like judgement of S. Ciril Alexandrinus, and manie others upon this place. [Edition of 1635.]

The descendants of Seth and Enos are here called sons of God, from their religion and piety, whereas the ungodly race of Cain, who by their carnal affec-

tions lay grovelling upon the earth, are called the children of men. The unhappy consequence of the former marrying with the latter, ought to be a warning to Christians to be very circumspect in their marriages: and not to suffer themselves to be determined in their choice by their carnal passion, to the prejudice of virtue or religion. [Editions of 1816 and 1843.]

The question of the right interpretation of our passage was briefly discussed in certain letters on "Hades," which appeared in the *Irish Ecclesiastical Gazette*, in 1867. One of the writers, advocating the view now to be examined, writes thus:—

Such unholy alliances, as those which I have supposed [viz., between Sethite men and Cainite women], were just what would be likely to bring about that fearful profligacy of manners, so painfully and terribly described in the sixth chapter of Genesis. The sons of God possessed the knowledge of God's truth, were probably educated in the fear of the Lord, and set as lights in the world, where moral and spiritual darkness was overshadowing multitudes of the human family: when these therefore, forsook the paths of rectitude, turned aside from the ways of God's commandments, and, allowing themselves to be seduced by those who, though they were fair in face, were foul in heart, formed the closest of all human relationships with them—what could be expected but abounding corruption and continually increasing wickedness? It fell out with the sons of God, as it did with Solomon in his old age, as it did with the Israelites, who loved and married strange women—they won not the wives—but the wives coorrupted them—and so the light was darkened, sin increased, judgment hastened, and the fire of hell, kindled on the earth, was at last extinguished in the waters of the Deluge.—(Letter of the Ven E. H. Brien, Archdeacon of Emly, I. E, G., May, 1867, p. 114.)

These extracts will enable the reader to understand the nature of an interpretation of our passage, which has been, perhaps, more generally accepted than any other. Extracts from the writings of two of the Fathers who understand the passage thus, and from some of the mediæval chronographers, who have highly embellished the story, will be found in Note L. The slightly altered form which the Sethite-interpretation has assumed, in the hands of some theologians of our day, resulting from a change in the application of the term *Bnoth-ha-Adam*, will be noticed in the concluding part of this chapter.

Previously to the latter part of the fourth century, this explanation of our passage appears to have been but little known, or at least to have had but few supporters, Christian writers, generally, to that time, having adhered to the old interpretation of *Bne-Elohim*. Dr. Kurtz mentions Ephraem Syrus (*ob.* 378) in the Syrian Church, Philastrius (*ob. circa* 390) in the Latin, and Chrysostom (*ob.* 407) in the Greek Church, as the first who

set forth, in their writings, the new interpretation, and condemned the other as absurd and heretical. It is, however, certain that the former had been propounded as early, at least, as the beginning of the third century: for Julius Africanus (*ob.* 232), as we learn from a fragment of his chronography, preserved by Syncellus, finding in the copies of the Septuagint the reading υιοι του Θεου, as well as that of αγγελοι του Θεου, in Gen. vi. 2, gives it as his opinion, that "the descendants of Seth are called the sons of God, on account of the righteous men and patriarchs who have sprung from him, even down to the Saviour himself: but that the descendants of Cain are named the seed of men, as having nothing divine in them," &c. (Fragments of Africanus and others, translated by the Rev. S. D. F. Salmond, in *Clarke's Ante-Nic. Lib.*, vol. ix.) This writer, however, as will be shown in a following section, seems to waver between this and the angel-explanation and hesitates decidedly to reject or adopt either of them.

From the close of the fourth century, the new explanation of Gen vi. 1–4, appears to have been preferred to every other, by the Christian writers, partly, no doubt, in consequence of the sanction given to it by several distinguished Fathers: but chiefly owing to certain other causes, which will be indicated presently. Amongst its earliest advocates, in addition to those already named, are to be reckoned Augustine (354–430)—although he does not, by any means, deny the possibility of such intercourse of demons and human beings, as that which our interpretation implies—Theodoret (386–457), Cyril of Alexandria (*ob.* 444), and Basil of Seleucia (*ob. circa* 458). Delitzsch adds Procopius (6th century) and Jerome, whom we mention last, because it is doubtful whether he can rightly be claimed as a supporter of either view, as he has not expressed a decided opinion on the subject. (See Kurtz, p. 3, note 9.) Throughout the period of the middle ages, if we exclude the Cabbalistic and other Jewish writers, the Sethite and Cainite explanation was approved of by all who attempted to expound the meaning of, or referred to, our passage, and met, indeed, with universal acceptance, both in the eastern and western churches. The Byzantine historians, George Syncellus (8th century), in his *Chronographia*; George Cedrenus (11th century), and John Zonaras (12th century) in their *Annals*; the Christian Arabic writers, Eutychius (10th century), whose Arabic name was Said Ibn Batrik, Patriarch of Alexandria, and George Elmacin (13th century), in their *Annals*: and, amongst the Syrian Christians, the maphrian or primate, Gregory Bar-Hebræus, or Abulpharagius (13th century), in his *Chronicon Syriacum*—all represent the occurrence related in Gen. vi. 2, in accordance with this interpretation, some of them largely embellishing the story. Amongst pre-Reformation expositors, may also be mentioned Nicolaus Lyranus, or De Lyra, of Jewish extraction, a Franciscan monk, and Master of Theology in Paris, A.D. 1320, His expositions of the Scriptures are said to have been far in advance of all others of that age, and contributed so much to promote an acquaintance with the Bible, that they have been regarded by some as amongst the causes which led to the Reformation.

Dr. Keil names, of the Rabbins, the eminent Abarbanel (15th century), as propounding the Sethite-interpretation, together with the traditional one of the later Jewish schools. The descendants of Seth, he says, *are called sons of God, "propter ipsius (sc. Sethi) pietatem, justitiam, ei fidem."* We may add Aben Ezra, who likewise notices this interpretation, although, like Raschi, giving the foremost place to the Jewish—*"Some say that the Bne-Elohim are sons of Seth, and the Bnoth-ha-Adam daughters of the families of Cain"*—Comm. on Gen. vi. 2, in *Pentat, Mosis, cum Targg. Comm. Raschi, Aben Ezra*, &c. Berolini, 1705.

Christian commentators, Protestant and Romish, from the time of the commencement of the Reformation, to the time when Rationalism made its appearance in the last century, and the greater number since that time, have adhered to this interpretation of *Bne-Elohim*, Luther, Calvin, and Melanchthon, are named by Delitzsch, and the older expositors, generally, on the Continent. We may mention specially Lambert De Daneau, or Danaeus, a learned French Calvinistic divine of the 16th century, who defends this view at some length, and with ability, in his book *De Prima Mundi Ætate*. The Douay translators offer a like explanation in their notes: as do also the notes to the Latin version of *Tremellius* and *Junius* (1585), where the angel-interpretation is not even alluded to. "The sons of God," says Bochart (*Phaleg.* I c. 10), "are opposed to the daughters of men, as believers to unbelievers;" and with regard to the Greek legend of the giants piling mountain upon mountain, in order to scale the heavens, he says, "Far be it from us to believe, with the apostate Julian, that the Mosaic narrative has anything in common with the fable of the Alöidæ." C. 13. Joh. Drusius, more strongly still, in his *Miscellanea*, printed 1586, where he says of the angel-explanation, "Nihil à religionis nostræ veritate magis alienum. Quod qui dubitat, haud sanè intelligo, cur non idem sol sit an nullus sit dubitare possit."—*Cent. Prima.* xxv. Calmet, author of the well-known *Dictionary of the Bible*—the Abbe Banier, in his *Mythology*,—Suicer (*ob.* 1684) *Thesaurus*, s. v. αγγελος—are amongst the upholders of the Cainite and Sethite interpretation: while of the older British commentators may be named Bishops Patrick and Kidder, Ainsworth, Whitby (on 2 Pet. ii. 5), Matthew Henry, who does not even notice either of the two older interpretations; Ridgeley, in his *Body of Divinity*, and the learned Dr. John Gill, in his Exposition of the Old Testament, published in the middle of last century. This writer says on Gen. vi. 2,

> Those sons of God were not angels, either good or bad, as many have thought, since they are incorporeal beings, and cannot be affected with fleshly lusts, or marry and be given in marriage, or generate and be generated, nor the sons of judges, magistrates, and great personages, nor they themselves, as the Targums of Onkelos and Jonathan, and so Jarchi and Aben-Ezra…but rather this is to be understood of the posterity of Seth, who

from the time of Enos, when men began to be called by the name of the Lord, ch. iv. 26, had the title of the sons of God, in distinction from the children of men.

To those already named, we may add Parkhurst (*Hebrew Lexicon*), Cruden (*Concordance*), Shuckford (*Sac. and Prof. Hist*), and amongst the poets, Milton.[13]

In most of the commentaries published, within a recent period, in these countries, we find this explanation of our passage approved of, either in its original form of Sethites and Cainites, or modified in the manner hereafter to be shown. Amongst these we include Dr. Adam Clarke's Bible—Henry and Scott (Religious Tract Soc.)—*Genesis expounded in a Series of Discourses*, by R. S. Candlish, D.D., 1868—*The Book of Genesis in Hebrew*, with notes, &c., by C. H. H. Wright, 1859—*Commentary on Genesis*, by Henry C. Groves, M.A., 1861. This writer, opposing the angel-interpretation, quotes these words of St. Chrysostom, "If the saints who had been partakers of the Holy Ghost, could not bear the sight of the angels, and Daniel himself lay lifeless by reason of such visitation, who would be so irrational as to suppose, that the immaterial and spiritual natures could ally themselves with the fleshly?"—*Commentary on Genesis*, with translation, by J. G. Murphy, D.D., 1863[14]—the Speaker's *Commentary*, 1871—and the Holy Bible, with notes, &c., by Chr. Wordsworth, D.D., Bishop of Lincoln, 1875. Those English writers who take a different view will be mentioned in another section.

Of Continental writers, advocates of this view now, or recently living, Delitzsch mentions:

Hengstenberg, Tiele, Hävernick, V. Gerlach, Schröder, Ebrard, Keil, J. P. Lange, Rampf (*Brief Judæ* 1854), Fr. de Rougemont (*Le Peuple Primitif*, 1855), Andr. Wagner (*Gesch. der Urwelt*), Bunsen, Philippi and Kahnis (in their dogmatic works), Keerl (Lehre von der Herrlichkeit Gottes, 1863, p. 87, where he maintains that sons of God is a common designation of those who do the will of God), Veith (*Anfänge des Menschengeschlechts*, 1865), and Paul Scholz (*Die Ehen der Söhne Gottes mit den Töchtern der Menschen*, 1865)—all these discover in our passage that, with the increase of the human race, the distinction between the two lines of Cain and Seth, which had hitherto existed, in a moral point of view, became obliterated, and the divine life swallowed up in the worldly.—*Delitzsch*, p. 191.

Were we able to ascertain the views entertained respecting the meaning of our passage, by all whose attention has been directed to the subject, whether these views have been committed to writing or not, it would probably appear that, while the Sethite-explanation was almost universally adopted in the past, from the time when it had completely usurped the place of the old one, it has still the largest number of adherents—so very reluctant are the many to admit the idea of any communication between the visible and the invisible world, the possibility of which they are unable to explain or conceive.

It will, however, naturally be supposed that the general abandonment of an interpretation of a passage of Scripture, which, up to a certain period, had been the commonly received one, and the general adoption of another of a very different kind, did not take place without some sufficient cause. Into the nature of this cause, it may be worth while inquiring. Dr. Keil, adverting to the question, assigns as the sole, or, at least, principal cause which led to the renunciation by Christian writers of what he regards as a heathenish interpretation, the fact that the reputation of the Book of Enoch, as a genuine and authentic writing, had been demolished in the third or fourth century, and the book itself consigned to the category of apocryphal and unauthentic documents: the consequence of which was, that the Fathers, whose belief in the marriage of angels had been founded solely, as he assumes, on the narratives contained in the apocryphal book, renounced the old interpretation of our passage, and adopted another. That the rejection of the ancient interpretation, however, cannot be explained on this ground, is abundantly manifest from the fact pointed out by Kurtz, that the angel-legend was still in repute—and we may add, the angel-interpretation, maintained by several Fathers, as Lactantius, Ambrose, and Sulpitius Severus—subsequently to the time when the Book of Enoch had ceased to be recognised as an authoritative writing, or, rather indeed, when it had become, in great measure, unknown.

The renouncing of the old interpretation must be attributed to causes of a different kind. The question has been discussed at length, by the writer just named, in his treatise, *Die Ehen*, &c., pp. 35, sqq.; and we should not do more than refer the reader to the passage, were the work extant in the form of an English translation, if, indeed, in such case, we had undertaken at all to write on the subject We are not aware that any translation has appeared, and as even the original may not be accessible to all, we offer here the substance of his remarks.

The causes which led to the adoption of the Sethite-interpretation of our passage are to be sought for, partly in opinions entertained by some of the Fathers relative to the nature of angels, but chiefly in the rise and spread of certain superstitions and unwarrantable practices in the Church.

That the Church Fathers, who first set forth the new explanation in their writings, and condemned the old one as absurd, or even blasphemous,—as Theodoret, Basil of Seleucia, and others—were influenced, in their rejection of the one, and their adoption of the other, not by any opinion they may have entertained respecting the authenticity or otherwise of the Book of Enoch, but solely by their views of the incorporeality of angels, and the impossibility of such intercourse as that implied in our passage, between angelic and human beings, appears plainly from their writings. They make, indeed, as Kurtz observes, no secret of the dogmatic considerations which influenced their exegesis. Thus Theodoret, (*Quast 47 in Genesin,*) says "*Qui*

ex Setho genus duxerunt, olim quidem, ut virtutis studiosi, filii Dei vocabantur," and he adds, "*oportebat eos* (qui angelos intelligunt) *inde perspicere naturam incorpoream non habere carnem, neque angelos vitam habere tempore definitam, immortales enim creati sunt.*"[15] Similarly Basil of Seleucia, (*Orat.* VI.) "*Filii quidem Sethi vocantur filii Dei, symbolum suæ cum Deo conjunctionis appellationem hanc ferentes*"—"*Quomodò carnis expers angelorum natura corporum amore capiebatur? Creator enim quamlibet naturam convenientibus legibus muniverat, et creaturas intra terminos et metam suam stabiliverat.*" And the author of *Quæst. ad Antiochum*, wrongly ascribed to Athanasius (*tom.* II, p. 352, Quæst 57)—"*Filii Dei sunt filii Sethi: natura enim corporis expers neque corpora amat, neque cum mulieribus miscetur.*"

These passages from the writings of those eminent Fathers show the nature of the considerations, by which they were influenced, when they applied themselves to the interpretation of Bne-Elohim. The sanction given by them to the Sethite-explanation, may have served to recommend it to others, and contributed largely towards its subsequent general reception. But belief in the incorporeality of angels was not the sole cause which induced theologians generally to abandon the old interpretation, and to adopt the new. Had it been so, that view of the angelic nature would be found to have been as universally prevalent in the Church, as was the Sethite-interpretation subsequently to the fourth century. This does not appear to have been the case. On the contrary, the opinion entertained by most of the Fathers, previously to the fifth century, that angels possess a subtile, ethereal corporeality—a certain material substance, of the nature of air or flame, occupying the place in the angelic constitution, which the fleshly body does in the human—in other words, that they are not wholly immaterial, but in part material also, possessing corporeal forms conformable to the mode of their being— this opinion prevailed, our author says, long after the belief in an antediluvian angel-fall had been condemned: and, although not so generally received as in the earlier centuries, was yet entertained by some of those who regarded the Sethite-interpretation of our passage, as the only admissible one.

As this interpretation thus appears to have been adopted by persons holding opposite views on the question of the nature of angels, some other ground, than that of the absolute immateriality of these beings, must be sought on which to account for its general reception in the centuries which followed the fourth. That Dr. Kurtz has discovered, in the practice of *angel-worships* the real ground, we have no doubt. In this religious corruption, which had been making progress in the Church from, at least, the second century, we can discern a cause amply sufficient to account for the substitution of a new interpretation in the room of the old.

The development of angel-worship, [he says,] progressing imperceptibly, but, for that reason, all the more irresistibly, could not continue without exerting a transforming influence on the historico-dogmatic opinions respecting angels. It could not continue without gradually, but surely, removing everything that might tend to shake confidence in the holiness of angels, or mar the gratification which their worship afforded: and hence, must exclude, as coming under this description, the dogmatic view of the *possibility*, as well as the *historical fact,* of a second angel-fall, inasmuch as these allowed, at least, the abstract possibility of such an event being repeated.

The idea of such a possibility, we may conceive, would be but little in accordance with the feelings of veneration entertained for angels, or with the devout adoration of which they were the objects in those centuries, during which Christianity was being overlaid with the superstitions and abominations, which constitute the distinctive features of the idolatrous Roman Church. Hence, it was found convenient to deny that the "Sons of God" were angels, or that any fall in the angelic world, save that of Satan and his host, had taken place, or could, subsequently to that revolt, take place—all those angels (it was assumed, in opposition to the views of the earlier Fathers), who had not suffered themselves to be involved in Satan's sin, having been then confirmed in their state of holiness, so that apostasy from it became, from that time, impossible.

The change made in the explanation of our passage, about the period indicated, is thus, as it appears to us, accounted for in a manner completely satisfactory. Dr. Kurtz, however, assigns a second cause, which he

31

seems to regard as having been equally influential with the other, in effecting this change. This cause he finds in the spread of monkery, and in the reverence with which it and celibacy in general, were regarded in, as well as after, the fourth century. In that century, the learned writer observes, the monastic life came, for the first time, to be designated, on the ground of the words in Matt xxii. 30, a *vita angelorum*, the monks, like the angels, neither marrying nor being given in marriage. The old interpretation of Gen.vi. 1–4, however, taught that, although the angels in heaven marry not, yet that, once, a portion of them, seduced by the beauty of womankind, came down from heaven to earth, for the purpose of gratifying their amorous propensities: and as angels in heaven had yielded to such a temptation, a weakness of the like kind in one of the "earthly angels" might be the more readily excused. That the passage in Genesis was actually so abused, and pleaded as an apology for monkish trangressions, Kurtz infers from expressions used by Theodoret and Cyril of Alexandria: and it was therefore, he thinks, a ready and natural expedient for preventing such abuse of the Bible passage,—an expedient suggested, no doubt, by the New Testament usage of the expression "Sons of God"—to convert angels of heaven into angels of earth: holy beings above, into pious men below: these pious men being drawn from the ranks of the Sethites, on the ground, we may feel assured, of Aquila's erroneous rendering of a clause in Gen. iv. 26, hereafter to be noticed. This expedient would be adopted the more willingly, as some change

in the old interpretation of "Sons of God," was imperatively demanded by the practice of angel-worship then gaining ground.

If we regard this second cause assigned for the change in question, as consisting merely in the desire to find a ground, on which allowance might be made for the frailty of monks, it may be doubted whether it was concerned, in an equal degree with that already mentioned, in effecting the substitution of the Sethite for the angel-explanation. The cases we conceive, would not be many, in which delinquents of this kind, however numerous they might be, and possibly were, would seek to excuse themselves on such a ground. It may be doubted also, whether it would have occurred to theologians in the fourth century, or been deemed advisable by them, to discard the interpretation of a passage of Scripture, till then generally received in the Church, and one which had the sanction of nearly all the Fathers of the first three centuries, and to substitute for it an explanation till then unheard of, merely for the purpose of meeting such cases, should they occur. At the same time, that the regard, then prevailing, for the monastic life and celibacy, had a share in bringing about the change, is probable, for this reason, that the newly-devised explanation of our passage (especially as it appears in the writings of some Sryian and other Oriental Christians, to whom chiefly is due the embellishment of the story) was evidently famed with the intention, not only of removing what might seem to be inconsistent with the purity and holiness of angels, but also with a view to give countenance and encouragement to the practice of celibacy and monkery.

Indeed the originators of the Sethite-explanation, and those who exhibited it in their writings, appear to have proceeded on a two-fold plan—that is to say, they naturally sought, in the first place, to produce a story, which might resemble the narrative of the sacred writer, or, rather perhaps, the version of it presented in the Book of Enoch, so far as the circumstances would allow: and secondly, they seem to have been desirous that their account of the occurrence should lend support to the unwarrantable practices which led to its introduction. Accordingly, as the angels came down from heaven to earth, to visit the daughters of men, and descended, according to the Book of Enoch, on Mount Hermon, so the new interpreters exhibit the sons of Seth as dwelling together on that mountain, and thence descending to the plain below, to converse with the daughters of Cain (Cedrenus, Eutychius, and Bar-Hebraeus.) The apocryphal book places the occurrence in the time of Jared—a view, however, for which there is some ground—and the Oriental writers make a like representation. Pseudo-Enoch fixes the number of angels at 200, and Syncellus and Bar-Hebraeus give the same as the number of the Sethites. The angels are called *watchers* in the apocryphal book, and the Sethites receive the same title from Syncellus and Cedrenus. Indeed the narrative of the latter (See Note L) bears a close resemblance throughout to that of Pseudo-Enoch. Finally, the giants are described by some of these writers in terms agreeable with what may be inferred respect-

ing them, from the sacred narrative, but regarded, of course, as nothing more than human. On the other hand, to suit the special purpose of the new interpreters, the pious Sethites appear as abstaining from marriage, leading lives of holiness and devotion to the service of God, and bearing the title of *angels of God* (Eutychius and Bar-Hebraeus), so long as they maintained their virginity and purity! Kurtz (*die Ehen, p.* 43) notes these features of the Sethite-explanation, and in Note 15 gives the legend as it is found in Ephraem Syrus, the Ethiopic Book of Adam, and the Chronicon Syriacum of Bar-Hebraeus.

From the time when this interpretation succeeded in supplanting the old one, it might not unfairly be said to have been the universally received one in the Church, so very small was the number of expositors, until within a period comparatively recent, who supported the claims of any other interpretation. Not until the rise of Rationalism, in the last century, did the angel-interpretation again find favour with Christian Theologians. From that time to the present, it has met with general approval from those who have entertained the opinion that the narratives of the Pentateuch partake in part of a mythical character. (Note C.) For this adoption of it by the Rationalists, Dr. Keil assigns as a reason, the opportunity thus afforded them of pointing to a piece of mythology (in which light only he and they regard the angel-story) in the pages of the Old Testament. It was probably one of the reasons which may have influenced them. The rationalists, however, are not the only ones who have adopted it, for, in our own times, a large number of divines on the Continent, and some in these countries, who acknowledge fully the claims of the Bible to be a Divine revelation, and desire not to explain away those uncommon or supernatural occurrences which it records, have also pronounced in its favour. This restoration to some extent of the ancient exposition to its former place in the favour of theologians is attributed by Kurtz chiefly to the revival of Biblical exegesis which took place in the last century. That this was the principal cause of a return to the true interpretation of the passage, not only in the case of orthodox, but also of rationalist divines, we may believe, although the latter abused the Sacred Record, thus correctly interpreted, to serve a purpose of their own. Grammar and lexicon, to use the words of the same writer, then assumed their rightful place in the exposition of Holy Writ, and the old dogmatic prejudices, which had induced so many, in past times, to set aside the angel-interpretation as heretical and absurd, were, in the case of not a few, triumphed over and removed.

Suppositions and Assumptions in Support of this View—Cainites and Sethites—Their Moral and Religious Character

Though no objection could be urged, on philological grounds, against the claims of this exposition to be regarded as the true one, we should still hesitate to adopt it, depending for support, as it does, on suppositions and assumptions, for which hardly any grounds exist. These have already, in some measure, been indicated in the remarks of Dr. Maitland; but may be here fully set before the reader, together with those Scriptural expressions and facts, which appear to have furnished for them a foundation of some sort. The Sethite and Cainite exposition of our passage assumes:—

1. That the posterity of Seth formed, for several generations, a community distinct and separate from the descendants of Cain, as well in point of moral and religious character, as of local habitation: that their devotion to the service of God was so warm and conspicuous, and their moral conduct so faultless, that not only did they themselves think it allowable to use the title "Sons of God," or "Sons of Jehovah," but that that title was so generally recognised as belonging peculiarly to them, that Moses having occasion to refer to them in his narrative, might with full propriety, designate them by it, as a title the application of which was not, in the least, liable to be mistaken.

2. That Cain's descendants, in the same period, constituted another community, equally distinct from that of Seth; that they were universally, but especially the female portion of them, characterised by irreligion, carnal-mindedness, and profligate life: that the Cainite women were further

distinguished by personal beauty—a quality in which, the exposition implies, the women of the race of Seth were wanting: and, finally, that Moses, making mention in the same historical writing of these female descendants of Cain, might, without any apprehension of being misunderstood, describe them as "the daughters of men," or "the daughters of Adam."[16]

For these assumptions the only grounds which appear to exist are:—

1. An erroneous translation of the last clause of Gen. iv. 26, hereafter to come under consideration, which represents Seth as having received the appellation of "Θεός," *God*, on account, it is explained, of his eminent piety—his descendants, it is added, having, on that ground, been known to their contemporaries as the υἱοὶ τοῦ Θεοῦ, *Sons of God*. The expositors—coupling this with the fact, that in some passages of the Old Testament, the chosen race are called "Sons of the Lord God," Deut. xiv. i, and "Sons of the living God," Hosea x. i: and that, in the New Testament, believers are sometimes called "the Sons of God"—arrive at the conclusion, that the *Bne-ha-Elohim* of Gen. vi. 2 were pious men, descendants of Seth, known to the men of their time as "the Sons of God."

2. The record, Gen. iv. 16, that "Cain went out from the presence of the Lord, and dwelt in the land of Nod, on the east of Eden"—the existence of separate genealogical tables for the families of Cain and Seth—the personal characters and brief history of Cain and Lamech—the inventions of Lamech's sons, indicative, as is imagined, of utter worldly-mindedness on the part of the Cainite race—and, finally, we may add, the signification, "lovely" or "graceful," attributed by some to the name Naamah. From these it is inferred that the two families constituted, for some generations, two distinct tribes, dwelling apart one from the other: and that not merely had Cain himself become an apostate from the service of God, but that all his descendants—especially the Cainite women, supposed to be eminently beautiful—followed in the course of estrangement from God on which their ancestor had entered, and were universally characterised by impiety and depravity of manners.

3. In addition to this somewhat slender Scriptural foundation for the superstructure which these expositors have raised upon it, some support for their views was, probably, afforded by Josephus, who writes (*Ant.* I. iii. i and II. ii., *Whiston's Transl.*) that "the posterity of Seth continued to esteem God as the Lord of the universe, and to have an entire regard to virtue for seven generations;" while, of Cain and his descendants, he records that the former, having travelled over many lands, finally settled at Nod: and that the latter "became exceedingly wicked, every one successively dying one

after another more wicked than the former: that they were intolerable in war, and vehement in robberies: and if any one were slow to murder people, yet was he bold in his profligate behaviour, in acting unjustly, and doing injuries for gain."

On these grounds it has been assumed that the Cainite and Sethite families formed two tribes, separate from each other in place, in character, and in name, continuing completely, or nearly so, to the time when the godless alliances took place. How far if at all, such an assumption is warranted by what the Biblical history or tradition relates, it may be worth while briefly to inquire.

That these families, if at any period they formed two distinct tribes, had, at all events, become blended together, for a considerable time previous to the Deluge, and that any distinction, religious or otherwise, originally existing between them, had long been obliterated, will be admitted, we suppose, even by advocates of the Sethite-interpretation. That any such distinction, however, did ever really exist, or that the Cainites and Sethites did, at any period of their history, form two tribes completely separate one from the other, we find nothing in the Sacred Volume to warrant us in concluding, and regard as more than doubtful. The geographical situation of the land of Nod, in which Cain settled after his departure from the place of the revealed presence of God, and which, no doubt, received its name from Cain himself, condemned to be a fugitive and an exile, cannot be determined,

though attempts have been made by Bochart, Huetius, and later writers to ascertain it. India, China, the territory known as Susiana, to the north of the Persian Gulf, Syria and Lydia—the last two indeed, lying west, not east of the primeval dwelling-place of man— each has been suggested by one or more writers, as probably the region in which Cain's settlement was made. Could it be shown that Cain, before he found an abiding-place, had travelled—as Josephus expresses it, "over many countries"—to a land so remote from the scenes of his early life, as the countries now called India or China must have been, we might readily believe that his descendants constituted a race, as widely separated from that of Seth in religion, and manners, as in the place of their habitation; and that a lengthened period must have elapsed before any sort of intercourse could have subsisted between them. But far more probable is the opinion—nor is it inconsistent with anything that appears in the Mosaic record, unless, indeed, we suppose that prolonged wandering on the part of Cain, was a necessary consequence of the Sentence pronounced upon him—that Cain effected a settlement in some land at no very great distance from Eden. Of this opinion the LXX. appear to have been, describing the land of Nod as κατεναντι Εδεμ,[17] "over against Eden." In this case the various intercourse sure at once to spring up between his descendants and those of Seth, would effectually prevent the possibility of any such distinction of races, as that which is supposed. Quite in accordance with this view is the statement quoted by Lambert de Daneau from Philo

Judaeus, that alliances in marriage between Cainites and Sethites, were first brought about by the former—Enoch, the son of Cain, having sought a wife of the daughters of Seth—and that the connexion of the two lines, thus formed at their very commencement was continued through succeeding generations. Whatever value may be attached to the statement of Philo, it shows, at all events, that tradition was not altogether on the side of the inventors of the Sethite-interpretation.

An opinion has been entertained by some divines (see Kurtz I. 91: Del. 173), founded on the identity and similarity of names in the two genealogical tables, ch. 4, 5, that these are only different forms or versions of one primary legend in which were set forth the origin and development of the primeval race: the one version placing Cain at the head of the series of Patriarchs, while the other places Seth. If the correctness of this view (entertained, we believe, for the most part by writers of rationalistic tendencies) could be established, the main ground on which the Sethite and Cainite interpretation rests would be removed: and, indeed, Dr. Keil, while rightly denying the identity of the genealogies, is constrained to admit that the identity and similarity of names may prove that the two branches of the human race did not keep entirely apart from each other—a fact, as he adds, established by their subsequent intermarrying. We must reject the opinion of the identity of the tables, however, were it only for the reason assigned by Dettinger (quoted by Kurtz and Delitzsch, p. 173), that the more detailed particulars furnished respecting the persons named Enoch

and Lamech in both genealogies, were, no doubt, designed, as they are sufficient, to prevent the possibility of these persons being regarded as identical. At the same time we do not think that the Sethite-exposition of our passage derives much support from the fact of the existence of separate genealogies. The intention of the Sethite table was, not only to furnish a chronology of the primeval age, but still more to afford the means of tracing that privileged line, to which Messiah was to belong, and in which the Church of God was to be maintained to the time of His appearing. There was thus special reason for keeping this line separate from that of Cain, while the latter serves a valuable end, in that it has left on record the names of distinguished inventors of arts, and probably furnished a key to a portion of the heathen mythology. We may thus discern a reason why the Sacred Writer, under the guidance of the Holy Spirit, or in accordance with His special revelation, kept these genealogies distinct; and we will be the less disposed to regard such distinction as a proof, that the two families constituted two tribes, dwelling completely apart from one another.

That long before the coming of the Deluge, the race of Cain, and, not less, that of Seth, were spread over regions far removed from the abode of the first human family, may be regarded as certain. And, in connexion with this fact we recognise one of the absurdities attaching to the Sethite-story, as it appears in the pages of some of the Oriental Christian writers—that of confining the Sethites to a lofty mountain, as their place of abode, and the Cainite race to the plain or valley beneath: and this, as they say, in the 40th year of the Patriarch Jared (=A.M. 500, Heb: A.M. 1000, Sept.)—a period at which (even though we follow the Hebrew computation) the human family must have spread itself over no inconsiderable part of Western Asia—an inference we are warranted in drawing from the fact, that the races descended from the sons of Noah spread themselves, in less than 500 years from the Flood, over regions extending from the Euphrates to the Mediterranean, and from Mount Ararat to the Nile.

The question is not, were all the branches of Adam's family so united at the period of the Deluge, as to form but one great family—the human race—for this is not denied; but were the Sethite and Cainite branches of that family at first, and for some centuries, so distinct from one another, not only in point of the localities which they occupied, but still more of their moral and religious character, and their generally recognised names, that Moses might speak of the Sethite men as the *Sons of God*, and of the Cainite women as the *Daughters of men*, without any apprehension that his words would be misunderstood. We do not think there is anything in the Sacred narrative to lead us to such a conclusion.

The question of the moral and religious character of these families deserves attention. Commentators generally, whatever their interpretation of our passage, appear to be agreed that wickedness and the worldly mind were as characteristic of the Cainite family, as piety and virtuous conduct were of the family of Seth. Indeed Dr. Kurtz (I. 91) says that undoubtedly the genealogy of Cain has been left on record for the purpose of showing more clearly the opposite direction in which the development of these two lines tended, and that, on this ground, it closes with Lamech, the sixth from Cain, in whom the ungodliness of the family reached its climax. That this view of the character of both families, is not without some foundation must be admitted. But that the character attributed to either belonged to the individuals of it, so generally as seems to be supposed by some, may well be doubted. We may admit that Cain lived and died in a state of alienation from God: but does it therefore follow that all his posterity through several generations, must have been in the like condition. Nay, who will affirm that even his own immediate family must certainly have been so? Subsequently to the fourth chapter of Genesis, no special reference is made to the race of Cain. His descendants flourished with the rest of mankind, to the time of the Deluge, and are included amongst those denoted by האדם (vi. I). Some of the race have been famous to this day, as the originators of certain arts and occupations indispensable to the maintenance of civilised life, or contributory to its enjoyment. Strange to say, this distinction has been generally alleged as an indisputable evidence of the worldly-mindedness of the entire race, as though an aptitude for artistic pursuits, and devotion to them, or to the peaceful occupations of pastoral life, were incompatible with devotion to the service of the Great Artificer, and Shepherd! With the exception of the recorded incidents in the lives of Cain and Lamech, the names of those who formed the intermediate links in the chain, and the notice of the Cainite inventions, nothing is related of the descendants of Cain, as distinguished from the rest of mankind—not a hint is given with regard to their character or their acts, their piety or their impiety—until we arrive at the period of the Deluge, when we gather from the narrative that they in common with the rest of the world—but not, so far as appears, in any greater degree—were grossly and daringly wicked.

Let us not ascribe, [says Dr. Kitto,] all the evil of the old world to the race of Cain, nor cast any needless stigma upon the great fathers of useful arts who are named as of his race. It was not until the times just before the Flood that the corruption became universal; and then it was not confined to the seed of Cain, but extended to all but one small family of the race of the righteous Seth, not to speak of the descendants, probably numerous, of the other sons and daughters whom the Scripture assigns to Adam. We may hope that, in the earlier ages, there were many, even in Cain's race, who lived and died in the fear of God.—(*Daily Bib. Illustr.*— *Antediluvians*, p. 99.)

We cannot but sympathise in the hope thus expressed by this writer, who at page 128 of the same volume has adverted to a circumstance eminently worthy of our regard, namely, the signification of the names borne by the Cainite Patriarchs, as suggestive of dis-

positions and aspirations not ordinarily associated in our minds with the people of that family.

It is clear, [he writes,] from the reasons assigned [in a former section of his book] for the names which Eve gave to her sons, and from that which the Sethite Lamech gave to his son Noah, that these names are all significant, and that they expressed the views and hopes with respect to their children, of those by whom these names were imposed. Many of them are holy and good names, and some of them contain the sacred name of God, and seeing that such names occur in the line of Cain, as well as in that of Seth, it may be questioned whether the opinion (founded chiefly on a doubtful interpretation respecting the 'sons of God' and 'daughters of men') that Cain's race were all unholy and evil-minded people, is founded in truth.

Having shown the significance of the several names in the Cainite genealogical table, he concludes thus—

Among these names, all that are not humble are holy, with the exception of one (Irad) which bears an indifferent local sense. Out of five names two contain the name of God; whereas out of eight names in the longer line of Seth, only one contains that name. We find not among these names, one that is arrogant, boastful or defiant—such as our notions respecting this family might lead us to expect. All are just the reverse, and are such as would not have disgraced the line of Seth. This is assuredly a point worthy of notice, with respect to an age in which names were facts and expressed sentiments.

The entire passage is worthy of perusal by those for whom the history of the primeval race possesses an interest, enabling us as it does to contemplate the race of Cain in a somewhat different light from that in which many have been accustomed to regard it.

But if we have not sufficient grounds for believing the race of Cain to have been universally irreligious and profligate, neither will we be justified in coming to a directly opposite conclusion respecting the descendants of Seth. The family of Seth was chosen, as the branch of the human race from which the Promised Seed, the Messiah, was to spring; and hence the descent of that family continues to be traced through Shem (Gen. v., &a, 1 Chr. i., &C.) after the almost universal destruction of mankind: the Cainite genealogy on the contrary extending not beyond the sixth generation from Cain, thus reaching perhaps nearly to the time of the Deluge. But while this honourable distinction attached to the family of Seth, it does not follow that all the members of that family, or the greater number of them, must have been God-fearing men, or even externally blameless in life and character. As well might we say, that the entire Jewish nation, of whom Christ came according to the

flesh, consisted of godly and virtuous individuals, at the time of the Incarnation. At all times there have been those who have preserved in the world the knowledge of the true God, and who showed, by their godly life, that they were children of God: but, the probability is, that, at all times, the many were "alienated from the life of God." That no exception in this respect would have been found in the case of the descendants of Seth, when they had become numerous in the world, we feel assured. There is nothing in the Sacred Record, from which we might infer that they were involved in a less degree, than Cain's posterity, in the prevailing corruption which preceded the judgment of the Flood: and while there could, no doubt, have been reckoned amongst them, during the course of their history, very many who were, not in name, but really, children of God, yet that at any period of their history, they were universally so remarkable for their attachment to true religion as these expositors suppose, and of such repute for virtue, as to be entitled to, and known by, the designation of the "Sons of God," is a supposition which the sacred narrative does not warrant, and which does not accord with human experience.

Rendering of Gen. iv. 26—(last clause)

It was observed, previously in this work, that amongst the grounds which have been alleged in support of the Sethite-exposition, and on which it has been supposed that *Bne-ha-Elohim* may lawfully be taken to denote pious men, descendants of Seth, the last clause of Genesis iv. 26, wrongly translated, occupies a place. The investigation of this portion of our subject would be incomplete, were we to omit all notice of this clause—translated, as we believe, correctly in our Authorized Version—because, not alone has Aquila's erroneous rendering of it been employed to support their interpretation of our passage, by Theodoret and other Fathers, and by many expositors since their time,[18] but also because other meanings have been assigned to this statement of the Sacred Writer, and especially one by some eminent Jewish commentators, no mean authorities in matters which concern their own language. As the passage has been adduced for the purpose of sustaining an objectionable explanation of Gen. vi. 1–4, though really having no connexion with the subject of the latter, an inquiry into its meaning cannot be deemed irrelevant.

Of the clause in question, which is, in the original, אז הוחל לקרא בשם יהוה, at least four renderings have been proposed:—

1. "Tunc coeptum est profanari in invocando nomine Jehovæ."—*Tremellius and Junius.* "Then began men profanely to call on the name of the Lord."—Ainsworth.[19]
2. "Then began men to call themselves by the name of the Lord."—*Marginal Reading,* A. V.
3. "Then was it begun to proclaim (or, prophesy) in the name of the Lord." —*Maitland.*

4. "Then it was begun to invoke (or, call on) the name, of the Lord."—*Vulgate, Syriac, etc.*

1. Of these several modes of rendering, the first has the support of Onkelos and Jonathan, of Maimonides and other rabbins, and of the Arabic version edited by Erpenius (Bp. Patrick). These suppose that the passage informs us of the introduction of false worship and idolatrous practice into the world. Ainsworth, in his commentary on this place, and the Abbe Banier (Mythology, I., p. 163) quote a long passage from Maimonides' Treatise on Idolatry, intended to shew that false worship had its origin in the days of Enos— the patriarch himself being one of those who erred—that the heavenly bodies were the first objects of religious adoration: and that the evil rose to so great a height, that, at length, except in the case of a few, "the glorious and fearful Name of God was forgotten, and men acknowledged Him not" Others, besides the rabbins, both in ancient and modern times, have likewise believed that false or idolatrous worship had its beginning in the antediluvian times. It was the opinion of the late Archbishop Whately, amongst others.

Whether false religion was introduced before the Flood, we are not, [he says,] expressly told, but there is every reason to think it must have been. For, we read that mankind had become excessively wicked, and that this brought on them that terrible judgment; And all experience shews that great moral depravity and gross religious corruption accompany each other.

Referring to the passage in Gen. iv. 26, the Archbishop says that it seems, although it be only an obscure hint, to relate to the first introduction of false gods in the times of Enos.

The sense of the passage, [he writes,] certainly cannot be, that Divine worship was then introduced for the first time: which, we know from the preceding history (ch. iv. 3), was not the case. But it probably means that, then, those who worshipped the true God, began to apply to Him some distinct name or title, such as *Adonai* or *Jehovah*, to distinguish Him from the pretended gods worshipped by others: and that they called themselves 'by His Name'—that is, described themselves as His worshippers—to distinguish themselves from those who served other gods.—(Lessons on the History of Religious Worship, pp. 38, 39.)

These opinions have been controverted. Dr. Maitland (Essay on False Worship) says that, while "the records of the antediluvian world furnish but little information respecting the worship of the true God, they say absolutely nothing, of idolatry or the worship of false gods." This, he adds, is a very remarkable fact, and one which the reader should keep in mind, when commentators tell him about the pious descendants of Seth, and the idolatrous progeny of Cain. This writer thinks that the language of the strong statements in verses 5, 11, 12 of Gen. vi. might be made to include the worship of false gods, if we found reason elsewhere for believing that it was then practised. But he does not know where any evidence of this can be found, and observes that, while "our Lord, in His reference to the days of Noah, speaks of the sinful carelessness and carnal security—perhaps of the sensual sin—of the antediluvians, he does not suggest any idea of idolatry." Another able writer of the present day says,

Though we know little of the impiety of the world before the Flood, further than that it was extreme in its violence socially, and in its presumption against God, we are not necessarily to infer, that idolatry had become its crime. There is no intimation of such crime, but simply of wickedness and violence between man and man, and of defiance of Divine warnings and judgments: so that it is *possible* that, till the age after the Flood, the worship of any created object, as God, was a thing not precedented, at known, or even conceived of. (*Ancient Empires*, Rel. Tract Soc., p. 96.)

Dr. Maitland connects the whole of the heathen belief with the events of which our passage contains the record. He believes that the first false worship was introduced by the sinning angels, and that they were themselves the first objects of it. It should, however, be observed that if, as tradition relates, and as is not improbable, the fallen angels appeared in the world some hundreds of years before the Deluge, false worship, admitting it to have been first introduced by them, might have been widely prevalent long before that event.

Some of those who hold the opinion of the general depravity of the Cainites, regard the statement in Gen. iv. 26, as having special reference to them, on the ground that a Sethite race could not, at the time, be said to exist: and, adopting this Jewish interpretation of the clause, conceive that they have thus an additional argument in favour of the Sethite and Cainite explanation of our passage. To us it appears that if the statement were to be restricted to a particular section of the human race, that section should be the family of Seth, inasmuch as it occurs in immediate connection with the first mention of that Patriarch and his son, and after the genealogy and special history of the Cainites had come to a close. But we do not believe that sufficient reason can be shewn for any restriction of the kind, or for supposing that the public adoration of Jehovah (the institution of which we think the words relate) was practised by the Sethites only. However that may be, the rabbinical interpretation of the clause is grammatically inadmissible. We have examined the usage of the sacred writers, in the case of the verb חלל, with a view to ascertaining whether it can bear, in this place, the signification which the Jewish interpreters assign to it: and we think that any reader, who might take the trouble of making a like examination, would, with us, come to the conclusion, that הוחל, in Gen. iv. 26, cannot have any such meaning as that

of *profane*, and consequently that there is no room for the interpretation which some rabbins have put upon the passage.

2. The second of the translations given above is found in the margin of our English Bible, as one which the translators thought the clause might bear. It is supported by the version of Aquila, and, on the ground of his rendering, by Theodoret (Quæst 47 in Gen.)—

When Moses had related, [says this Father,] that Seth was born to Adam, and Enos to Seth, he added, Ουτος ηλτισεν εκικαλεισθαι το ονομα Κυριου του νοεΘ. Aquila has interpreted this passage, Τοτε ηρχθη του καλεισθαι τω ονοματι Κυριου—intimating that he (Seth or Enos) first received, on account of his piety, a Divine appellation, and was, by his kindred, styled Θεος; hence those sprung from him were called '*Sons of God*' even as we are called *Christians* from the name of our Lord Christ. [The original may be read in Suicer's Thesaurus, s.v. αγγελος, and is quoted by Kurtz, p. 34.]

Cyril of Alexandria (cont. Jul, lib. 9) and others, who defend the Sethite-interpretation of our passage, understand the clause in Gen. iv. 26, in a similar way, and suppose that the posterity of Seth, so styled *Sons of God*, were the *Bne-ha-Elohim* of Gen. vi. Even were such a rendering of the clause allowable, it might still be objected that the title in Gen. vi, in order to be in keeping with it, should be, not

Bne-Elohim, but *Bne-Jehovah*. But the rendering is not admissible. The verb קרא is used, in conjunction with the noun שם, very frequently throughout the Hebrew Scriptures—sometimes, to express the idea of *invoking or calling on*, the name of another—sometimes, to express the very different notion of *calling*, or *being called by*, or *after the name of anyone*. The forms of expression in these two cases, different enough in English, are even more so in Hebrew, as anyone will see, who may inspect, as we have done, the passages in the Hebrew Bible in which such expressions occur. It will, we think, be evident to him, that such translation of the clause in Gen. iv. 26, as that which the marginal reading of our English Bible exhibits, is at variance with the grammar and usage of the Hebrew language: and that, had Moses intended to say, in this place, that men "began to call themselves by the name of the Lord," the construction of the sentence would have been very different from what it actually is.

3. The explanation of this passage proposed by Dr. Maitland, in his essay on False Worship, is, in our judgment, deserving of attention. Rejecting the notion, that mankind had lived to the time of Enos, without prayer to God, or the invocation of His Name, he gives it as his opinion that we are here informed that, then, for the first time, men were commissioned to take upon them the office of prophet—meaning, by the term *prophet*, one who either predicted future events, or announced Divine commands, or performed a miracle—doing these things under supernatural, that is. Divine influence—and who, in virtue of this Divine commission or authority, formed the link between the visible and the unseen world.

It seems, [he says,] as if there had been prophets from the days of Enos, for so I think we must understand, 'Then began men to call upon the name of the Lord'—Gen. iv. 26. Who can believe that mankind lived on for centuries without prayer to God, or the invocation of His Name? and yet I know not what else our translators would have us to understand by the words which I have just quoted. Can they mean anything but that hitherto men had not been wont to 'call upon the Name of the Lord'?

Having referred to the Jewish interpretation of the clause, as if possible still more unsatisfactory, he says,

As to the passage of Scripture itself, surely we may say that, simply construed, it means that from that time forth men began to speak, or proclaim, in the Name of the Lord. It is barely possible, that if we had not the long sacred history which follows, we might be more or less in doubt, as to the meaning of the phrase; but what can be more plain, when we are expressly told that Enoch, the seventh from Adam, prophesied (προεφήτευσε, Jude 14), when Noah is described as a preacher of righteousness (δικαιοσυνης κηρυκα, 2 Pet. ii. 5), and these early prophets are followed, in Scripture history, by a long line of chosen and inspired men, crying to one generation after another, "Thus saith the Lord"?

Considerable grounds exist for this interpretation. The verb קרא is undoubtedly used in the sense of proclaiming as a herald or prophet (Prov. i. 21; Isa. xl. 6; ixi. i; Jer. xxxiv. 8; Jon. iii. 4), and often rendered by the LXX. by κηρυσσω, the usual Greek word in such cases. That בשם יהוה may denote "in the name of," *i.e.*, "by the authority of," the Lord, will be evident from a consideration of such passages as Deut. xviii. 5, 7, 22; I Sam. xvii. 45; xxv. 9.

4. The rendering of our Authorized Version—"Then began men to call upon the name of the Lord," or as it might, more accurately, be, "Then was it begun to call on the name of Jehovah," has the support of the Arabic (Saadias), Syriaq, Samaritan, and Vulgate versions, and is entirely in accordance with the usage of the Hebrew language. Commentators, however, who approve of this translation, are not agreed as to its meaning. Parkhurst (Heb. Lex.) explains the passage as does Archbishop Whately. The Bishop of Ely (Speaker's Comm.), who understands the words as referring specially to Seth, says that there is not any good ground for the notion that emphasis is to be laid on the special name of God, Jehovah, as though then, for the first time. He was invoked under that name: he thinks the most natural sense of the Hebrew is, that when Enos was born, Seth in gratitude and hope began to call on the Lord, with reassured hope in His mercy and His promises. Dr. Murphy (*Comm. in loc*) advances the

opinion that not until the time of Enos did men venture to offer *audible* prayer to God—that while the pious in all the preceding years from the Fall, no doubt trusted in, and conversed with each other in humble hope respecting the mercy of the most High, they were yet restrained by a sense of guilt from making any advances—beyond the bringing of an offering—towards the Infinitely Holy God; but that now, at length, in the days of Enos, they began to call on the name of the Lord—they ventured to express, in audible voice, the desires and feelings that had long been pent up within them.

To us, the meaning attached to this passage by many commentators—namely, that it records the institution, in the time of Enos,[20] of public united Divine Service, over and above that private invocation of the Deity, by individuals, and most probably by families also, which we cannot but think was practised from the first—commends itself as a probable one. Whether this explanation be adopted, or that of Dr. Maitland, which also appears to be consistent with the usage of the language, we must, in any case, reject both the Jewish interpretation, and that of Theodoret, founded on the version of Aquila.

Bne-Ha-Elohim, not pious men, but angels

We have endeavoured, in Sections VII. and VIII., to show what slender grounds exist for the assumptions on which the Sethite-explanation of our passage is founded: but even though these assumptions could be shown to have a more substantial basis than they appear to have, and the families of Cain and Seth to have been, in all respects, as distinct from each other, as has been assumed—this should not be allowed to affect the interpretation of the text, which ought to be determined, not by considerations of this kind, but on the grounds of exegesis, in accordance with the rules of grammar, and the usage of the Hebrew language. Especially, if we have reason to conclude that the term Bne-ha-Elohim can be intended only to denote angels, then all such considerations as those referred to, must be regarded as entirely beside the question.

Dr. Keil, having referred (Pent. 128) to the use of *Bne-ha-Elohim* in the book of Job, where, he admits, the term unquestionably designates angels, and to the antithesis "sons of God" and "daughters of men," in Gen. vi. 2, goes on to say, that "apart from the context and tenor of the passage, these two points would lead us most naturally to regard the sons of God as angels, in distinction from men and the daughters of men."

"But this explanation," he continues, "though the first to suggest itself, can only lay claim to be received as the correct one, provided the language itself admits of no other." He then adduces certain passages of Scripture, as proof that godly men are sometimes called "Sons of Elohim," and arrives at the conclusion, that this title is not to be restricted to celestial spirits, but is applicable to all beings which bear the image of God, or by virtue of their likeness to God, participate in the glory, power, and blessedness of the Divine life—and therefore, that the expression, *Bne-ha-Elohim*, "cannot be elucidated by philological means, but must be interpreted by theology alone." He thus makes it manifest that, with him, as with all who reject the angel-interpretation, dogmatic considerations, respecting the nature of angels, are allowed to govern exegesis. As we cannot but recognize the soundness of the principle now generally maintained by interpreters, that we should arrive at the meaning of a passage of Scripture, not by means of any preconceived opinions respecting it, but chiefly or solely on exegetical grounds, as well as of the further principle, that we should not assign to a word or phrase, any signification which is not supported by the *usus loquéndi* of the sacred writers, when a signification, which is so supported, yields a good and appropriate sense—so do we fully concur in the opinion expressed by Dr. Kurtz, with regard to *Bne-ha-Elohim*, that the exegete is not at liberty to put upon it, in Gen. vi., any other meaning, than that which confessedly belongs to it in those other places, in the Bible, in which it is found, "unless he can show that the idea of *angels* is utterly inapplicable there, that it is clearly and unmistakably excluded by the context." "This (he adds) is so far from being the case, that it is imperatively demanded, both by the nature of the passage itself, and by the context."

It does not appear to us to be necessary, for the purpose of ascertaining the meaning of this term, to enter on any inquiry respecting the derivation or radical signification of *Elo-*

him, or the grounds on which the title of *Bne-Elohim* is given to angels. The latter inquiry, indeed—whether Moses may here have used *Bne-ha-Elohim* as a *nomen naturae*, applicable alike to holy and fallen angels, instead of Maleachim, their *nomen officii*, as messengers of God[21]—would, of necessity, assume that the signification of *Bne-ha-Elohim* had been already determined: whereas the question for the interpreter of Gen. vi. 2 is, What is the signification of the term in this place? Is it applied by Moses to angels, and can they only be intended by it? The answer to this question can be furnished only by an examination of the *usus loquendi* of the writers of the Hebrew Scriptures; but when we have thus ascertained the signification of the term, our belief in the correctness of that signification will be strongly confirmed by considering the general tenor of the passage, and the connection in which it stands.

The expression בני האלהים translated in our Authorized Version, "the sons of God," is found (in addition to Gen. vi. 2, 4) in three places in the book of Job, viz., i. 6, and ii. I.—"There was a day when the sons of God (בני האלהים) came to present themselves before the Lord"—and xxxviii. 7, "All the sons of God (בני האלהים) shouted for joy." In these passages the LXX. render the Hebrew by ἄγγελοι, and all commentators, ancient and modern, we believe, concur in the opinion that only angels can be meant. It appears, therefore, to be as reasonable as it is natural that we should understand the expression similarly in our passage. Nay, more, unless convincing reason be shown to the contrary,

we are bound, on every principle of right interpretation, to assign to it precisely the same signification, namely, that of angels. Dr. Keil, indeed, objects to this, and says that *Bne-ha-Elohim* may have had, in the time of Solomon, (the period to which he and some others assign the composition of the Book of Job), a very different meaning from that which it had at the time when Genesis was written. But this objection is sufficiently met by his opponent, on the ground that the Hebrew language underwent but little change—as, indeed, the other allows—from the Mosaic age to the time of the captivity, at least, as compared with that to which the languages of the West have been subjected: and that it is, therefore, only reasonable to believe that the signification of *Bne-Elohim* remained unchanged. It should, however, be observed here, that solid grounds, exist for the opinion, that the Book of Job—which both these writers assign to the age of Solomon—belongs to a very much earlier period: that its composition was not later, at all events, than the time of Moses, and, not improbably, prior to that of the Exodus from Egypt. These grounds have been often pointed out.[22] If the authorship of Job, as well as of Genesis, may be ascribed to Moses himself, as some Rabbinical and other writers, have, not without reason, supposed, the argument, in favour of our interpretation of *Bne-ha-Elohim*, derived from the *usus loquendi*, possesses, it will be seen, still greater force than it would have in the case of different, even though contemporary, writers.

It has been well observed by E. H. Engelhardt, that, in the case of a narrative so brief, as that in Gen. vi. 1–4—one which barely indicates the events—it was all-important that the meanings of the terms employed should be so definite, as to preclude all possibility of their being misunderstood. "If the term *Bne-ha-Elohim* might have a two-fold signification—an ethical as well as a physical—and thus admit of an application, not only to angels, but to men, the writer should have expressed himself so, as to guard against the danger of the term being wrongly applied."

But, inasmuch as Moses has simply used this term, without explanation or addition of any kind, "it must have had, in his view, a perfectly exclusive and well-defined meaning, and one which he felt would be obvious to the mind of every reader." That this way was so, we entertain no doubt. The expression *Bne-ha-Elohim* must have been, at least at the time of the writing of Genesis and Job—whether these were composed in the same or in different periods—an established and recognized term for designating a particular class—a title so generally known, that the historian takes it for granted (See Kurtz, 48) that his readers, happening on the word, would, at once, and as matter of course, know who were the persons intended by it.

There are two other expressions, met with in the Hebrew Bible, similar in form to *Bne-Elohim*, and probably kindred in point of etymology (See Gesenius, Lexicon, אל, and Nägelsb. 51), which have been adduced in support of the rendering of Bne-ha-Elohim, for which we contend. These are בכי אלים (Psalm xxix. I, and Ixxxix. 7), and בו אלהין (Dan. iii. 25). Dr. Kurtz believes that, if we take these expressions into account, in conjunction with those in the Book of Job, the proof of the correctness of our rendering becomes complete, inasmuch as in all the passages (as he feels assured) angels are unquestionably meant; and, in all of them, expressions are employed, wholly or almost identical—אלים being substantially the same as אלהים, and the Chaldee אלהין not only substantially, but literally, the same word, conveying the same idea as the Hebrew אלהים. We are not disposed to attach, to the terms in the Psalms, so much importance, in reference to our interpretation of Bne-ha-Elohim, as the learned writer does: because, however similar in form to the latter, they are still different expressions, and also because they do, at least, admit of another rendering than that of *angels*, and have, by some interpreters, been understood to mean *the great* or *mighty ones of earth*. Bishops Patrick and Horne, Ainsworth, and the translators of the English Bible understand them so [23]: and it may be observed that even the seventy do not use ἄγγελοι in these Psalms, as they do in the passages of Job, in which *Bne-Elohim* occurs. With regard to בו אלהין the case is somewhat different; and although, as has been objected, the expression is not Hebrew, but Chaldee, yet it may fairly be taken into account in an inquiry respecting the meaning of *Bne-ha-Elohim*, not alone on the ground assigned by Kurtz, that it is literally the same with Elohim, but also, we may add, because there can be no doubt that, whether it was the Second Person of Deity, who should in the fulness of time become incarnate, or else a created angel, that appeared with the Hebrew youths in the burning furnace, the term denotes, at all events, a superhuman being.

The more closely we have examined the subject presented to us in this passage of Holy Scripture—the more that we have pondered the recorded facts, and the various circumstances connected with, or bearing upon, them—and the more that we have investigated the meaning of the language employed by the sacred writer—the more decided has become our conviction, that the *Bne-ha-Elohim* could have been no other than angels. When we find that, in the four passages in which it occurs, the expression meets us without any explanation of its meaning—this, at least, in the time of the writer, being well understood—and that, in three of these, it can designate only angels: when we see that to assign to it, in the remaining passage, the same signification, is consistent at once with the facts which are there related, and with the connexion in which the passage stands—that it accords with all the circumstances, and meets the requirements, of the case—and that, only when we thus understand the term, can these ends be attained—we cannot but think that, to reject this signification, and substitute for it that of *pious men*, is, not merely to set aside the true and natural meaning, but it is, further, to propose an interpretation, which is not supported by the *usus loquendi*, and which, moreover, involves not only improbabilities, but even some absurdities.

Amongst the arguments advanced by the defenders of the Sethite-interpretation, in support of their view, a principal one is derived from the fact that, in the Old Testament, the Israelites are spoken of as the "first-born son of Jehovah" (Exod. iv. 22), "the children of the Lord God" (Deut xiv. i), and "sons of the Living God" (Hosea i. 10—in the Hebrew Bible, ii, I): and that believers are sometimes, in the New Testament, styled "sons of God:" and, also, that in Psalm lxxiii. 15, the writer addressing Elohim, speaks of the righteous as דּוֹר בָּנֶיךָ, "the generation of thy (*i.e.*, Elohim's) children," whom he is supposed thus indirectly to call *Bne-Elohim*, This passage in the Psalm, Dr. Keil regards as strongly supporting his interpretation of *Bne-ha-Elohim* in our passage. Advocates, generally, of the Sethite-exposition maintain that it is erroneous to suppose, that such titles as Sons of God, or Sons of Jehovah, were introduced for the first time when Israel was chosen to be the covenant nation.

They deem it probable—proof is out of the question—that they were applied to pious men, even in the antediluvian times. The following extract from Keil's Commentary on the Pentateuch will exhibit to the reader the views entertained on the subject:—

So much is true, indeed, that before the adoption of Israel, as the firstborn son of Jehovah (Ex. iv. 22), it would have been out of place to speak of Sons of Jehovah: but the notion is false, or at least incapable of proof, that there were not children of God in the olden time, long before Abraham's call, and that, if there were, they could not have been called 'Sons of Elohim.' The idea was not first introduced in connection with the Theocracy, and extended thence to a more universal signification. It had its roots in the Divine image, and therefore was general in its application from the very first: and it was not till God, in the character of Jehovah, chose Abraham and his seed to be the vehicles of salvation, and left the heathen nations to go their own way, that the expression received the specifically theocratic signification of 'Son of Jehovah,' to be again liberated and expanded into the more comprehensive idea of Elohim, at the coming of Christ, the Saviour of all nations. If, in the olden time, there were pious men, who, like Enoch and Noah, walked with Elohim, or who, even if they did not stand in this close priestly relation to God, made the Divine image a reality, through their piety and fear of God, then there were sons (children) of God, for whom the only correct appellation was 'Sons of Elohim,' since sonship to Jehovah was introduced with the call of Israel, so that it could only have been proleptically that the children of God in the old world could be called 'Sons of Jehovah.'

It is, undoubtedly, true that Enoch and Noah walked with God, and were "Sons of God" in the highest sense—in that sense, in which the expression is used in the New Testament: but there is no proof, nor any reason to believe, that they, or any of the posterity of Seth, or, indeed, any other of mankind, were ever styled "Sons of Elohim"—nay, rather, we may assume with tolerable certainty, that they never were. To say, that there *may* have been pious men, in the antediluvian age, on whom that title was bestowed, and to assume that the *Bne-ha-Elohim* of Gen. vi. *may* have been of the number, is a mode of argument not very convincing.

Dr. Kurtz has discussed, at some length, the question of Divine sonship, both in his treatise, "Die Ehen," etc., pp. 52–54, and in his History of the Old Covenant, II., 193–6, and has pointed out what he conceives to be the idea involved in the term "Son of God." To us it does not appear to be necessary, for the purpose of elucidating our text, to enter on an examination of the subject: nor can we, indeed, wholly avoid thinking that, to speak of *generation*, with reference to the origin of angels,[24] savours somewhat, as Keil has hinted, of the Gnostic doctrine of Æons; or else it does not convey any definite idea to the mind. It is sufficient, we think, to say, that the terms used in Scripture to express the filial relation between the chosen race, or the pious, and God, are not the same with that in our passage: and the fact of their being applied to such persons, does not warrant a like application in the case of *Bne-ha-Elohim*, nor does it furnish any ground for the interpretation which the Sethite expositors have adopted: Expressions such as בכים ליהוה אלהים (Deut. xiv. I) and בבי אל חי (Hosea ii. I, Heb.) may be employed to denote the children of God in the ethical sense: but these expressions are very different from that in our text, and an argument, founded on the use or application of the former, cannot avail to determine the meaning of the latter, and; in fact, such argument is inadmissible.

It may not, perhaps, be unimportant also to observe—as tending to illustrate the difference in the use of these expressions in the Hebrew Scriptures, and to shew that the idea of using *Bne-ha-Elohim* in the ethical sense, never occurred to the sacred writers—that those terms which are confessedly used in that sense, are never found in a situation analogous to that which *Bne-ha-Elohim* occupies in Gen. vi. In other words, the expressions which denote Divine sonship, in the ethical sense, whether in the Old or New Testament, never stand in the place of subject, but always in that of predicate, in the sentence. When such appellations as *Bne-El-chai* (Hosea ii. I), or *Banim la-Jehovah* (Deut. xiv. I), or υιοτ Θεου, in the New Testament, are applied to men, the persons so entitled appear, not in the character of actors, as do the *Bne-ha-Elohim* in Gen. and Job, but only as passively concerned in the matter or event, in connection with which they are mentioned—indeed, generally, or always, as recipients of spiritual blessings.[25]

If these titles, then, might not be applied to the people of God, when they are presented in the former capacity, does it not seem strange that *Bne-ha-Elohim* should never have been used in such cases? It is, certainly, unaccountable that the latter term has not been employed in any one of the many passages, in which it might thus have been fitly introduced, if, as we are told, it may have the signification of holy men, or believing children of God. Amongst passages of the kind to which we refer, may be mentioned Ps. xxxvii. 29, and Prov. xi. 28, in which צדיקים occurs, and,

as specially to our purpose, Ezra ix. 2, "They have taken of their daughters for themselves, and for their sons, so that the holy seed (הקדשׁ זרע) have mingled themselves with the people of those lands: yea, the hand of the princes and rulers hath been chief in this trespass." The singular analogy which may be traced between this passage, and verses 1 and 2 of Gen. vi., as the latter are understood by the Sethite and Filii-magnatum interpreters, is very worthy of notice in connection with our present remarks. If *Bne-ha-Elohim* could, properly, be used, in the ethical sense, might it not have been employed, with entire fitness, in this passage of Ezra, to designate "the holy seed"?

The Antithesis—"Sons of God"— "Daughters of Men"

Whatever may be the signification assigned to the terms Bne-ha-Elohim and Bnoth-ha-Adam, it must be evident to a reader of the passage, that, in verse 2, a contrast between the former and the latter was intended by the writer—Sons of Elohim: Daughters of Adam. So long as the Bne-ha-Elohim were regarded as angels, and Bnoth-ha-Adam taken in its natural and obvious signification, this contrast was plainly apparent—Angels of God: Daughters of Men. But when the old interpretation came to be discarded, and pious men, descendants of Seth, to be substituted for angels, it was seen that if the Bne-ha-Elohim were men, the plain signification of the other term failed to convey the idea of contrast evidently intended, and, therefore, that some more suitable antithesis must be found than "daughters of men," that is, womankind in general. Hence the meaning of Bnoth-ha-Adam was adapted to that newly assigned to the other term; instead of being allowed to retain its old and proper signification, it was now restricted to the women of the race of Cain; and the required antithesis then appeared—Sons of God, *i.e.*, pious Sethite men: Daughters of Men, *i.e.*, ungodly Cainite women.

This interpretation of Bnoth-ha-Adam, adopted by Christian writers, when the angel-explanation was abandoned, was the all but universally received one in the Church, for centuries, and has supporters still. The inconsistency, however, involved in taking האדם in different senses in verses I and 2, has been already (III.) noticed, and must have been apparent to all. "The supposition that the Sons of God were the sons of Seth, and the daughters of men (Heb. Adam) were the daughters of Cain, to whom great numbers of very beautiful women were born (it is supposed), has no foundation in Scripture: nay, it is against Scripture, for Seth was not God, and Cain was not Adam." (Rev. Theoph. Campbell, in *Irish Eccl. Gazette*, April, 1867.) Were the expression to be translated, as it might be, "Daughters of Adam," or, as Dr. Murphy renders it in his Translation, "Daughters of Man," it would perhaps be more likely to make, on the mind of the English reader, the impression which Moses assuredly meant to convey, namely, that the parties to these unlawful alliances were of earthly origin, on the one side, but not on the other: that the one were human beings, denizens of earth, the other, superhuman, belonging to another sphere.

Accordingly, some theologians, as Hengstenberg, Hävemick, C. F. Keil, perceiving the inconsistency referred to, have exchanged this interpretation for another, not open, as is imagined, to a similar objection. This modification of the Sethite-exposition has been alluded to (VI.), and may now be more fully explained. Dr. Keil, in his essay on our passage (Zeit, p. 242), quoting the words of an opponent of the Sethite-interpretation, that "Bnoth-ha-Adam, in verse 2, cannot mean daughters of the family of Cain, inasmuch as, just before, in ver. I, האדם is used to denote the whole human race, without any distinction"—pronounces the remark to be just, but observes that it had been long before made by supporters themselves of the Sethite view, and adduces in proof a passage from the *Dubia Vexata* of Augustus Pfeiffer—a treatise, we may add, on difficult passages of Scripture, printed at Dresden, in 1679. Dr. Keil remarks that the objection of his opponents lies, not against the interpretation which he approves, and which he styles that of the Church; but only against that which rendered Bnoth-ha-Adam, Cainite women, and which, he says, has been given up, as untenable, by more accurate Biblical investigators.

For the purpose of setting before the reader this explanation of Bnoth-ha-Adam, together with the argument advanced in support of it, we quote a passage from Dr. Keil's Commentary on the

Pentateuch (I. 130)—

The antithesis, *Sons of God* and *daughters of men*, [he says,] does not prove that the former were angels. It by no means follows that, because in ver. I האדם denotes man as a genus, *i.e.*, the whole human race, it must do the same in ver. 2, where the expression "daughters of men" is determined by the antithesis "Sons of God." And, with reasons existing for understanding, by the Sons of God and the daughters of men, two species of the genus האדם, mentioned in verse I, no valid objection can be offered to the restriction of האדם, through the antithesis Elohim, to all men with the exception of the Sons of God, since this mode of expression is by no means unusual in Hebrew.

From the expression 'daughters of *men*,' [as Dettinger observes,] it by no means follows that the Sons of God were not men: any more than it follows from Jer. xxxii. 20, where it is said that God had done miracles 'in Israel and among *men*, or from Isa. xliii. 4, where God says He will give men for the Israelites, or from Judges xvi. 7, where Samson says, that if he is bound with seven green withs, he shall be as weak as a *man*, or from Ps. lxxiii. 5, where it is said of the ungodly, they are not in trouble as *men*, that the Israelites, or Samson, or the ungodly, were not men at all. In all these passages אדם (men) denotes the remainder of mankind, in distinction from those who are especially named.

Dr. Keil adds that cases occur, even in simple prose, in which the same term is used, first in a general, and then directly afterwards in a more restricted sense; and having cited one from the Book of Judges, in which the expression "tribes of Israel" means the rest of the tribes, with the exception of Benjamin, although the Benjaminites also were Israelites,[26] he draws the conclusion, that the fact of the Sons of God being distinguished from the daughters of men in Gen. vi. 2, does not prove that the former could not be men.

According to this explanation, it would appear that, while האדם in verse I designates the *whole human race*, in verse 2 the Bne-ha-Elohim and Bnoth-ha-Adam are two distinct portions of the race, the former being men of the family of Seth; the latter, daughters of the rest of mankind, *i.e.*, women belonging to the Cainite and all other branches of the human family, with the exception of the Sethite only. The Sethite men, captivated by the remarkable beauty (of which they are supposed to have been possessed) of these daughters of the rest of men, chose wives from amongst them, in preference to the women of their own tribe.

This view is approved of by the Bishop of Ely, in his notes on our passage in the Speaker's Commentary. He thinks it probable that, of the various interpretations which have been proposed, the right one is a modification of the old Cainite and Sethite-explanation—this modification being that which has been noticed, viz., the inter-marriage of *godly Sethites* with *women of the rest of mankind*. We are not justified, he remarks, in saying that there were only *two* races, those of Cain and Seth, descended from Adam: and, supposing that the Sethites were then *the Church of God*, he thinks they "may well have been called 'the children of God,' a term by no means limited in Scripture to the holy angels."

While this interpretation of Bnoth-ha-Adam gets rid of one inconsistency, that of taking it to mean the women of the race of Cain, it involves another hardly less glaring. "What right have we," says Kurtz, p. 60, "to understand Bnoth-ha-Adam in verses I and 3 as referring to the whole of the human race, including the pious Sethites, and in verses 2 and 4, as referring to the whole race, exclusive of those Sethites?" The right, however, thus to limit the meaning of the term is not merely defended, as we have seen, on the ground of the antithesis *Elohim*: but such limitation is said to be "the more natural, as one member of the antithesis is far more insignificant than the other—the number of the sons of God being so small, compared with the great corrupt mass of mankind, that the essential idea contained in Ha-Adam remains unchanged"—*Hengstenberg, Beiträge z. Einleitung ins* A. T. 11., p. 331, quoted by Kurtz, p. 59, and by Keil. (*Zeit* p. 242, n.)

Without dwelling on the assumption that the Sons of God, or pious Sethites, formed only a very small body in comparison with the rest of mankind—only one, indeed, of the many groundless and arbitrary assumptions, by which the whole of the Sethite-hypothe-

sis is supported—it is sufficient to say that, to assign to האדם, in verse 2, the signification which these commentators thus propose, is a proceeding, for which the cases adduced by Dr. Keil do not afford sufficient authority. In none of these cases could any doubt exist as to the meaning or application of the various terms—Israelites, the ungodly, &c.—no necessity to inquire, who or what are the persons they are intended to designate. But it is otherwise in our passage, where the question to be determined, before all others, is, who or what are the Bne-ha-Elohim? The interpretation put upon Bnoth-ha-Adam, takes for granted what needs to be proved, namely, that the Bne-ha-Elohim were *men*—a point which Dr. Hofmann observes (I. p. 86) should have been previously established by better proof than a reference to chap. iv. 26. Besides, it is merely a delusion to suppose that, interpreting *Bnoth-ha-Adam* thus, the essential idea in *Ha-Adam* remains unchanged. The idea conveyed by האדם, in verse I, that of the *whole human race*, and the idea which we are required to annex to it in verse 2, that of the greater portion of the race, are very different ideas: and to understand this term, in verse I, in the former sense, and in the following verse as denoting, either the family of Cain, or all mankind with the exception of the Sethites, is to proceed on a principle opposed to all true exegesis. (See Kurtz, 59–61, and Keil, Zeit, 242.) The inconsistency of taking האדם in different senses in verses I and 2, is avoided by one of the latest commentators on Genesis, Dr. Murphy, whose explanation of Bnoth-ha-Adam agrees with ours: but inasmuch as he believes the other parties to the alliances to be but men, the result is not more satisfactory. "Some," he says, p. 178, "take the *daughters of man* to be the daughters of the Cainites only. But it is sufficient to understand by this phrase the daughters of man in general, without any distinction of a moral or spiritual kind, and therefore, including both Cainite and Sethite females." But in this case, all contrast disappears, and as the question of moral and religious character is, in great measure excluded, even the slender and insufficient grounds, which the *Cainite*-interpretation assigned for the increased moral corruption of the human race, are, in a proportionate measure, taken away.

We have already, in examining the Jewish-interpretation of the passage, inquired into the meaning of *Bnoth-ha-Adam*: we only add, that the antithesis "Sons of God" and "daughters of men" appears to us, as we think it must to every unprejudiced person, to militate strongly against the Sethite-explanation. Even Dr. Keil, probably the ablest defender of the latter, allows to it, as we have seen, some weight. The *Sons of God* appear in contrast with the daughters of men, and the natural inference undoubtedly is, that the former belonged to another order in creation, than that of human beings.

Improbabilities involved in this view

It is almost unnecessary to call attention to the several improbabilities—we might even say, absurdities—which the Sethite-explanation

of our passage involves, analogous, as they are, with those already (III.) pointed out as attaching to the Jewish-interpretation. As in that case, however, we may remark how utterly improbable it is, that alliances so incongruous should have been so extensively formed. Let us assume, with the expositors, that the men of the race of Seth were entitled to the virtuous and godly character ascribed to them, and must it not appear incredible that they should so generally, indeed universally, as it seems, have united themselves with persons of such opposite character, as the daughters of Cain, and of the rest of mankind, are represented to have been? Were there fewer women in the Sethite, than in any other branch of the human family, in proportion to their respective numbers, that they were thus obliged to look beyond the limits of their own tribe? We might rather infer the contrary from chapters iv. and v., as we find frequent mention of daughters in the line of Seth, while in that of Cain there is only one whom we can affirm to be of Cainite origin. (Note D.) There is, indeed, a reason assigned in the Scripture— "the Sons of God saw the daughters of men that *they were fair*"—but that the characteristic of personal beauty belonged to Cainite women exclusively, or to all the female descendants of Adam, at that time, excepting only those of the family of Seth, is an idea not to be seriously entertained—one, for which the history of the antediluvian age furnishes not the slightest foundation, unless, indeed, we suppose it to be found in the signification of the name of Lamech's daughter, Naamah or Nöema, = fair or *graceful*, as it is interpreted by some. The narrative simply declares that the daughters of Adam—the female members, not of the Cainite, or any family in particular, but of the race in general, the women then in the world—were regarded as beautiful by some of the angels, who, under the influence of that attraction, left their proper habitation, and, having come down to earth, went "after strange flesh"—formed unlawful connections with beings who belonged to an order different from their own.

Amongst considerations of minor importance, which should incline us to reject the Sethite-explanation, Dr. Kurtz suggests one, which may be fitly mentioned here, as showing further the unreasonableness of that exposition. We refer to the fact, that the marriages in question were those of *Sons of God* with *daughters of men*, but in no instance, of *sons of men* with *daughters of God*.

In other words, the unholy alliances were sought and contracted (on the Sethite hypothesis) by pious Sethite *men*, but none by pious Sethite women. Undoubtedly, this must be viewed as a strange and anomalous fact (Kurtz refers to Gen. xxxiv. i6, and Judges iii. 6), and one for which it is impossible to account: but the difficulty vanishes at once, when we believe that the Sons of God were not descendants of Seth, nor men of any tribe, but angels who lusted after the beauty of daughters of men. (Kurtz, p. 63.)

Probably, however, the most astonishing fact, connected with the (supposed) marriage of pious men with fair, but godless, women, was that it resulted in the production of a race of giants—"mighty men which were of old, men of renown"—a result, indeed; as little to be expected in this case; as in that of the *Filii-Magnatum* and their lowly wives, and one which, in either case, it requires no small effort of faith to realize. (See Maitland, *Fallen Angels*, 134.) We need not, here, dwell upon this point, as we shall, presently, have occasion to advert to it again. We purpose, also, in a later section, to take notice of the supposition, that the unequalled moral corruption, impiety, and deeds of violence, which characterized the antediluvian time, and rendered necessary the awful Divine visitation of the Deluge, were the necessary effects of those intermarriages of the virtuous with the profligate—a supposition which we cannot but regard as utterly erroneous, the cause thus assigned for the existence of that enormous evil, being quite inadequate to the production of such an effect.

CHAPTER THREE

THE ANGEL-INTERPRETATION

Alleged Impossibility

Of the history of this, the oldest interpretation of our passage, some particulars may be gathered from the preceding pages. What further we may be able to impart on the subject, we reserve to the close of chapter iv. Should the arguments which have been, or may yet be, advanced in support of the angel-explanation, so weigh with the reader, as to incline him to believe in its correctness, the knowledge that this view was maintained by the ancient Jewish synagogue, by Hellenistic Jews at, and before, the time of our Saviour's sojourn on earth, and by the greater number of the early Christian writers—may serve to give confirmation to his belief. Meanwhile, we proceed to consider the grand objection urged against our view,—that which constitutes the real

cause of its rejection by the many—namely, that we are not able to explain or comprehend how such an occurrence as that which we suppose could take place.

We have already examined, at some length, the Sethite-interpretation, and shown, as we cannot but think, sufficient reason for concluding it to be inadmissible. We took notice, in the first place, of the causes which led to its substitution for the old explanation of the passage—causes which induced theologians to disregard philological and exegetical considerations, in obedience to preconceived dogmatic views. We pointed out some reasons for doubting whether such distinctions, as those which the expositors assume, ever really existed between the Cainite and Sethite branches of the human family. We sought to prove that *Bne-ha-Elohim* and *Bnoth-ha-Adam* cannot have the significations which the Sethite-interpreters affix to them—that the former, in the only other places in the Old Testament, in which it is found, can denote only angels: and that, unless some better reason for rejecting it can be shown, than the impossibility of fully comprehending the nature and mode of the occurrence, the same signification should be given to it in Gen. vi. We showed further, that there is no reason to suppose, but rather the contrary, that such a title as that of "Sons of God" was ever borne by the posterity of Seth, or by any, in antediluvian times—that the expression "daughters of men" denotes not women belonging to one family or class, but simply women, in general, without distinction of any kind—and that this term does not convey any idea of contrast, if the sons of God be regarded as nothing more than men. Finally, we noted certain improbabilities which the Sethite-exposition involves. It will be our object, in this and the following chapter, to offer other arguments in support of our interpretation—to show, that the circumstance of the angelic intercourse being incomprehensible or inexplicable by us, is not a proof of its impossibility—and, in a word, to advance whatever further grounds we may, for believing that the *Bne-Elohim* were angels, and the *Gibborim* something more than men.

The fourth verse of Gen. vi. says, according to our Authorized Version, "There were giants in the earth in those days: and also, after that, when the sons of God came in unto the daughters of men, and they bare children to them, the same became mighty, men which were of old, men of renown." We have already remarked, that this result of the inter-marriage—according to the view so long and so generally entertained—of pious sons of Seth with ungodly Cainite women, namely, the production of a noted race—"mighty men of name"—famous in all ages—is a result for which we would hardly be prepared. Who would not be surprised to find that a race of mighty heroes, of gigantic proportions too, had sprung from the unions of pious men with godless women; and that—not in the case of some few of these alliances, but of all! Nor indeed would such a result be less unexpected in the case of the alliance of men of exalted rank with women of humble station; or men of the family of Seth with daughters of the rest of mankind; or of any other of those incongruous unions which some expositors imagine Moses meant to record. But such a result would not be so improbable, or, we may add, under the circumstances so unnatural if the fact was, that an extraordinary intercourse had been carried on between angelic and human beings—between inhabitants of the visible, and of the invisible world. In this case, we would look for something extraordinary as the result. Such a result the Sacred Record announces—"When the sons of God came in to the daughters of men, and they bare to them, the same became mighty men, which from ancient times have been of distinguished name."—the writer evidently intending to convey to the mind of the reader that the offspring of the Sons of God and daughters of men were so pre-eminently raised in power and might, above others who were then on the earth, that they were still famous in his own time. And this, indeed, is only what we would expect. It could not create in us any surprise, were we told that the progeny, in part, of superhuman beings—mighty, though fallen—had exhibited marks of their superhuman origin, and that these had appeared in the form of gigantic physical proportions, prodigious strength of body, violent, malignant, or sanguinary disposition, or of vast intellectual power—in short, that they had borne, in some shape, the impress of the higher nature—of the might and power of the spiritual beings, to whom they partly owed their existence. And this very fact, that these "mighty men" of the antediluvian age were possessed of such attributes as those referred to—a fact to shew that they differed widely from those who, in modern times, have been reputed giants," the latter, we believe, having usually exhibited a feebleness and inactivity both of mind and body.

This fact, then, which appears from the record, that from these unnatural unions proceeded a race so remarkable, as to be described in the terms of verse 4, is of itself a strong presumptive proof of the correctness of our interpretation: while the general tradition, respecting the gigantic size, vicious propensities, and deeds of violence, of the *giants*, tends to confirm our belief of its truth. "For the tradition," says Josephus, "is, that these men did, what resembled the acts of those whom the Grecians call giants."[27] Accordingly, the fact has been adverted to by several of those who defend the angel-hypothesis (Engelhardt, Kurtz, and others), and that that view derives from it no small support, appears to us to be undeniable. "The gigantic dimensions," says Nägelsbach, "are not human: it is not the Adamic image, created after the Divine type, which shews itself in such colossal corporeal development"—p. 399. Nevertheless, it is objected, that however probable such a result, in the way of offspring, might be, if the supposed union of angels with womankind were a reality, yet that we cannot believe the latter to have been the case, inasmuch as, not only has our Lord declared that angels neither marry nor are given in marriage; but such a union must be concluded to be an impossibility, in consequence of the different natures of these classes of creatures. The nature of angels, it is alleged, is spiritual and immaterial, and therefore renders impracticable any conjunction of the kind supposed.[28]

It might be sufficient to say, in answer to this, that we know too little of the nature, essence, powers, or capabilities of angels, to warrant us in making a positive assertion as to what they can or cannot do: and that, in such case, everything must be regarded as possible, until the absolute impossibility of it be demonstrated.

I know so little of the nature of angels, says Dr. Maitland, replying to an objection of the kind, and of the limits of possibility, that I feel it safest to borrow the language of St. Augustine on this point, and say 'non hic aliquid audeo temerè definire.' (See Note G.) It does not appear to me more incredible, or more remote from my ideas of a spirit, than that angels should assume the human form, and eat the calf of Abraham,[29] and the unleavened bread of Lot. When the objector has explained these facts he will perhaps be able to explain the other. This however is not the point. All that I contend for is, that credible or incredible to man's wisdom—whether congenial or foreign to his conceptions of things in which a pretence to knowledge is mere folly—whether apparently possible or impossible—the fact is stated in the Bible, and that so plainly that the wisest commentators have been reduced to childish absurdities in attempting to evade it. (*Eruvin*, 135.)

This is true. All reasoning and preconceived opinions must give way to opposing facts: and these facts are plainly presented in the only legitimate interpretation of our passage. We find it stated that the *Bne-ha-Elohim* (whom we cannot but conclude to be angels, for this point we regard as established even by what has been already advanced), did, in the days before the Flood, form such alliances with human beings, as the objectors declare to be impossible: and this being so, we are bound to believe the fact, however difficult it may be to understand, or to explain, how such an extraordinary union could take place. It is worth while, however, more fully to consider the objection, which appears to rest on two distinct grounds—1. The declaration of Christ, Matt. xxii. 30.—2. The spiritual nature of angels, and their supposed incorporeality.

Declaration of Christ, Matthew xxii. 30.—Objection from the supposed Immaterial Nature of Angels

From the statement of our Saviour, recorded in Matt. xxii. 30, and also in Mark xii. 25, and Luke xx. 35, 36, it is inferred that the acts, which our explanation of Gen. vi. 2, 4 attributes to angels, are impossible. This inference is thus met by Kurtz—"The statement of our Lord amounts only to this, that all sexual intercourse is plainly contrary to the nature of the *holy* angels, from which it is by no means to be concluded that angels, fallen from their original, holy state, may not be capable of wicked action contrary to their proper nature"—and briefly, but forcibly, by Nägelsbach—"The angels do not marry in *heaven*, and therefore our passage does not contradict the declaration of the Lord." (See Kurtz, 88.) This might suffice for a reply to the objection. At all events, that our view is absolutely irreconcilable with the words of Christ, is what the objectors can by no means prove.

But we are not disposed to lay too much stress on the argument which the writers named, and especially the former, have advanced, with regard to the sexlessness of angels, or their capability of acquiring sexual power. That angels are, in their original state, sexless, appears to be the unavoidable conclusion, not only from the Saviour's statement referred to, but also from the fact—regarded by Dr. Nägelsbach (67) as furnishing even more ground for the opinion—that they always appear in the Bible as of the masculine, the higher gender (used in the case of beings in whom sexual distinctions do not exist, and where no such distinction is implied or intended), and with masculine names. We meet with *Bne-Elohim*, sons of Elohim, but never with *Bnoth-Elohim*, daughters of Elohim. Nowhere is there mention of female angels; while the idea of the marriage of angels, or of their propagation, is an idea absolutely unknown to Scripture. These writers, however, think it is not inconceivable that, although created without distinction of, or reference to sex, and destined by the Creator neither to "marry nor be given in marriage," they may yet have, latent in their nature, the power or capacity for the latter, rendering sexual intercourse not, in all circumstances, impossible—may have in their constitution the germ of a sexuality (if we may term it so) capable, under peculiar conditions, of being developed—just as the first man, though not created to sin, had in his original constitution the latent power or capability of sinning—a power which came into operation, in his departing from the ordinance of the Creator. In a like way might the unfolding of such latent power, in the angels, as that referred to—the development of such sexual distinction—be effected, as these writers suppose, by a wilful departure from their original

condition of existence, and their sinking to a lower and unnatural state, in their apostasy from God. From the fact that mankind, to whom in the present life belongs the distinction of sex, shall, in the resurrection, attain to that higher life, in which they neither marry, nor are given in marriage, and in this respect be equal to the angels—Dr. Kurtz thinks it not unlawful to infer that, in the event of angels falling, by their own wilful act, from the higher to the lower sphere of existence, a degradation of their nature, analogous to the elevation in the other case, may take place, and that thus may be developed that sexuality and procreative power, which pertained to the lower grade of life, but of which the principle or germ had always existed in the angelic nature.[30] (Kurtz, 96, 97—Nägelsb, 66, 67.)

However possible this may be—and, with our very limited knowledge, the possibility, at least, is not to be denied—it is, after all, but conjecture, and cannot be regarded as contributing anything to the support of our interpretation of Gen. vi. 2. The converse is rather the case. Our belief in the truth of the interpretation, and in the fact of the connexion between angels and human beings, which it implies, leads us to regard these conjectures as not unreasonable, or wholly groundless.

Accordingly, our opponents have some shew of reason on their side, when they refuse to admit that arguments of this kind possess any force—indeed, some even say they are meaningless—and maintain that the words of Christ must be held to apply to angels, under all circumstances, and in every condition. Dr.

Keil, referring to the statement in Matt. xxii. 30, and the parallel passages, says,

> When Kurtz endeavours to weaken the force of these words of Christ, by arguing that they do not prove that it is impossible for angels so to fall from their original holiness as to sink into an unnatural state: this phrase has no meaning unless, by conclusive analogies, or the clear testimony of Scripture, it can be proved that the angels either possess by nature a material corporeality, adequate to the contraction of a human marriage, or that by rebellion against their Creator they can acquire it: or that there are some creatures in heaven, and on earth, which, through sinful degeneracy, or by sinking into an unnatural state, can become possessed of the power, which they have not by nature, of generating and propagating their species. As man could indeed destroy by sin the nature which he had received from his Creator, but could not by his own power restore it when destroyed, to say nothing of implanting an organ or a power that was wanting before: so we cannot believe that angels, through apostasy from God, could acquire sexual power, of which they had previously been destitute.—*Pent.*, pp. 131–134.

The conclusive analogies, or clear testimonies of Scripture, which the writer requires, it is not possible to bring forward: but the fact of the intercourse of angels with women, and of the result of that intercourse, the production of a distinguished race, has been recorded by the inspired writer: and this alone affords a presumption in favour of the possibility suggested by Kurtz.

It is our part, at all events, to believe, simply on the ground of the record, that not only was such an occurrence possible, as that which our passage relates, and not contradictory of the statement of Christ, but also that it actually took place. The remark of Dr. Engelhardt is just—that we should not make our belief of such an event conditional on being shown the possibility of it: our conviction of the possibility must spring from our belief of the fact.

> The possibility of a thing, [says Kurtz,] remains, until the impossibility of it has been shown: but the impossibility can never be shown in this case, until we have a completely exhaustive knowledge of all that is possible to angels, in the way of sinful or unnatural degeneracy, within the limits of those powers and capabilities which may have been bestowed on them in their creation, and within those bounds which may be prescribed by the Supreme Ruler.

Of the difficulty supposed to stand in the way of our explanation of the passage, arising from the alleged incorporeality and purely spiritual nature of angels, which forms the second part of the objection which we are now considering, several solutions may be offered. We do not ourselves believe in the *purely* spiritual nature of angels: nor do we suppose that there is any being in the universe simply spiritual and immaterial save the One Infinite, who is above and beyond all time and space. We are disposed to ascribe, with some of the earlier Church Fathers, and some divines in modern times, a certain corporeality to angels.

We adopt the view of those who hold that the spiritual part of the angel is clothed with a body of subtile, refined, ethereal substance, analogous to that of air, or flame, and not perceptible by our gross powers of vision.[31] No one however supposes that the original angelic corporeality is of a nature adequate to the purpose implied in our interpretation of the passage: and hence one solution, at least, of the difficulty, which has been suggested is not dependent on the determination of this question, but available (so far as any value attaches to it) whether we regard angels as pure spirits, or as possessing, besides, from their creation, a corporeal form of some sort.

(I.) "Even though we should feel constrained," says Kurtz, "on biblical grounds, to decide in favour of the view of the absolute immateriality of angels, still there is nothing against the assumption, that angels, if they leave their heavenly habitation, for the purpose of taking up their abode on earth, are able, owing to the power of a spirit, even a created one, over matter, to fashion for themselves, out of the earthly elements into which they sink, a body analogous to the human." (p. 91.) There is certainly nothing against such an assumption, and there may even some grounds for it appear: but we cannot follow the writer, when he says, that, in the several appearances of angels mentioned in the Bible, we have evidence, not merely of the possibility of their doing this, but of the fact itself—because this is the very point which it would be desirable to have proved.

That the bodies in which angels appeared to Abraham and Lot (if real bodies, and not merely the appearances of them) were provided directly by the Divine Power, is quite possible: and hence, as already said, we do not care to maintain our cause by arguments founded on the appearance or acts of angels sent by God to execute His purposes. At the same time, when we know that, on these occasions, angels conversed with men, in forms which men themselves could not distinguish from human bodies[32]—that, in these, they could speak, eat, drink, as men do, and that, as Milton at least thinks—

—Not seemingly,
—Nor in mist, the common gloss
Of theologians—

and that, on these occasions, they are also called *men*—we might feel that even these circumstances afford *some* ground for our views respecting the Bne-Elohim. Besides, that bodies were, on such occasions as those mentioned in Genesis xviii. and xix., provided by the immediate power of God, and not by the power of the angels themselves, is an idea that does not commend itself to us, as we believe (what, indeed, is generally admitted) that the exercise, by the Divine Being, of miraculous power is reserved for those emergencies, in which there exists for it an absolute necessity, the end in view not being attainable in any other way. That no such necessity existed in these cases is clear. Angelic power is adequate—however inadequate ours may be—to the production of miracles. "For man to affirm," says Dr. Chalmers, "that nothing short of Omnipotence can suspend the laws of visible nature, would seem to presume a far more extended acquaintance with nature, and with the universe, than in fact belongs to him. For ourselves, we can perceive nothing like self-evidence in such an assertion. We cannot tell what may be the orders of power and of intelligence between us and God. We do not know either the limits or the extent of their agency in the affairs of this lower world. It appears to us a monstrous presumption to affirm, that no archangel, no secondary or intermediate being whatever, can perform a miracle. We, in fact, transgress the line of separation between the known and the unknown, when we make either a confident affirmation, or a confident denial, upon this subject. It is one of those things which are placed on the *terra incognita* beyond us: and it would comport more with the soundness and modesty of true science, just to acknowledge that we cannot say. What do we know about the constitution of the universe, or the concatenations of universal being: and, though warranted to believe in a Supreme and All-powerful God, is it for us to define the amount of permission, or of delegated power. He may have vested in the creatures who are beneath Him?"—*Evidences of the Christian Revelation*. By Thos. Chalmers, D.D., 1855, Book II., Chap, viii.

There is much sense in these observations:

and when we call to mind the assumption of the body of a serpent by Satan in the Garden—the feats of the magicians in Egypt—Satan's affliction of Job with bodily disease and other evils—and the New Testament cases of possession by demons of the bodies of men and beasts—all showing the exercise of miraculous power by evil spirits, in which it will not be pretended they were aided by Divine Power—and when we know that angels are "mighty" and "excel in Strength"—it appears to us not incredible, that the *Bne-Elohim*, who possessed, in the first instance, power sufficient to enable them to reach the earth—an orb remote beyond, perhaps, our conception, from "their own habitation"—might also possess the power, not to create out of nothing—a power belonging to God only—but so to combine existing elements[33], as to form for themselves bodies similar to the human: and if, in another period of the world's history, spirits of great force and intelligence could so take possession of the bodies and minds of living men, as, at one time, well-nigh to deprive them of life, at another, to impart to them a preternatural strength, and preternatural knowledge—it is not wholly inconceivable, that even to quicken an inanimate frame, which he had chosen to inhabit, and to invest it with ability to move and act, might not be utterly beyond the reach of a spirit of equal, or, perhaps, greater power.

(2.) Professor Kurtz, while he thinks it allowable to conceive of the acquisition by the Bne-Elohim of bodies, in the manner suggested above, prefers, nevertheless, accounting for it on other grounds. His views on the subject have been partly explained already, and may be further exhibited here. Believing that angels were, at their creation, invested with corporeal forms, he supposes that these are of a highly refined, ethereal substance, resembling light in appearance and rapidity of movement—that they "are not so crude and inflexible as ours, nor are they so well-defined and fixed in their outline, but rather possessed of a high degree of fluidity and mobility—that they do not oppose to the wishes of the eager spirit, the clumsiness and inertia of human bodies: but are rather the willing instruments of the spirit, subordinate to all its wishes, and completely adequate to all the wants and exigencies of spiritual life"[34]—in short, that they are possessed of a corporeality, so completely subject to the spirit within, that it yields unconditionally to the latter, not only when its desires are in harmony with the nature and Divine destination of angels, but even when they happen to be in opposition to these.

These subtile, yielding, corporeal forms, belonging originally to angels, constituted. Dr. Kurtz believes, the basis, ground, or condition of their embodiment in that earthly, fleshly corporeality, which he rightly regards as essential to the accomplishment of their ends. He thus recognizes, not the construction or assumption of a body wholly new, but only a change in the nature of the original corporeality—this change consisting in the condensation, the further materializing, and carnalization of their heavenly pneumatic substance—a change rendered possible by virtue of the power of angels, and realized by their volition, and consequent also, as he seems to say, on their wilful apostasy from God, and their fall from a higher to a lower state.

In accordance with this are also the views of Engelhardt and Nägelsbach. "How could the Bne-Elohim," says the latter, "appear on earth in the condition of earthly corporeality, capable of generation, if there had not been in their nature the germ of, or an adaptability for, it? Hence, to the like effect, Tertullian says (*De Carne Christi*, cap. 6), 'It is evident that angels do not, in their proper nature, bear a fleshly body, as being of a spiritual nature, and if possessed of a body at all, certainly of a body *sui generis*—yet such, nevertheless, that it may, when occasion requires, be converted to a fleshly substance like the human, so that they can appear to, and have intercourse with, human beings. And, as we are not informed from what source they derive this fleshly substance, we are at liberty to suppose, that it is one of the properties of angels, *ex nulla materia corpus sibi sumere*'"—that is, to acquire a fleshly body, not from any matter foreign to themselves, but simply from a change in their original corporeal forms—p. 278.

(3.) Should these views, or these modes of accounting for the acquisition of bodies by the Bne-Elohim be deemed unsatisfactory, there remains yet another way in which the difficulty may be removed: and this is a mode not open to some objections that might be urged against the others, inasmuch as it assumes only what most readers of the Bible admit has already taken place, though at a different period from that with which we have here to do. We refer to the possession of the bodies of men by evil spirits, at the time of our Saviour's sojourn on the earth. We do not discuss the question of the reality of the New Testament cases of demon-possession. We think Dr. Maitland does not put the case too strongly, when he says, that to deny this reality, amounts to a denial of Christianity; and that it is worse than a waste of time to argue the matter with one, who, professing to believe the Bible, refuses to admit that it tells us of the actual possession by evil spirits of human bodies. Those, however, who believe in the fact of demon-possession, will readily admit that what happened in the later period, might also have happened in the earlier: and that it is not absurd to suppose that, through the medium of human bodies, thus possessed, the Bne-Elohim may have had intercourse with the daughters of men. (Note F.) We have, in this way, a simple, but sufficient solution of the difficulty, which, undoubtedly, does present itself to the mind, when one is asked to believe that angels had carnal connexion with women. It rids us of the difficulty arising from a consideration of the spiritual nature of angels, or even of their spiritualized corporeality: while the result of the unnatural and extraordinary connexion is only in proportion to the cause.

We learn in the Gospels the effects which spirits were able to produce in human beings—how entirely they gained possession of both mind (Matt. viii. 28, Mark v. 5), and body (Matt ix. 32—xii. 22)—the more than human strength, which they imparted to the bodily frame (Luke viii. 29)—and in a word, how completely the powers and faculties of the human being were controlled, intensified, and directed by the demon—the former being, as it were, merely an instrument through which the latter worked—a garment with which the evil spirit was clothed—or else the two natures, in some incomprehensible manner, interfused, and the weaker overborne by the stronger. So likewise, in this case, the remarkable physical proportions, the superhuman strength, or the evil disposition of the *Nephilim*, would be but the natural effects of the influence exerted upon, or the power imparted to, the human beings, by strong but fallen spirits. It should be remembered, too, that possession by the Bne-Elohim (supposing it to have been) would not necessarily involve either the suffering, on the part of the possessed, of such physical or mental evils, as those to which the demoniacs of the Gospels were subjected, or the exhibition of that maniacal disposition and conduct which appeared in the case of some of the latter. Satan transforms himself into an angel of light, and adapts himself to the circumstances of the case: and these angels, in like manner, whether actuated by the old serpent, or proceeding on an impulse of their own, would act, of course, in a manner the most likely to accomplish the objects which they had in view.

It may be asked, indeed, whether Moses would not have related the occurrence quite otherwise than he has done, if the Bne-Elohim had really taken possession, as we have supposed, of living bodies, in order to attain their ends: and whether, in short, he would not have plainly informed us of the fact? We can only reply that every attempt to explain this strange event, must be more or less attended with difficulties: and if we are convinced of the reality of the occurrence, we must either adopt that explanation of it, which appears to be the most satisfactory, or else we must be contented to receive it as one of those mysterious things which we believe, but which we do not fully comprehend.

It must be added, that some of those who hold the Bne-Elohim to be angels, suppose that they did not become incarnate, or from any source possessed of *real* bodies; but that in their purely spiritual nature, or, at the most, in a subtile ethereal body, or with the appearance of a human body, they, in some incomprehensible manner, effected what our passage relates. Augustine (City of God, b. xv.), though he does not pronounce a decided opinion on the point, appears to think this not impossible. D. Henry More, also, a learned English divine and philosopher of the 17th century (a defender, indeed, of certain Platonic and Pythagorean notions, which, however, he believed to have been derived from the Hebrews, and to be of Divine origin), expresses (*Mystery of Godliness*, b. iii., c. 18.) the opinion, of which he offers some curious illustrations, that "an aery spirit, transforming himself into the shape of a man," may, in the circumstances referred to, supply his place, without being obliged to play the parts of the *Succubus* and *Incubus* (Note G.) Rev. Theophilus Campbell, writing in the *Irish Eccl. Gazette* (July, 1867), does not believe that the angels became incarnate. This hypothesis, while it may avoid difficulties of one kind, involves others as great: for

it is certainly as easy to conceive the assumption of a real body by a powerful spirit, as to comprehend how a purely spiritual influence could effect what is implied in our interpretation of the passage.

The Nephilim and the Gibborim

Whether we have succeeded, or not, in removing the grounds of the objections to our view, founded on the words of Christ, and on the nature of angels, the fact remains that an extraordinary race was brought into existence by the union of the Bne-Elohim with the daughters of men: and this alone affords, as observed, a presumptive proof, that the Bne-Elohim were more than human.

The reader will see that this presumptive evidence is, in no degree, affected by another difficulty which meets us, viz, that of determining with certainty the relations subsisting between all the classes of beings mentioned in verse 4. One of the most difficult, as it is one of the most important, questions to be answered by the interpreter of this portion of Scripture is, Are the *giants* (Nephilim), the *Sons of God* (Bne-Elohim), and the *mighty men* (Gibborim), three distinct classes? or, can the first-mentioned be shewn to be identical with either of the others?

That the Bne-Elohim and the Gibborim are not identical, is tolerably clear. But the latter question, it must be confessed, cannot be answered in a manner completely satisfactory. Dr. Kurtz remarks (what may be regarded as certain), that the first readers of Genesis had an advantage over those of the present day in this, that they understood exactly what Moses intended by the several terms. The constantly recurring article before each of them,—*the* Nephilim, *the* Bne-Elohim, *the* Gibborim, gives ground for believing that Moses speaks of what was well-known to his contemporaries, and that they, at least, had no difficulty in rightly applying these names: with us, the case is different, we have not the knowledge which they possessed, and therefore hesitate as to the meaning of words which they comprehended at a glance.

We think, however, that conclusions on the subject, in a high degree probable, may be arrived at: but, before proceeding further, it will be well to inquire into the etymology and signification of the terms כפלים and גורים. The word כפילים occurs in the Hebrew Bible only in Genesis vi. 4, and Num. xiii. 33. Some have concluded that the meaning of the term—*giants*, in the common acceptation of the word—is determined by the latter passage: a conclusion which has been arrived at on insufficient grounds.

The LXX. and Theodotion have rendered this word by γιγαντες. Onkelos, גבריא, *mighty* men. The Vulgate, *gigantes*, in Gen. vi. 4: *monstra, de genere giganteo*, in Num. xiii. 33. The Syriac, and Arabic of Saadias, by terms equivalent to *gigantes*. Symmachus, ßiāio, violent men. Aquila, επιπιπτοντες = those who fall, or rush, with impetuosity upon others. Those earlier Church Fathers, who denied

the superhuman nature of the Sons of God, as Augustine, Chrysostom, Theodoret, Cyril of Alexandria, seem to have understood the term in verse 4, in much the same sense as did Aquila and Symmachus. Amongst modern versions, that of Junius and Tremellius, for many years the most popular Latin translation in use amongst the Protestants, reads *defectores, i.e.* apostates from the truth: while the German of Luther has *tyrannen*, tyrants, because they were supposed to have oppressed the people.

The etymology of the word, Gesenius says, is uncertain. Some derive it from פלא or פלה to *separate* or *distinguish*, taking it to denote those who were in some way distinguished above other men: but, by the greater number כפל is regarded as the root, different significations, however, being affixed to the term *Nephilim*, according to the various senses in which that verb may be taken.

Thus Hofmann, (I. 86) supposed that *Nephilim* might be derived from כפל according to its signification in Isa. Xxvi. 19, and so denote those who were *cast forth* or *born* in an extraordinary way—a view which he is stated to have afterwards exchanged for another. Gesenius and Parkhurst derive from כפל, in the sense of falling on, or attacking an enemy, and regard the word as suitably translated by Aquila, επιπιπτοντες = *irruentes*.

Wholly improbable is the origin assigned to this term by the rabbins David Kimchi and Aben Ezra, and approved of by some moderns. These derive the word כפלים from כפבל, *to fall*, on the ground that men fell through terror at sight of those who were so called. Thus Aben

Ezra, on the word, in Gen. vi. 4—"Because the heart of one beholding them falls (אותם יפול לב הרואה), astonished at the height of their stature"—quoted in the Hebrew Thesaurus of Pagninus; and, in the "Concordantiae Sacr. Bibliorum Hebr." (Rome, 1621) of Calasius, "כפילים gigantes, homines magni, et inusitatae staturae aut magnitudinis sive altitudinis, quòd illorum timore homines cadant, ut R. Dav. Kimchi," &c.

Professor Kurtz, having noticed some of the derivations suggested, declares himself in favour of that from כפל, in the signification of falling from a higher place to a lower, and thinks that we may take it as denoting "the fallen down," i.e., from heaven—the Nephilim having been themselves originally inhabitants of heaven, or sprung from those who were such. This etymology and signification are approved of by Dr. J. Richers, who believes the Nephilim to be identical with the Bne-ha-Elohim, Mr. Garland, also, in the new translation which accompanies his "Genesis with Notes," renders Nephilim "the fallen ones." Delitzsch, having adverted to the general heathen tradition of the descent of unearthly beings to have intercourse with mortals, and especially to the Hesiodic legend respecting the origin of the giants from the blood which fell from Uranus, says that we might, in accordance with these traditions, interpret Nephilim "the fallen" from heaven; unless, he adds, Hesiod's description of the third or brazen race,[35] who were destroyed by each other's hands (or, according to Apollodorus, perished in the Deluge), should lead us to prefer the interpretation of

Aquila, taking Naphal in the sense of attack or fall upon.

To the explanation of the word Nephilim, "fallen" from heaven, it is objected in a note on the passage in Dr. Keil's Comm. on Pent., that the main element in it—"from heaven"—is a purely arbitrary addition, and that, therefore, the explanation needs not to be refuted. This is to misconceive the matter. It is not maintained that Nephilim means "fallen from heaven" but only "fallen"—but the beings designated by the term were so called on account of a fall of angels from heaven, with which angels these beings were identical or connected—this fall of angels being referred to in our passage, and believed, on sufficient grounds, to be a real event by those who first employed the name Nephilim.

It may be added, that this derivation of Nephilim, which we regard as the true one, has the support of R. S. L. Jarchi (Comm. Num. xiii. 33) and of the Targum of Jonathan (Gen. vi. 4), both of whom say, "Schamchazzai and Uzzael fell (כפלך—Jarchi) from heaven, and were on earth," &c.—these being the names of two of the angels in the Book of Enoch.

The term גבורים (from גבר, to be strong) applied in the latter part of verse 4 to the offspring of the Bne-Elohim and the daughters of men, is used sometimes as an adjective—strong, mighty—sometimes as a substantive—a hero, chief man. "גבוך, fortis, potens, robustus, heros, vir bellicâ virtute et auctoritate praeditus, illustris, princeps, gigas"—Calasius. Concordant. Sometimes, though rarely, it has a bad sense—tyrant, overbearing.

Hence, Josephus describes the sons of the

angels as "insolent (υβριστας) and despisers of everything good." The Seventy render, γιγαντες: Onkelos, גבריא, *mighty men*: the Vulgate, *potentes*: the Targum of Jonathan, דמעלמא גברין, "men who are of the world," (*Etheridge*)—though what the author meant precisely by this is not so clear. The Syriac and Arabic of Saadias use terms equivalent to *gigantes*: Junius and Tremellius—*potentissimi illi*. The writer of the apocryphal book of Baruch says (III. 26, Eng. Version), "These were the giants, famous from the beginning, that were of so great stature, and so expert in war"—a sort of paraphrase of the last clause of verse 4, and which Augustine has introduced (from the Vulgate) into his *City of God*—Ibi fuerunt gigantes, illi nominati qui ab initio fuerunt, staturosi, scientes proelium"—b. 15., c. 23.

The term גבורים, says Kurtz, "denotes strong men, champions, heroes, and, in Gen. vi., by reason of the article attached, it designates, not *any* heroes, or heroes in general, but those called *the heroes* κατ ἐξοχην, the well-known heroes of antiquity—in short, the Ηρώες or ἡμιθεοι of the Greeks." "We are warranted in supposing," he adds, "that the heroes or demigods of mythology are here spoken of, not only by the fact that these were said to be of heavenly origin, but also by the express intimation of the historian, 'These are the men of might, who have had a name from times of old.'"

Who were the Nephilim?

Any one reading, for the first time, in our English Version, the fourth verse of Genesis vi., would, not unnaturally, suppose that the *giants* there spoken of constituted a class of beings distinct from *the Sons of God*, and also from the *mighty men of renown*. The original itself leaves room for such a supposition, not alone in the distinction of names—*Nephilim, Bne-Elohim, Gibborim*—but in the fact, that the attempt to identify the giants or *Nephilim* with either of the others, is attended with no small difficulty.

At the same time, it is not easy to see what purpose is served by the mention of the *Nephilim*, or why they should appear in the narrative, on the supposition that they were a different class, as well from those who are called the *Gibborim*, as from the *Sons of Elohim*, Those, indeed, who reject the idea of any of these classes being of a nature above the human, suppose that they have, in the mention of the *Nephilim*, a powerful argument in support of their views. Observing the distinction of names, and that not only is there no direct statement made that the Nephilim (*giants*, in the ordinary sense, as they say) sprang from the union of the Sons of God with daughters of men; but that, on the contrary, to an unprejudiced mind the words of verse 4 represent them as in existence before the marriages of the Sons of God—they maintain that no ground exists for supposing these Nephilim to have been otherwise than of human origin: that their existence in the world, at the time when the Sons of God came in to the daughters of men, cannot therefore "afford the slightest evidence that the Sons of God were angels, by whom a family of monsters were begotten, whether demigods, demons, or angel-men:" and that, consequently, the *Gibborim*, sprung from the marriages of the Sons of God with daughters of men, could only have been human beings, though they may have been distinguished by gigantic size.

Believing, however, as we do, that everything recorded in this brief passage of Holy Writ, has more or less connection with the judgment of the Deluge, and, indeed, has been left on record by the Holy Spirit, chiefly for the purpose of showing the causes of that terrible visitation, we may ask, with Engelhardt and Kurtz, Why should any mention of the Nephilim have been made, if there were no better reason for it, than that they happened to be contemporaneous with certain pious Sethite men who married godless women, or merely that they should furnish ground for a comparison with the heroic sons of the latter? If this be the case, it is impossible to discern any special relation between them and the event of the Deluge, or any share they could have had in bringing it about. And if, as alleged, they are thus distinct from the other beings who are named in this verse, then we ask. Who or what are they? or, whence did they derive their origin?

It appears, therefore, desirable that we should be able to show that the Nephilim are not a third race, distinct from the Bne-Elohim, and from their mighty offspring, but identical with one or other of these. Adopting the derivation of the word, according to which it may mean "the fallen ones," and taking the Nephilim, with Sol. Jarchi and Jonathan, to be fallen spirits, we might believe them to be

one and the same with the Bne-Elohim. This view of the question which presented itself when first we entered on an examination of the passage, has, we find, been taken by Drs. Kurtz and Richers, the former regarding it as one of the only two which he thinks allowable, the latter as the sole admissible one.

Let us suppose, then, that the sinning angels, called in the first instance, in our passage as in the book of Job, Bne-Elohim, Sons of God, had come, at the time when Moses was writing, to be distinguished, on account of their fall from "their own habitation," by the name of Nephilim, fallers—and the entire passage may be explained as follows:—

When men had begun to multiply on the earth, and daughters had been born to them, the Sons of God, *i.e.*, angels, beheld these daughters, and fascinated with their beauty, chose wives from amongst them. From these unnatural alliances proceeded a mighty race, the members of which were known in after ages, as the *giants* and *the heroes*. Gross wickedness then prevailed in the world, owing to the presence and agency of these fallen spirits: and sentence of condemnation was pronounced by Jehovah on the wicked race, a respite, however, of 120 years being granted, in order to their repentance. But, then, as if to explain the cause of the abounding evil—to show that the Sons of God were concerned in its production—and to leave no room for doubt as to who the Sons of God might be— the historian observes (as it were, in a parenthesis), that "the Nephilim" were then in the earth—thus designing to inform his readers, in a manner, no doubt, intelligible at least to the earliest of them, that the Sons of God, of whom he had spoken, were no others than those known as the *Nephilim*—this being the established and recognized designation of certain angels, who left their heavenly habitation, for the purpose of companying with women. It may be observed, too, that as sinners of mankind had been specially brought into view in verse 3, by the use of the term *flesh*, (Note H.) the reference to the Nephilim would be the more in place, reminding, as it would, those readers, that other beings, besides the human, were responsible for the existence of the evil, the greatness of which the Divine Being had observed. And not only were the Nephilim (whom the writer now again, in verse 4, calls by the former name of *Sons of God*) on earth before, and at, the time when God condemned the world: but they remained there even after sentence of condemnation had been pronounced, and continued to hold intercourse with the daughters of men, in consequence of which the gigantic race became increased.

This view, as we remarked, and as the following extract will show, is approved of by Dr. Richers, who thinks that, only thus, can the passage be rightly understood.

The natural signification of *Nephilim* may be held, [he says,] to be that of the 'fallen,' the 'apostate,' and, having regard to the connexion of the whole passage, only the apostate angels who burned in fleshly lust towards the daughters of men. Beings, so far fallen could not well continue to be called Bne-Elohim (Sons of God), but rather Nephilim (fallen). But just as little could they, or would they be with *Elohim* in 'their own habitation' (Jude 6.), but only 'on earth' (Gen. vi. 4)—and, forsooth, 'in those days,' *i.e.*, the days of respite. They were thus 'fallen *down*'—and is not the whole ancient world acquainted with the idea of deities fallen or cast down from heaven? Jonathan speaks of Schamchazzai, *i.e.*, '*appeared*' and of Uzziel, *i.e.*, '*fled from God*' while the Book of Enoch tells of some who fell from heaven. Only when we believe the Nephilim to be the angels, who were cast out of heaven, and afterwards reserved in chains under darkness, does there appear to be any connexion in the passage, verses 1–4, or indeed 1–8: but, understanding it thus, verses 1–4 deal with the fallen angels, and verses 5–8 with the fallen and depraved human beings.

While offering this explanation to the reader, we cannot avoid feeling that it is unsatisfactory. Though we may assume (what, nevertheless, cannot be proved) that *Nephilim* was a name appropriated, in the days of Moses, to the fallen angels, we must be sensible of the difficulty involved in the supposition, that the historian has, within the compass of less than two lines, and without any intimation of the fact, designated *one* class of beings by two names, entirely different in form, etymology, and signification, and which, undoubtedly, seem at first sight to denote distinct classes. This has been remarked by Dr. Kurtz, and is obvious to every one. Had it been the intention of the writer to apply to the same persons these different names, he would probably have said, "The Nephilim were on earth in those days, and also after those days, for they are the Sons of God who came to the daughters of men, and begat the race of heroes," &c.

The better explanation of verse 4, is, perhaps, that which identifies the Nephilim with the Gibborim: or, more accurately, which regards the latter term as descriptive of the Nephilim, and the latter part of the verse as explanatory of the first clause. It may be admitted that the Sacred Record does not say expressly, that the Nephilim were the offspring of the union of the Bne-Elohim with women: but it should, at the same time, be observed that it does not state the contrary. Indeed, the natural inference from the language of the writer appears to be, that to that source their origin is to be assigned.[36] It may be remarked, too, in connection with this, that it is a proceeding of an entirely arbitrary kind, to assume that those who are called *Gibborim*—if a distinct race from the Nephilim—must, nevertheless, have been of like nature: for, only when we believe them to have been identical, have we ground for arriving at such a conclusion.

Accordingly, some able theological writers, who support the angel-hypothesis, have endeavoured to show that the terms *Nephilim* and *Gibborim* are both applied to those who owed their origin, immediately or otherwise, to the unnatural alliances of the Sons of God and daughters of men. These writers, however, while agreeing on the main point, that of the superhuman descent of the gigantic race, dif-fer from each other in some particulars—this difference consisting in the meaning which they respectively attach to the expression אשר וגם אחרי כן [37] translated in our version, "and also after that, when"—and in the fact that some regard the *Nephilim* as the earlier and more powerful generations of the race, the *Gibborim* as the later and weaker: while others suppose the race, in its later generations, to have been propagated by the Nephilim themselves: and others, again, that the terms *Nephilim* and *Gibborim* are both appellative of the entire race of beings, who proceeded immediately from the marriages of the Bne-Elohim, without distinction of earlier or later generations, and without reference to the times of their appearance in the world.

Dr. Delitzsch, who believes that the beings called *Nephilim* and *Gibborim* were, all, the sons of the Bne-Elohim, although brought into existence at different periods, and who takes the Hebrew expression, or combination of particles above referred to, in the signification of posteà, quùm = *afterwards, when*, not postquàm = *after that*, gives the following as his translation of the verse—a translation, it may be observed, which agrees with that of the Authorized Version—"The giants were (*i.e.*, were living, were present) on the earth in those days (*i.e.*, at the time when God appointed the respite of 120 years); and also, after that (*i.e.*, after sentence of condemnation had been pronounced, and during the progress of those years), when the Sons of God joined themselves to the daughters of men, and they bare children to them (giants arose likewise): and these (*i.e.*, the later-born) are the heroes, who from old time have been men of name." The firstborn of the unnatural unions, as he concludes, both on the ground of the connexion, and in view of the extra-Israelitish tradition, were the Nephilim: these he supposes to have been the more powerful, and to have come into existence before the commencement of the 120 years: but the intercourse between angels and human beings continuing subsequently to, and notwithstanding the Divine warning, *the heroes* (Gibborim) were born, a second and less gigantic, but still very powerful race.

The objections to this explanation of verse 4, are, that it seems to represent the connexion of the Sons of God and daughters of men as having had its commencement, not until after the giving of the Divine warning, and thus to make the origin of the Nephilim independent of that connexion: also, that there is no sufficient ground for making a distinction, in point of might or gigantic size, between the earlier and the later progeny of the Bne-Elohim. If both originated in the same source, as this writer believes, we should rather infer their equality in these respects, and indeed the very signification of the term *Gibborim* seems opposed to the other opinion.

Accordingly, Mr. E. H. Engelhardt rightly says that he cannot agree with Delitzsch, when he discovers in the *Gibborim*, a later race of giants, less gigantic than the first. He adds truly that the המה introduces an explanation of the name or character of the Nephilim. Engelhardt's own explanation is to this effect:—

The famous Nephilim were on the earth in those days (*i.e.*, at the time when the Sons of God, having made choice of daughters of men, began to have offspring of them: they were, consequently, in full activity, when the Divine wrath was first denounced against the wicked: they were connected, as in part its cause, with that denunciation: and they had sprang, as appears from what follows, from the union of angels with human kind), and also after the time when [he takes the Hebrew particles as equivalent to postquàm = *after-that*] this carnal intercourse of the Sons of God with daughters of men had taken place, and the latter had borne to them, they (the Nephilim) were still there—now, indeed, in consequence of propagation by themselves, and no longer by the Sons of God, as at first. The continuance of the unnatural intercourse of the Bne-Elohim and women God did not permit. The beings of higher nature, who had sinned, received immediate doom, as we learn from the Epistle of St. Peter: but to the human beings who were, not the seducers, but the seduced, God graciously gave time for repentance. *These Nephilim* (as well those who sprung from the union of angels and women, as those later ones who derived their origin, not immediately from the angels, but from the progeny of the latter) *were the Heroes* whose fame, as men of renown, has come down to us from ancient times.

There is nothing improbable in supposing that the sons of the angels propagated their race.[38] Such a circumstance would go to account for the necessity for a destruction so general as that of the Deluge. The evil, physical as well as moral—the mixture of different kinds, not less than the corruption of manners—would thus have been increased and perpetuated, until nothing short of the almost total extermination of the race could remedy the evil.

The marriages of the Sons of God, [says Kurtz,] with the daughters of men being, as verse 4 expressly tells us, fruitful, the offspring of these may, in their turn, have united themselves with the sons and daughters of other men, and thus might the evil have gradually pervaded the entire race. The 120 years which intervened between the time of the announcement of the Divine purpose, and that of its execution, afforded sufficient space for the bringing about of that corruption of all flesh, described in Gen. vi. 5, *sqq.*

There was, indeed, a much longer space, if the fall of the angels took place, as the Jewish tradition relates, and as appears to be probable, as early as the time of the patriarch Jared.

Some interpreters of our passage, who maintain the superhuman origin of the giants, are of opinion that the angelic intercourse with human beings, spoken of in ver. 4, is not to be understood as confined to antediluvian times.

Of this number are Dr. M. Drechsler and Dr. Nägelsbach, connecting אחרי כן immediately with the preceding sentence, and taking it to mean "*afterwards*" i.e., after those days in which the Nephilim first appeared: and rendering אשר, "*whenever*," (Gen. xxx. 38; Lev. iv. 22.) Drechsler translates the verse, "The Nephilim were on the earth in those days, and also afterwards: indeed, as often as the Sons of God came to the daughters of men, and the latter bare children: these (the Nephilim, the children thus borne) are the heroes, who from old time have been men of great name."

We concur in thinking with some of the principal advocates of our interpretation, that the sojourn of the angels on earth was a lengthened one, rendering possible an oft-repeated intercourse, and the appearance of successions of Nephilim, to the close of the antediluvian period. Accordingly, if it appear that Dr. Drechsler's interpretation of כן אשר אחרי is allowable, this rendering of the passage, which, we may remark, seems to be supported by the Syriac and Arabic versions, would be a satisfactory one, enabling us to identify the Nephilim and Gibborim—to shew that these terms are applied by the historian to one race, the offspring of the union of Bne-Elohim with daughters of men. But we cannot, by any means, adopt the view of the writer, that Moses, in this verse, refers to post-diluvian times. Rightly regarding verses 1 and 2 as relating to the period between the Fall and the Deluge, he supposes it declared in the fourth verse, that the unlawful intercourse was again carried on after the termination of that period, and consequently after the Flood—in short, that the meaning of the verse is, that certain beings of superhuman nature were on earth in the antediluvian age, until they were destroyed by the Deluge; that, *after* that event, beings of like nature were again on earth, the like intercourse of angels with daughters of men having again taken place—and that the object of the historian in imparting this information, was, to account for the origin of the giant-races of Canaan, in order that the Israelites, when they came to enter on the conquest of that land, might be the less disheartened at the sight of these gigantic foes, being aware of the source from which they had proceeded.

This explanation of the passage is approved of, and defended on grammatical grounds, by Dr. Nägelsbach. Rejecting the notion of Aben-Ezra, that the Nephilim (*giants*, Num. xiii. 33) whom the spies discovered in Palestine, were *descendants* of the *first* Nephilim, he thinks that the origin of these Palestinensian Nephilim is directly accounted for in verse 4, interpreted as above. The adoption of this view he holds to be the more indispensable, in consequence of the use by the historian of the imperfect tense יבאו. If, he says, only that intercourse which is spoken of in ver. 2, as an accomplished fact, be intended, he is unable to comprehend why Moses should not have written באו: but if, on the other hand, it be meant to express, not an intercourse once had and completed, but a continued intercourse, or one often repeated in past time—then must the imperfect be used (as it actually is), according to the known usage of the Hebrew language. On this point he refers to Ewald's

Ausführliches Lehrbuch der Hebr. Sprache, &c., 136: and concludes that we are warranted by the text in supposing the births of Nephilim in later times (*i.e.*, after the Deluge) as often as the Bne Elohim had intercourse with daughters of men.

An insuperable objection appears to lie against the notion, that demon-intercourse of the kind in question was carried on subsequently to the Deluge. The purpose of God in bringing on the world that widespread destruction, was, we believe, not merely to punish transgressors, but, quite as much or more, to put a period to the unnatural intercourse of angels with daughters of men—to prevent the further commingling of different classes of creatures—to obliterate all traces of such intercourse, and to exterminate the monstrous offspring to which it had given rise. We entirely coincide in the opinion of those who think that, only for such a purpose, and only in consequence of the existence of an evil so extraordinary, would a remedy like that of the Deluge have been resorted to. A visitation, more limited in extent, and less terrible in its effects, would, otherwise, have probably appeared sufficient, in the view of the Supreme. The intention of Jehovah, of course, was not to be frustrated: and hence we are compelled to reject the notion, that a like connexion, between angelic and human beings, was formed in the period which succeeded the Flood.

Another rendering of the verse remains to be noticed. Regarding אחרי כן אשר as a conjunction, equivalent to the Latin *postquam*, or to the English *after-that, after it so happened that*—and understanding גם, not in its cumulative sense, as introducing something new or additional to what had been mentioned, but in its intensive or emphatic signification—*yea, even, just*—Dr. Kurtz would identify the Nephilim and Gibborim by translating thus:—"The Nephilim were on earth in those days, even after that the Sons of God had been coming to the daughters of men, and had begotten children: these (the Nephilim, the children thus begotten) are the heroes who," &c. This translation agrees substantially with that of the Vulgate, and the author offers it as one of the only two[39] explanations of the passage which he holds to be admissible—admitting, at the same time, that he is unable to decide between this, and that already noticed, and which is adopted by Richers in preference to all others.

Were it not for the difficulty arising from וגם (Note I.) we would not hesitate to accept this explanation as at once the simplest, and serving to identify, perhaps more clearly than any other, the Nephilim and Gibborim, as one race, the progeny of the Sons of God. Should the difficulty referred to be thought insurmountable, we give the preference, in the next place, to the rendering of the verse proposed by Drechsler, rejecting, of course, the idea of a post-diluvian intercourse.

The following paraphrase of verse 4 accords with those translations of it, which appear to us best to express the meaning of the sacred writer:—

In the days preceding the Deluge there were living on the earth a superhuman and powerful race of beings, called the Nephilim, a race which owed its origin to an unnatural connexion of certain angels with human females. In consequence of the presence and agency of these beings, gross wickedness prevailed in the world; and although sentence of destruction was pronounced by God upon all flesh, yet even after, and notwithstanding this, the unnatural intercourse between angelic and human beings was continued, and *Nephilim* were brought into existence, to the time of the irruption of the Deluge—as often, indeed, as the angels may have come to the daughters of men, or the Nephilim themselves may have propagated the race. These Nephilim, whether sprung immediately or otherwise from the angels, are the demigods or heroes of the heathen mythology, famous from that primeval age to the present day.

Gigantic Races.—Report of the Spies (Numbers xiii.)

The opinion has been commonly entertained that, in the earliest ages of the world, the physical proportions and endowments of mankind were vastly greater than those which pertain to the race at the present day—that the men, generally, of those ages were characterized by a stature, size, and strength, which have not been found in men of later times—and that, in these respects, the human race has degenerated greatly. This belief was based, partly on the testimony of ancient writers, and partly on the discovery of colossal bones, supposed to be human, but which in reality were those of elephants or other animals of large size. Homer, Hesiod, Herodotus, Plutarch, Pliny, Virgil, and others of the Greek and Latin poets and historians—some of the Old Testament apocryphal (2 Esdras v. 54; Bar. iii. 26), and other ancient Jewish writers—besides some of the monkish historians, and Christian writers in modern times, have countenanced this opinion.[40] Homer draws, more than once, a contrast between the mighty heroes of the Trojan war, and "such men as live in those degenerate days." Hesiod, likewise, tells of the brazen race, "terrible and strong, formed from ash trees," and of "the race of heroes called demigods, who perished, some fighting before the seven-gated Thebes, and others at Troy, for the sake of the fair-haired Helen." But it has been observed by recent writers on the subject, that, from all the facts and circumstances which can be adduced, as bearing on the point, we should rather infer that the notion of diminished strength and size, in the case of mankind generally, is not well founded: and whilst we must admit the existence in early times of races of men, and, in both ancient and modern times, of individuals, whose physical proportions certainly exceeded the present standard, yet these appear to be exceptions to the general rule, and to have been regarded as wonders even in their own days.

If we be asked, [says Dr. Kitto,] whether the race of men were, in early times, taller than at present, we must answer frankly that we do not know. No facts in favour of that conclusion have been found. All the facts in history, and art, and human discovery, are against, rather than for, that notion, and tend to show that the stature of men in general has not been greater than at present, within any period to which any kinds of monuments extend. What may be said to be, at the first view, the most striking argument in its support, is the impression that the stature of men in the olden time may have borne some proportion to the duration of their lives. But the supposition rests on an analogy which has no foundation in nature, for it is not seen that long-lived animals are generally larger than short-lived ones: and if the conjecture had all the force that could be assigned to it, it would not account for the Canaanites, or any tribes of them, being taller than the Israelites, or than the Egyptians, who were their contemporaries; seeing that among them all the average duration of life, for aught that appears, was the same.

But if we be asked, whether there might not be gigantic races, which, however originated, increased, and multiplied? We answer, yes—because the Scripture affirms it in the case before us [that of the giants seen by the spies—Num. xiii.] and in other cases; and because the facts of human experience are in favour of it. We see that stature is somewhat influenced by climate, and that men are taller, generally, in moist and temperate climes, than in those which are very hot, or very cold, or very dry: and it is on record that tall parents have tall children born to them; and if they cared, by their intermarriages, to preserve the distinction, they might keep up a race of giants: but not generally caring for this, the stature of their descendants dwindles, sooner or later, down to the common standard. Such races the Anakim, and others mentioned in Scripture, seem to have been.—*Daily Bib. Illust.—Moses and the Judges*, pp. 183–4.

That there have been individuals, and races of men, of a stature much above the common standard, is not to be denied. Several instances have been mentioned, by writers on the subject, of individuals both in ancient and modern times, who attained to the height of 8 and 8 1/2 feet: and human skeletons are, or lately were, preserved in museums, in these islands, and on the continent, varying in height from 8 feet to 8 feet 6 inches. We read, in Deut, iii. 11, of Og, king of Bashan, that he alone "remained of the remnant of the giants: behold, his bedstead was a bedstead of iron—nine cubits was the length thereof, and four cubits the breadth thereof, after the cubit of a man."

This length, [says the writer last named,] we take to be 13 1/2 feet, at the rate of half a yard to a cubit. But a man's bedstead is usually larger than himself, yet not so much larger but that it may be taken as affording some indication of his stature. It is so intended in the text,

which clearly shews that then, as now, bedsteads were not much longer than the person who lay in them. If, therefore, the bedstead were 13 1/2 feet, the man may have been about ten or eleven feet high—a very great stature—higher than that of Goliath, but not incredible or unexampled.[41]

Of Goliath he says, reckoning the cubit as above, "his stature, which may be taken at about nine feet, is a good measure by which to estimate that of the Anakim, whose appearance so alarmed the Israelites." Goliath's height, however, has been variously calculated, some reckoning him to have been nearly 12 feet.[42] Pliny (Nat. Hist. vii. 16), who refers to Homer, as having a thousand years before lamented the degeneracy of the human race in point of physical qualities, relates that the body of Orestes, son of Agamemnon, having been dug up—the story of its finding may be read in Herodotus, lib. I.—was found to measure seven cubits. He further mentions one Gabbaras, who came from Arabia in the time of Claudius, whose height was 9 feet 9 inches: and two others, Pusio and Secundilla, in the time of Augustus, each of whom exceeded the Arabian in stature by half a foot. Josephus (Ant. xviii. 4, 5) tells us that, amongst other hostages sent on one occasion to the Emperor Tiberius, was a Jew named Eleazar, whose height was 7 cubits. It may be added that Cæsar and Hirtius Pansa speak of the great size of the Gauls and Germans, as compared with that of the Roman soldiers. "Homines (sc. Romani) tantulæ staturæ," says the former, *De Bel. Gal.* II. 30, "nam plerisque hominibus Gallis, præ magnitudine corporum suorum, brevitas nostra contemptui est," &c. The other writes, "Horum (sc. Gallorum Germanorumque) corpora, mirificâ specie amplitudineque, cæsa toto campo jacebant"—*De Bel. Afric.* 37.

We know, from the Old Testament, that not alone individuals, but whole races of gigantic men, existed in Palestine, in early times. Moses informs the Israelites, when they were about to take possession of the promised land, that they would encounter there "a people great and tall, the children of the Anakim," of whom it was said, "Who can stand before the children of Anak?" (Deut. ix. 2.) In a preceding part of the same book, he describes other gigantic tribes who, in by-gone days, had dwelt in the land of the Moabites. "The Emims dwelt therein in times past, a people great, and many, and tall as the Anakim, which also were accounted giants as the Anakim: but the Moabites call them Emims" (ch. ii. 10, II); and, verses 20, 21, the ancient inhabitants of the territory of the children of Ammon—"That also was accounted a land of giants: giants dwelt therein in old time: and the Ammonites call them Zamzum-mims: a people great, and many, and tall as the Anakims: but the Lord destroyed them before them, and they succeeded them, and dwelt in their stead." Long after the days of Moses, another sacred writer (Amos ii. 9) refers to the gigantic stature and might of one of the ancient tribes of Canaan—"Yet destroyed I the Amorite before them, whose height was like the height of the cedars, and

who was strong as the oaks." Josephus adds his testimony, and says (Ant. v. 2, 3), that when the Israelites took Hebron—a town of the Amorites—(Joshua xiv. 15, and xv. 13; Judges i. 10)—there was still in existence the race of giants, "who had bodies so large, and countenances so entirely different from other men, that they were surprising to the sight, and terrible to hear of."

Of the spies, who were sent by Moses to explore the land of Canaan, some brought an evil report, declaring, amongst other things, that they had seen "the giants, the sons of Anak, *which come* of the giants"—adding that they were in their own sight, as well as in that of the giants, only "as grasshoppers," in size, in comparison with them. This application of the term *Nephilim* to the giants of Palestine, has been confidently alleged as conclusive evidence, that the word denotes nothing more than *giants*, in the usual sense: and that *Nephilim* were to be found, not only in the antediluvian days, but long afterwards, forming merely a portion, though remarkable one, of the human race.

This conclusion is not warranted. That the spies made a true report, so far as regards the appearance of the persons whom they saw, and that they were not led, as some have supposed, by any feeling of terror which may have seized upon them, to exaggerate the physical proportions of the Anakim, we feel assured. The question is not, whether they saw gigantic persons, for that, we think, must be admitted: but whether they made a proper application of the term *Nephilim*, in bestowing it on these persons.

Having regard to the words of Gen. vi. 4, we must conclude that they did not. "The Nephilim," says Moses, "were in the earth in those days"—from which the inference is, that whoever the Nephilim may have been, they were on earth *in those days only* (the days before the Flood), and not at any other time. Why, then, did the spies apply the name to the giants of Palestine? We reply that, in doing so, they merely recognised the claim of the Anakim themselves, who professed to be descended from the real Nephilim, and were generally reputed (Delitzsch, 197, Kurtz, 80) so to be—an opinion which Aben-Ezra and Raschi appear from their commentaries, to have adopted, the former taking אחרי כן, Gen. vi. 4, to mean "after the Deluge," and pointing to the "sons of Anak as descended from the families of the Bne-Elohim"—בתחלה היו ממשפחת בגי האלהים:—אחר המבול והכה בכי צגק, while the latter says (Gen. vi. 4) that the Nephilim were on earth "in the days of the generations of Enos and the sons of Cain"—and tells us (Num. xiii. 33) that the Nephilim, whom the spies saw, were "Anakim, of the sons of Schamchazzai and Uzzael, who fell from heaven in the days of the generations of Enos."—מבכי שמחזאי ועוזאל שכפלו מן השמים— בימי דור אגוש:—דכפלים צגקים.

The notion that the Anakim of Palestine were *descendants* of the Nephilim, or of the Bne-Elohim, must be at once rejected, involving, as it does, the necessity of believing, either that some, besides those who were in the Ark, must have survived the Deluge, as the Jewish tradition relates was the case with Og, the King of Bashan, who alone "remained of the remnant of the giants," and who, according to some of the rabbins, escaped the general destruction by climbing to the roof of the Ark! or else, that Noah, his wife, or some of his sons' wives, must have had *giant* blood in their veins. The latter supposition Dr. Maitland regards as probable, and although we are not able to adopt such a view, yet, as his opinion on any question connected with our passage is worthy of all attention, we insert here his observations on the subject.

Having referred in his Essay on False Worship (IV., on *the Descendants of the Giants*, to the almost total destruction by the Flood of those who were living on the earth, he says—

Perhaps we are liable, rather hastily to take up the notion that by this catastrophe the race of the giants became extinct. When in the history of later times we read that 'Og King of Basan remained of the remnant of the giants;' and still later of 'Ishbi-benob which was of the sons of the giant;' we may perhaps be satisfied, as to the former, with Bishop Patrick's remark, that the Rephaim were 'a very ancient people in that country;' and for the latter by his suggestion that Ishbi-benob was a son of Goliath, 'though Bochartus thinks the Hebrew word Rapha signifies any giant.' Perhaps I say, we may take this for commentary, without further enquiry as to what 'giants' had to do with the matter at all: or if we are not satisfied with this, and think that we see reason for believing that the word here translated 'giants' has reference to antediluvians (Note J), it

81

may be suggested that, as those original 'giants' or their offspring were 'men of renown,' there might probably be warriors in after ages who would profess to be the descendants of those heroes, and whose pretensions were not likely to be questioned while they were prepared to support them by spears like weavers' beams.

For my own part however, I see no reason why Ishbi-benob may not have been personally and lineally descended from 'the Sons of God,' whosoever they may have been. Some people were, I suppose, and why not he? We must consider, that though the Ark contained only one family, consisting of but eight souls, yet in all probability that family represented five lines of pedigree. The Patriarch Noah, it may be remembered, was himself of the family of Seth. Whatever idea we may have of his personal holiness, and of the antediluvian piety of his sons, we are not, I suppose, authorised to assume that by something amounting almost to a miracle, the several lines of Noah himself, of his wife, and of his three daughters-in-law—lines going back perhaps through many ages and generations—were all kept pure from any mixture of giant blood. Those who imagine that the originators of all the evil which was raging in this world of violence and furious sin, were the descendants of Seth, and persons so eminent for holiness as to have been called, on that account alone, 'the Sons of God,' cannot fairly insist on a

more rigid and scrupulous selection of partners by the sons of Noah.

We cannot coincide in this opinion. That there were descendants of the sons of God, is clear—the giants (*Nephilim* or *Gibborim*) of verse 4—and as it has often been observed that a particular style of face, or some peculiar form of feature, or other physical characteristics, are handed down in families, from one generation to another, or perhaps, passing over one or two generations, revive in a third: so if we could believe that, in any of those who were saved in the Ark, the giant blood had been preserved, we might readily enough conceive that the gigantic physical proportions of the "mighty men" of the antediluvian age might reappear in some of their descendants. We feel, however, that all the circumstances of the case, at least as they appear to us, allow no other supposition than that all of the gigantic race, and all who may have had even remote relationship with it, in existence at the time of the commencement of the Deluge, were destroyed: and that that peculiar race became extinct, no trace or remnant of it remaining. We think it is not an unwarrantable assumption, that "the several lines of Noah himself, of his wife, and of his three daughters-in-law—lines going back perhaps through many ages and generations—were all kept pure from any mixture of giant blood." We think so, because the purpose of God—the extermination of a mixed race, and the preservation of the pure Adamic seed—required it. And it will not be denied that it was an easy matter for that All-seeing and Almighty Power, who ordains and disposes even the minutest circumstances of the lives of all, to ensure that it would be so, without any extraordinary effort, or any apparent deviation from His ordinary providential course. Dr. Nägelsbach, who rejects the notion of Aben-Ezra, that the Anakim were descended from the Bne-Elohim, justly remarks that if Moses intended to convey such an idea, he has not by any means clearly expressed it.

Our own impression is, that Moses himself attached to the words the same meaning, which the two rabbins named have put upon them, and which we believe to have been the meaning of the spies also, viz., that the giants whom they saw were descended (מן used, as in Gen. ii. 23; xv. 4, to express the notion of *origin*) from the Bne-Elohim, or their offspring the Nephilim: and as no mention of such beings had been previously made in the Pentateuch, except in Gen. vi., the reader would be reminded of the *Nephilim* who are mentioned there: and these antediluvian *Nephilim*, of whom alone tradition as well as the Sacred History has preserved the remembrance, we conceive to have been likewise present to the mind of the spies. Not, indeed, that the Sacred Writer meant to sanction any such erroneous notion, as that entertained by the spies: he has simply recorded the words of the latter, who, in thus applying the name *Nephilim* to those who had no title to it, gave expression to a belief which appears to have been then received. The pretensions, however groundless, of the Anakim to an origin of a superhuman kind were admitted by some of their contemporaries.

The word *Nephilim*, as Dr. Maitland remarks, is not that which is "generally used, to signify what we understand by the word *giant*, in the Scriptures, though giants are often enough spoken of" there. The term *giant* or *giants* occurs in the English Version seventeen times. Once the Hebrew is גבור (Job xvi. 14)—thrice, כפילים (Gen. vi. 4; Num. xiii 33, bis.) and in the remaining thirteen instances, the Hebrew is רפא or רפאים. These latter, therefore, being the terms usually employed by the sacred writers, when they mean to designate persons of great stature and bodily power, it may fairly be inferred that, when the word *Nephilim* is used, it denotes those who were possessed of some other distinguishing characteristics than those just mentioned. We do not mean that the *Nephilim* of Gen. vi. were not giants, in the ordinary sense, though we cannot agree with Nägelsbach, when he says that this is undoubtedly clear from Num. xiii. 33. The latter passage shows that the persons whom the spies beheld, and to whom they applied the name *Nephilim*, were persons of gigantic stature: but we are not, as a matter of course, to apply the description given of them to the Nephilim of Gen. vi. 4, the original word signifying a gigantic person, and those to whom it is bestowed in Numbers being, as we have reason to conclude, of a nature essentially different from the others. The *Nephilim* of Gen. vi., supposing them to be identical with the *Gibborim*, are represented to us as mighty and renowned: but these characters might be possessed in the absence of gigantic size. At the same time, we believe this characteristic did belong to the *Nephilim* of Gen. vi.

They are universally represented as possessed of gigantic physical proportions—in the Jewish tradition, in the ancient versions, and in the writings of Church Fathers. We only say that, if giants, they were something else besides. Gigantic stature was not their most remarkable or distinguishing quality, as that, we believe, consisted in their superhuman nature.

It is highly probable that the idea of gigantic stature was that, which the mention of the *Nephilim* would most readily suggest to men's minds, in the days of Moses and afterwards. Indeed, the fact of the Anakim claiming, on the ground, no doubt, of their gigantic size, to be descended from them, is an evidence of this. It appears also, we think, from the remarkable fact, that the Hebrew word *Rephaim*, although ordinarily applied to men distinguished merely by gigantic size, is, in certain passages of the Books of Job and Proverbs, evidently used to designate the giants who perished in the Deluge, and who, in these places, are represented as being in the abode of the unrighteous dead. So, at least, the LXX understood the passages (Note J), and their interpretation is, decidedly, a more natural one than that of the authors of our English Version. Indeed, the original words in Job xxvi. 5 do not seem to admit of any other interpretation than that which the Greek translators have assigned to them, and which has been followed in the Vulgate. The English translation, in this instance, is void of meaning. When, therefore, we find the authors of Job and Proverbs applying the term *Rephaim*, the usual Hebrew word for giants, to those who, in Gen. vi., are called Nephilim: and when, on the other hand, we find the spies designating by the latter title men of the class elsewhere called Rephaim—we cannot avoid the conclusion, that the idea with which the *Nephilim* of Gen. vi. were associated in the minds of men, in later times, was that of gigantic stature, from which, however, it does not follow that the real Nephilim of the antediluvian age had no more remarkable or distinctive characteristic.

CHAPTER FOUR

THE ANGEL-INTERPRETATION
(CONTINUED)

Probable Period of the Descent of the Angels to Earth—Whence the Necessity for the Deluge?

We are reminded by Dr. Maitland, at p. 24 of his Essay on False Worship, that the sin which occasioned the destruction of the antediluvian world was not one "criminal act committed by certain parties at a certain time, but rather a course of transgression extending over an undefined, and perhaps protracted, period, growing worse and worse, and reaching to the day of vengeance."

This is true. The evil which led to the awful catastrophe was a continued evil, and one which became more and more aggravated and widely spread, until at length the moral and social condition of the world was such, as Moses has described in Genesis vi. verses 11, 12.

The general causes which produced the gross moral corruption, prevalent in the period preceding the Deluge, and which led to the perpetration of those deeds of violence by which its history was marked, must be sought for in the fallen condition of man, and his natural proneness to evil. To another and special cause, however, operating in that period only, must be ascribed the existence of the peculiar evil, which rendered necessary a judgment so exterminating as that of the Flood. We refer, of course, to the presence on earth of fallen angels, their unnatural connexion with human beings, and the results of such connexion—the reality of which has been evinced, we think, in the preceding pages. To determine the precise time at which the descent to this world of the angels took place, or to ascertain the exact duration of their abode on earth is not possible: but it may not be uninteresting to notice some traditions, bearing on the subject, which have been preserved by Josephus and others.

The author of the Book of Enoch (ch. 105) represents Enoch as saying to his son Methusaleh, "I have shewn thee that in the generations of Jared my father, those who were from heaven disregarded the word of the Lord. Behold they committed crimes, laid aside their class, and intermingled with women. With them also they transgressed: married with them and begot children."

An old writer, Lambert de Daneau, already mentioned, page 38—although not a supporter of the angel-interpretation—quotes in his book a passage from Epiphanius, *contr. Hær.* lib. I, to the effect that the corruption and violence which distinguished the antediluvian time, had been specially prevalent from the days of Jared. Epiphanius says,

The son of Adam was Seth: the son of Seth, Enos: after him successively, Cainan, Malaleel, and Jared. From the time of this last, according to the tradition which has come down to us, is to be dated the rise of the gross wickedness which prevailed in the world (εντευθεν ηρξατο ή κακομηχανια εν κοσμω γινεσθαι). This, indeed, had its commencement in the sin of Adam, followed by the fratricidal act of Cain; but now, in the times of Jared and afterwards, sorcery, magic, unclean-ness, adultery, and all unrighteousness abounded (νυν δε εν χρονις του Ιαρεδ, και επεκεινα, ραρμακεια, και μαγεια, ασελγεια, μοιχεια, τε, και αδιπια).

In accordance with these is the account of Josephus (Ant I. 3, I), that the "posterity of Seth continued to esteem God as the Lord of the universe, and to have an entire regard to virtue for seven generations" (επτα γενεας),— in other words, to the time of Enoch, who was contemporary with Jared, and with Methuselah, and was translated 669 (LXX. 775, Sam. 420) years before the Deluge—but, then, he tells us, they forsook this good path, in consequence, as his language implies, of the descent of the angels, and the birth of the giants—"for many angels of God companied with women, and begat sons that proved unjust, and despisers of all that was good." (See Note M.)

The Byzantine and Syrian writers, Syncellus, Cedrenus, and Bar-Hebræus, follow what seems to be the general tradition, and represent the intercourse between the Sons of God and the daughters of men, as having had its commencement in the time of the patriarch Jared. These writers, however, approve of the Sethite-interpretation, and reject the idea of the sons of God having been angels.

The tradition, thus preserved by Jewish and Christian writers, relative to the time at which the Sons of God associated themselves with the daughters of men, when gross wickedness began to abound, whatever its value may be, is, at the least, not inconsistent with the statements of Moses. That, for some ages preceding the Deluge, the moral and spiritual condition of the posterity of Seth, amongst whom, at first, we believe religion and virtue to have flourished, had been declining, and the family in general, in common with the rest of mankind, becoming more and more alienated from the knowledge and service of God, seems certain.

There is nothing in the sacred narrative to forbid our supposing that this declension had been in progress, prior to the sinning of the Sons of God, and that, in this respect, the world had reached a low stage, as early at least as the days of Enoch. On the contrary, such appears to be a legitimate inference from the circumstance mentioned by Moses, in his brief notice of the patriarch, that he "walked with God."

> These words, [says Kurtz,] which express the intimate communion of Enoch, and of Noah, with God, shew—what every unprejudiced person will allow—a wholly exceptional state of things in the case of these two: not exceptional for the first time, when the moral corruption had become great and general [*i.e.*, in the time of Noah], but exceptional even so far back as the days of Enoch, who died [?] 669 years before the Flood.

The prevailing evil would, naturally, be increased by means of the fallen Sons of God. "God saw the wickedness of man"—great before, but greater after, the arrival of these unearthly beings. And if we suppose—a supposition not at all improbable—their coming to the daughters of men to have had its begin-ning in the time of Enoch, there is room for the suggestion, that the extraordinary removal of that patriarch from the world, may have had a further meaning, than that of the righteous being taken away from the evil to come. It is not impossible that it may have had some connexion with the descent to earth of those who had been inhabitants of heaven. Just as the extirpation of the evil which led to the ruin of the old world, and the complete removal of its cause, were effected in the days of one righteous man, who "walked with God," and who was singled out from the rest of the world, as having "found grace in the eyes of the Lord," so the commencement of that evil, and the introduction of its special cause, may have been in the days of another righteous man, who, likewise, "walked with God," and who, like the other, was, by Divine grace, preserved from the general contamination, and from perishing with the transgressors.

When we remember that the giants or mighty men, the sons of the angels, have acquired a fame which is likely to endure to the end of time: and that, for this, they are indebted to their lawless deeds—to the rapine, wars, destruction of life, the impurities or debaucheries, to which their daring and malevolent disposition, or their incontinent desires, may have prompted them, as well as to their impiety and rebellion against the Most High—as in these, we feel assured, consisted, in great measure, the "violence and corruption with which the earth was filled"—when we know that the evil had risen to such a height, that God saw fit to announce a period of 120 years as the term of the Divine forbearance—and further, when we have regard, not merely to the length of time required in the antediluvian age, as compared with ours, before men could attain to the maturity of their powers, but still more to that which must have elapsed, before that enormous amount of evil could have been accomplished, which we must, on the several grounds of Scripture, tradition, arid reason, attribute to the giants—when we take these various circumstances into account, we will be of opinion, that these beings must have been in the world for a considerable time before the commencement of the 120 years, and that tradition has, perhaps, not greatly erred in fixing the descent of the angels to earth, and the origin of the giant-race, in the times of Jared or of Enoch. R. Solomon Jarchi, indeed, places the fall of the angels even earlier: for he says that "Schamchazzai and Uzzael fell from heaven in the days of the generation of Enos and the sons of Cain."

We have already, more than once, intimated our belief that, only on the ground of the interpretation which renders *Bne-ha-Elohim* by *angels*, have we a rational explanation of the fact, that the destruction of the old world by the Deluge was absolutely necessary. To this topic we may here further advert.

No one who reads the first twelve or thirteen verses of Gen. vi. can avoid coming to the conclusion that Moses designed to represent the age immediately preceding the Deluge, as surpassing in point of moral corruption, social wrong, and outrageous crimes, any that had gone before it: and also, that, between this unprecedented evil, and the alli-

ances of the Sons of God with daughters of men, recorded in verse 2, a close connexion subsisted—indeed, that the former was, in a great degree, the consequence of the latter. All interpreters recognize this connexion, and are agreed that the necessity for a judgment such as that of the Deluge arose out of these alliances. The advocates of the Sethite-interpretation, however, while admitting the connexion, deny that it furnishes any ground for regarding the Bne-Elohim as angels. They say that the Bible is concerned not with the history of angels, but with that of mankind, so far as it is connected with the economy of Redemption—that "we are here in the region of humanity, and not in the sphere of superhuman spirits" (Murphy, *comment. in loc.*)—and that the awful judgment is to be accounted for, solely on the ground of the "wickedness of man" (ver. 5) and the "corruption of all flesh" (ver. 12) that is, of the human race.

It is, undoubtedly, true that it is not any part of the design of Holy Scripture to record the history, or relate the doings of angels, except in so far as these may bear upon the history of mankind in this world, or their destiny in the next. This principle is maintained throughout the Bible.

To whom, [says Engelhardt,] has it not been a matter of wonder, how suddenly and without the least previous allusion to his existence, Satan is brought before us as invading the life of the first human beings? Who does not also see that the punishment of that adversary for the seduction of our first parents, is mentioned only so far as it is of significance in connexion with the history of Redemption? And who is not surprised at learning, in the Epistles of Peter and Jude, events which had taken place in the spirit-world, about which, nevertheless, Scripture is silent in that connexion to which they belong chronologically? In truth we perceive throughout the sacred volume, the existence of the principle of taking up only so much of occurrences in the spirit-world, as is absolutely necessary for the carrying on, and for the understanding of, the history of Redemption.

Accordingly, Moses has not, in the preceding narrative, informed us of the creation of angels, nor has he taught, directly, even the existence of such beings. The latter fact, however, we learn in the mention of the cherubim (iii. 24), whom some, indeed, would have us believe are simply the creations of symbolic and destitute of all objective reality—in short, a sort of poetical creation—but whom we cannot but regard as part of that spiritual world of creatures, whom we commonly designate by the general term of angels (see Kurtz, *Old Cov*. I. 80): while from the account of the Temptation, and the sentence pronounced on the Tempter, the reflecting reader would be likely to infer the existence of an evil spiritual being or beings, opposed to God and man, who should attack and, to some extent, succeed in injuring the latter, but be eventually overcome.

Allusions to the spirit-world, or its events, are made thus sparingly in the Bible, and only when the occasion imperatively demands it. Such an occasion presented itself in connexion with the history of the Deluge, the Holy Spirit designing to show the causes which led to the infliction of that tremendous judgment, and thus to vindicate the ways of God. If the angelic intercourse and its result, the production of a new race, together with the violence and corruption with which the world was filled by their means, constituted the chief and special causes which rendered such a visitation indispensable—then it was not only within the scope of the sacred narrative, but on many grounds expedient that these causes should be revealed; and if Moses has not expressly told us that the Bne-ha-Elohim were angels, it is only because, as has been already observed, the meaning of the term was, when he wrote, established and well known.

We look upon it, indeed, as an argument of no small weight, in favour of the angel-interpretation, that only on such a ground does there appear a necessity for the almost total destruction of the human race. If the great men of the time—the rulers, judges, chiefs—chose to form alliances with women of inferior rank—if the elder descendants of Adam formed unions with the women of a later generation—or if Sethite men conspicuous for piety, united themselves with godless Cainite women—these unions might be incongruous and productive of unhappiness enough to the parties themselves: but they could not be the means of producing the great and general corruption of manners, and forgetfulness of God which characterized the age preceding the Deluge, nor do they afford any sufficient explanation of the cause which drew down upon the world a judgment so terrific.

But if the Sons of God were not men, but angels, who about the period indicated left their "proper habitation," and came to earth for the purpose of gratifying unlawful and unnatural desires, we have, in this, a cause at once adequate and likely to produce the unparalleled evil, which led to the ruin of the old world. Were not fallen spirits, dwelling amongst mankind, and intimately associated with them, very capable of producing the gross and widely-spread depravity of conduct and morals, which prevailed in those times? And was not this depravity a natural result of the abode on earth, not only of these fallen but powerful beings, but also of another mighty and lawless race, who owed their origin to them? When we reflect on the evil which fallen spirits have wrought in this world—of the untold miseries which one successful act of an evil angel has caused to our race—of the power exercised by such spirits, and the ills which they inflicted on individuals, at the time of the sojourn on earth of Him, who will eventually bruise the serpent's head—we discern in the character and degree of the evil prevalent in the antediluvian age, the strongest reason for believing that fallen angels, and their offspring, were the prime cause and authors of it.

The opponents of our interpretation say, on the other hand, that such a view is "decidedly at variance with those statements of the Scriptures, which speak of the corruption of *the men whom God had created*, and not of a race

that had arisen through an unnatural connexion of angels and men, and forced their way into God's creation." (Keil, *Pent.* 139, *n.*) The determination, on the part of God, to destroy, and the motive assigned for it, that *every imagination of the thoughts of his heart was evil*, are supposed to be irreconcilable with the angel-theory. "Had the godless race," says Philippi, quoted by Keil, "which God destroyed by the Flood, sprung either entirely or in part from the marriage of angels to the daughters of men, it would no longer have been the race first created by God in Adam, but a grotesque product of the Adamitic factor created by God, and an entirely foreign and angelic factor." True. It would have been, as we have already described it, a race of monstrous beings, outside the limits of creation prescribed by the Creator: and, therefore, to put a period to the existence of such a race, and to preserve, in its purity, that which had been originally created in Adam, the greater portion of which had probably become contaminated by means of connexion with the mongrel brood[43], no way, perhaps, remained, except the extermination of the whole race then in the world, one family only being preserved in the ark.

When the advocates of the Sethite-interpretation maintain that the moral corruption of man was as great after, as it was before, the Deluge, and refer to ch. viii. 21, where, as they allege, it is described in the same words as in vi. 5: and when they further say that "if the race destroyed had been one that sprang from angel-fathers, it is difficult to understand why no improvement was to be looked for after the Flood; for the repetition of any such unnatural angel-tragedy was certainly not probable, and still less inevitable"—(*see Keil*, l c.)—we reply that, while the natural disposition of man, and his proneness to evil, remained the same, the causes were removed, to which were chiefly owing the peculiar character and enormity of the evil which had existed in the old world, viz, the visible presence and agency amongst men of fallen angels and their progeny. An "improvement" *was* naturally "to be looked for" after the terrible visitation of the Flood: and, accordingly, an improvement appears in the fact, that those who had not alone disturbed the limits of creation, but who also had been instrumental in producing a state of lawless behaviour and moral depravity, to which no other age presents a parallel, were now no longer in the world. "The Nephilim were in the earth" in the antediluvian period, and also the fallen "Sons of God"—and only in that period—and the condition of the world, socially and morally, was in consequence, as we infer from the language of the historian, worse then, than in the times succeeding the Deluge. No "such unnatural angel-tragedy" has since been enacted in this world, and, probably, never again will be: and this fact, evident to the Divine foreknowledge, was the ground and reason of the Divine resolve that the judgment of the Flood should never be repeated; rather than that suggested by Dr. Keil, that God, expecting no change in human nature, would, simply from motives of pure mercy and long-suffering, forbear again to execute such judgment on the race.

Indeed, Dr. Keil himself admits, in a following section, that this is hardly an appropriate reason, and mentions Luther and Calvin as expressing a like thought. In truth, as the words are translated in our version, and in the Septuagint and Vulgate, the same reason which, in ch. vi., had been assigned for sending the Deluge, is alleged, in ch. viii., as a reason for its never being repeated. But, if we render the particle כִּי, as it is in the margin of the Authorised Version, by the English "though" (as in Ex. xiii. 17, Deut. xxix. 19) then the words convey an appropriate meaning, for then the Divine Being is represented as resolving that "He will not again destroy every living thing, *even although the imaginations of men are only evil,* because no such necessity, for a general destruction of life, as that which existed in the antediluvian time, will again arise."

The fact of the general destruction of living beings in the Deluge affords, undoubtedly, one of the weightiest arguments in support of the angel-interpretation: and, accordingly, it is urged by Kurtz and others, that only on the ground of that interpretation, can we explain the necessity for the almost universal extermination of the antediluvian race.

We call attention to the fact, [says the writer named, in his Hist, of the Old Cov.,] that it seemed to be necessary to destroy all mankind, and to commence, as it were, a new race—a circumstance which can only be accounted for on the view which we have advocated. It surely cannot have been an arbitrary arrangement, that when a new development of grace commenced with Abraham, the rest of mankind were allowed to continue, while, in this case, it seems to have been necessary that they should be destroyed, although (as he elsewhere observes) the sin of the builders of the Tower of Babel might well be supposed to be a more heinous one, than the marriage of pious men with godless women.

I do not comprehend, [he writes at p. 71 of his treatise, *Die Ehen*, etc.,] how the espousal of some pious Sethites with fair women for the sake of their beauty, could have caused a disturbance, in the development of human history, so terrible and so irreparable, that the evil could be remedied in no way, but by the extirpation of the human race. Espousals of that kind have often, and to a large extent, taken place; and, if, on every such occasion, a deluge must have followed, the world would have numbered as many deluges as years. That the fair daughters of men, spoken of in Gen. vi., were also godless, is only assumed: but, admitting that they were, however blameworthy we may believe such marriages to be, that they should, of necessity, draw after them the judgment of the Deluge, is inconceivable.

The real cause of that judgment he explains in a way which, to us at least, appears to be completely satisfactory.

We may easily conceive that the commingling of two classes of creatures, so widely separated from each other, and so different in their nature and destination, as are angels and human beings, must be an act by which the limits of creation, ordained by God, would be displaced—a displacement which must, of course, be the more hurtful in its consequences, the higher and more important, in the scale of being, the transgressors on either side[44]. We will see that if such commingling were universal—that is, if the unnatural influence had then pervaded the entire human race—the Divine plan would thereby be thrown into disorder, and, in fact, destroyed: and that, in such case, no resource would remain, but either to allow things to take their course, to the absolute and irretrievable ruin of the parties: or else, in order to save the earth, and the germ of the race, for a new development of human history, to exterminate the whole infected generation, with the exception of eight souls. The circumstance of a respite of 120 years being allowed, as a warning to those not yet involved in the corruption, who, at the date of its announcement, may have formed the larger portion of mankind, is, on our theory, quite natural and comprehensible.

Dr. Kurtz further quotes, as coinciding with his own view, the striking remark of Hofmann, that the evil to be met, in this case, was, not an excess of ordinary sinning—not simply a depraved condition of things within the established limits of creation,—but it was, that humanity was no longer propagated from itself, as God had ordained, and that the power of the beings who were brought into existence in a preternatural way, surpassed the limits allowed to human kind: hence, the essential conditions of the existence of mankind as a distinct race being thus unsettled and endangered, there was no way open for the counteraction of the evil, but that of terminating abruptly the history, in the course of which the race was being divested of its humanity.

The learned and able writer concludes this part of his subject with some observations respecting the manner, in which such violations of the established order of things are regarded by the Mosaic Law, and the abhorrence which that Law expresses of any intermingling of what the Creator designed to remain separate and distinct. We content ourselves with merely mentioning the passages, Lev. xix. 19; xx. 13, 15, 16 (Note K), to which he refers: and only add that, long prior to the promulgation of the Levitical Law, as will probably occur to the mind of some reader, the Divine abhorrence of such transgressions of the law of nature, was expressed in an unmistakable manner, in the awful punishment of the inhabitants of the cities of the plain.

The conjecture of De Zezschwitz will, probably, appear to be not wholly groundless, that the angels of Genesis vi. 2 were instigated by Satan to the commission of their sin, in order that he might thus be enabled to effect what we may, not inappropriately perhaps, term the adulteration of the Adamite race—that the race, for the salvation of which the promised seed of the woman should come, should be no longer purely Adam's, but a race impure and mixed, partly of demon origin—attempting thus to overthrow the counsel, and defeat the purpose of God.

Cujus rei (*scil.* humani generis per angelos corruptionis) rationem, si conjecturâ uti licet, hanc fuisse conjicias, ut quam Deus O. M. per procreandum ex humano genere salvatorem aperuisset salutis liberationisque e satanicâ potestate viam, eam diabolus *corrumpenda ac pervertenda generatione humana* voluerit praecludere, venturoque Dei filio *sui quasi seminis* homines opponere. Certè quae carnis voluptas in Genesi angelis imputari videtur non efficit, ut alia magis occulta criminis ratio, quae si non omnes, qui ita peccaverunt angelos, diabolum certè commoverit, omninò neganda sit.— (*De Christi ad Inferos Descensu, etc. Diss. Scripsit C. A. G. de Zezschwitz Lipsiae.* 1857. p. 66.)

Supporters of the Angel-Interpretation (Ancient Jewish)

We bring our review of the angel-interpretation to a close, with a brief notice of the several authorities which may be cited in support of it.

Not only does this interpretation appear to have been the first which suggested itself to readers of Gen. vi., as the natural and obvious meaning of our passage, but it was very anciently received both by Jews and Christians, no motive being fairly assignable for their adoption of it, except their belief that it was the true one. Indeed, no other explanation of the passage would, probably, have ever been thought of, had it not been for the influence of causes already adverted to. Of course, the worth of any interpretation of Scripture must be estimated on other grounds than that of the number or reputation of its supporters: but the opinion of many eminent Jewish and Christian writers, that the "Sons of God" were angels, will hardly be reckoned as of no account; and if it be shewn that the writings of two inspired Apostles contain a reference to the passage, and that they took a like view of the nature of the Sons of God, then we must conclude that all doubt as to the truth of the angel-interpretation has been removed.

The Septuagint.—The earliest authority, so far as we know, which can be adduced in support of this interpretation, is the version of the Seventy. The right, however, to claim these translators as favourable to our view, is disputed. The matter stands thus:—The Codex Alexandrinus (in the British Museum) and three later MSS. are said to render Bne-ha-Elohim, in verse 2, by αγγελοι το υΘεου, angels of God. All other MSS. of this version, including the Vatican, are stated to have υίοι του Θεου, sons of God, in this verse, as well as in verse 4: and even the Codex Alexandrinus reads υίοι in the latter verse. (See Kurtz, p.

12; Keil, p. 222.) Opponents of our view say that αγγελοι, in verse 2, is an alteration of the original reading, the interpolator having forgotten to introduce a like reading into verse 4: and that the Septuagint cannot, therefore, be brought forward as supporting the notion of the Bne-Elohim having been angels. This, however, is merely a conjecture, while the supposition, that any such alteration, had the idea of it been conceived, would have been omitted in verse 4, is utterly improbable. Dr. Kurtz has remarked that in Job i. 6, ii. I, xxxviii. 7, where the interpretation is not liable to be affected, as in Gen. vi. 2, by dogmatic prejudice, these translators have rendered Bne-Elohim by αγγελοι, and here the MSS. all agree. He has also pointed out (what it is of high importance to observe) that all the MSS. of the Septuagint, which we possess, date from a period when the angel-interpretation had fallen into disrepute—indeed, had come to be deemed impious and heretical—and that it is not, therefore, at all improbable, that transcribers of MSS. would, of their own accord, substitute the literal and then more acceptable rendering, υίοι του Θεου, for the original but condemned one.—*Vide infra*, p. 158.

It is worthy of note that Philo Judaeus (*vide inf.* p. 141) and Eusebius (Ev. Praep. 1. v. c 4), citing the passage Gen. vi. 2, appear to have been unacquainted with—at least, they do not make mention of—any other reading than that of αγγελοι του Θεου. It may be remarked that Eusebius adds, that of these angels "were begotten the giants, famous from old time" (—αφ' ων εγεννηθησαν οι γιγαντες οἱ ὀνομασςοι ἐξ αιωνος.) The same observations are applicable in the case of Josephus, although he does not quote the words of our passage: and Suicer (*Thes.* s. v. αγγελος) remarks that the Latin version must, at least, in some copies, have read *angeli Dei*, as Augustine, Ambrose, and Procopius testify.

What the views of the Seventy were, respecting the origin and nature of the *Nephilim* or *Gibborim*, they have intimated, not obscurely, in the fact that they have rendered these terms by γιγαντες. Dr. Maitland, asking how the authors of the English Version came to use the term *giants*, as the translation of *Nephilim*, replies that it was because the LXX. had used γιγαντες, and reminds his reader of the original meaning of that word, and of the idea which οἱ γιγαντες would have conveyed to the mind of a Greek, or of a Hellenistic Jew—a Jew acquainted with the Greek language, such as those who made, and those who subsequently used, the Greek version. Every school-book of heathen mythology, [he says,] will tell him. Let him, for instance, turn to Lempriere's *Classical Dictionary*, and he will find 'Giants, the sons of Coelus and Terra, who, according to Hesiod, sprang from the blood of the wound which Coelus received from his son Saturn: while Hyginus calls them the sons of Tartarus and Terra,' (Note A.) The giants, it is notorious, were a mixed race, of an origin partly celestial, and partly terrestrial: and it will be obvious that, supposing

the Seventy Interpreters to have understood *angels* by *Bne-Elohim* (which I have endeavoured to show they did), they could not have better expressed in Greek, that which they must have supposed the Hebrew word *Nephilim* to mean.—*The Fallen Angels*, p. 143.

The writer of the article Giants, in Dr. Smith's *Dictionary of the Bible*, referred to in a former section, remarking how closely allied the angel-story is to the Greek legends respecting the sons of gods and the giants, observes that "the Greek translators of the Bible made the resemblance still more close, by introducing such words as θςομαχοι, γηγενεις, and even Τιτανες." And it is true that such terms have been employed by the Seventy, and also by later Greek interpreters, as in Prov. ix, 18, where we read in our English version, of the house of a loose woman, that "the dead (*Heb.* Rephaim) are there," the LXX. have γηγενεις, "the earth-born," Theodotion, γιγαντες, and Symmachus, θςομαχοι, "fighters against God:" while, in 2 Sam. v. 18, 22, "the valley of the giants" (Rephaim) is, in the Septuagint, κοιλας των Τιτανων, "the valley of the Titans." But why may we not believe that their reason for using these terms, was, that they regarded the Rephaim, spoken of in these passages, as identical with the *Gibborim*, of Gen. vi. 4, and, consequently, with the γιγαντες of the Grecian mythology—in other words, that they viewed the "earth-born giants," and "the Titans," as representing in heathen tradition a race which they believed to have once been in existence, and whose origin they supposed to have been recorded by Moses? If the Greek translators were able to trace—as many since their day have done—not a few vestiges of the Mosaic history in the legends of the pagan mythology—if they discerned in the circumstances of the uncommon strength and stature, the ambitious and warlike disposition, of the giants—in their piling mountain upon mountain for the purpose of scaling the heavens—in their hurling rocks, trees, and mountains against the gods—and in their final overthrow by the latter—an unmistakable reference not only to the "mighty men of name," who flourished in the antediluvian times, and the "violence with which the earth was filled" in their day: but also to the tradition of the Tower of Babel, and the defeat of the impious purpose of its builders: and, if they further believed that these "mighty men which were of old" have been designated in Scripture by the several names of *Nephilim*, *Gibborim*, and *Rephaim*—then it was natural that, in translating these, they should employ the Greek terms best fitted to represent the ideas with which they associated the Hebrew words.

BOOK OF ENOCH.—Whether the version of the Seventy can be claimed, or not, as favouring our interpretation, the story of the angel-intercourse with daughters of men is set forth at length, but with additions and embellishments for which the Mosaic narrative does not supply ground, in the apocryphal Book of Enoch, a document in which is preserved, amongst other matter, the tradition of the ancient Jewish Church, relative to the meaning of Gen. vi. 1–4. The book is maintained, indeed, by Dr. Keil and others to have been the source from which Josephus and Philo, as well as certain Fathers and Rabbins, derived their views, for which, it is said, no foundation can be shown in Scripture. This famous book is supposed by its English translator, Dr. Lawrence, Regius Professor of Hebrew at Oxford, and afterwards Archbishop of Cashel, to have been composed about 30 years B.C.: but Dr. Dillmann, the latest editor, believes it to have been written so early as 110 B.C. The author was an unknown Jew, who borrowed the name of Enoch, and the book, originally written in Hebrew, Chaldee, or Syriac, refers to the fall of the angels, to their posterity, the giants, the crimes which occasioned the Deluge, visions of Enoch relating to various parts of the universe, revolutions of the heavenly bodies, and phenomena of the seasons, and to some of the leading events in Sacred History. Portions of it are sufficiently tedious. The work was current, in the form of a Greek translation, in the primitive Church, and until about the eighth century, when it was lost sight of, and known only by extracts preserved by Syncellus and some of the Fathers. Towards the close of the last century, however, the traveller Bruce discovered, in Abyssinia, three MSS., containing an Ethiopic version of the Book of Enoch, evidently made from the Greek one in use among the Fathers. Archbishop Lawrence's translation, published in 1821, was made from the MS. Deposited by Bruce in the Bodleian Library, Oxford, and follows the arrangement of chapters and verses observed in that MS[45].

The following is Pseudo-Enoch's representation, according to the translation of Lawrence, of the occurrence related in our passage:—

CHAPTER VII.—SECT. II.

1. It happened after the sons of men had multiplied in those days, that daughters were born to them elegant and beautiful.

2. And when the angels, the sons of heaven, beheld them, they became enamoured of them, saying to each other. Come, let us select for ourselves wives from the progeny of men, and let us beget children.

3. Then their leader Samyaza said to them, I fear that you may perhaps be indisposed to the performance of this enterprise:

4. And that I alone shall suffer for so grievous a crime.

5. But they answered him and said, We all swear,

6. And bind ourselves by mutual execrations, that we will not change our intention, but execute our projected undertaking,

7. Then they swore all together, and all bound themselves by mutual execrations. Their whole number was two hundred, who descended upon Ardis, which is the top of Mount Armon.

8. That mountain, therefore, was called Armon, because they had sworn upon it, and bound themselves by mutual execrations.

9. These are the names of their chiefs: Samyaza, who was their leader, Urakabarameel, Akibeel, Tamiel, Ramuel, Danel, Azkeel, Sarakuyal, Asael, Armers, Batraal, Anane, Zavebe, Samsaveel, Ertael, Turel, Yomyael, Arazyal. These were the prefects of the two hundred angels, and the remainder were all with them.

10. Then they took wives, each choosing for himself, whom they began to approach, and with whom they cohabited: teaching them sorcery, incantations, and the dividing of roots and trees.

11. And the women conceiving brought forth giants,

12. Whose stature was each three hundred cubits. These devoured all *which* the labour of men *produced*, until it became impossible to feed them:

13. When they turned themselves against men, in order to devour them:

14. And began to injure birds, beasts, reptiles, and fishes, to eat their flesh one after another, and to drink their blood. [46]

15. Then the earth reproved the unrighteous.

In the following chapter are enumerated the various arts, &c., in which tradition represents the Angels as having instructed mankind:—

CHAPTER VIII

1. Moreover, Azazyal taught men to make swords, knives, shields, breastplates,

the fabrication of mirrors, and the workmanship of bracelets and ornaments, the use of paint, the beautifying of the eyebrows, *the use of* stones of every valuable and select kind, and of all sorts of dyes, so that the world became altered.

2. Impiety increased: fornication multiplied: and they transgressed and corrupted all their ways.

3. Amazarak taught all the sorcerers and dividers of roots.

4. Armers *taught* the solution of sorcery:

5. Barkayal *taught* the observers of the stars....

[In chapter xv., verses 8, 9, the giants are thus spoken of:—]

8. Now the giants, who have been born of spirit and of flesh, shall be called upon earth evil spirits, and on earth shall be their habitation. Evil spirits shall proceed from their flesh, because they were created from above: from the holy watchers was their beginning and primary foundation. Evil spirits shall they be upon earth, and the spirits of the wicked shall they be called. The habitation of the spirits of heaven shall be in heaven; but upon earth shall be the habitation of terrestrial spirits who are born on earth.

9. The spirits of the giants *shall be like* clouds, which shall oppress, corrupt, fall, contend, and bruise upon earth[47].

It may be observed that, in a fragment of the Greek version of the Book of Enoch, preserved by Syncellus (pp. 24–26, ed. Paris, 1652), the progeny of the angels are designated, not only as the γιγαντες, but also as the ναφιλείμ, και ισχυροι της γης, οἱ μεγαλοι ονομαστοι—terms nearly identical with some of those in Gen. vi. 4.

It is justly remarked by Dr. Lawrence, in his Preliminary Discourse, that apocrophal books, although they may have no claims to inspiration, are yet of considerable value, when they indicate the theological opinions of the periods at which they were composed. He regards this as being the case, in no small measure, with the Book of Enoch, and observes that, although it may abound with fiction and fable—and, we may add, although it may contain some things that are extravagant and unreasonable—yet, it ought not, therefore, to be stigmatized as containing only error, but may fairly be regarded as a correct standard of the doctrine of the time in which it was written, so far as the subjects of which it treats are concerned. The advocates of the Sethite-interpretation, not unconscious of this truth, and perceiving the value of the testimony which the Book of Enoch thus affords, not merely to the antiquity of our explanation of Gen. vi. 1–4, but also to the fact of its having been the traditional one in the ancient Synagogue, have endeavoured to shew that the doctrine of the writer, relative to angels and angel-offspring, is to be ascribed, not at all to a Biblical, but to a heathen source. They have thus sought to bring into disrepute the interpretation which, they assert, has been derived from the apocryphal book exclusively. Dr. Keil, for example, maintains that the notion of a race sprung from the union of angels and women, has been borrowed from that of the demigods and heroes of the Grecian mythology: and the doctrine of the "watchers" from the paganism of Babylonia. But, his opponent, Kurtz, has pointed out that the latter objection applies with equal force to the angel-doctrine of the Book of Daniel: while, with respect to the former, he observes, that if the author of the Book of Enoch discovered, from an examination of the passage itself, and from the Biblical *usus loquendi*, that by the term *Bne-ha-Elohim*, in Gen. vi. 2, nothing but *angels* can be understood—then he must be allowed to have derived his views of the nature and origin of the *giants*, not from any pagan notions respecting demigods or heroes, but from Holy Scripture itself. He further shews, on the authority of Dillmann, that the intention of Pseudo-Enoch was, to oppose the heathenish opinions and tendencies of his time: and that, while he may have been indebted to heathen tradition for his embellishments of the story of the angel-fall—albeit these are few in number—yet that his knowledge of the event itself was derived from a different source; and that so far as his relation does not transgress the plain, verbal meaning of our passage it may be regarded as a not unfair representation of the opinion entertained on the subject by the ancient Synagogue. Both he and Dr. J. Richers refer to Eisenmenger's Entdecktes Judenthum (Judaism Unmasked), Vol. I., p. 380, as shewing that most of the Rabbins believed the *Bne-Elohim* to be angels.

PHILO JUDAEUS.—Additional testimony as to what the Jewish Church, about the time of Christ, understood by the expression "Sons of God," in our passage, is supplied by the Hellenistic Jews, Philo and Josephus. The former, quoting verse 2, in the treatise *De Gigantibus* (ed. Pfeiffer, 1786, Vol. II, page 358), and verse 4, in that which follows (*Liber, quòd Deus sit immutabilis*, page 388), reads, in both cases, αγγελοι του Θεου. On the former verse he says, "Those whom other philosophers call demons, Moses is wont to call angels. They are souls (ψυχαι) flitting through the air." In another passage from the *De Gigant.* quoted by Dr. Keil, he says, "Some of these (aerial beings) came down into human bodies, and could not separate themselves from them." Dr. Maitland's remark is to our purpose:

Whether it was (as Mangey suggests) from following the reading of the Septuagint version, as it appeared at least in his copy of it, or from his own idea of what was meant by the title *Sons of God*, it is clear that Philo Judaeus understood the passage as relating to angels. In either case, his testimony is worthy of notice. In the former, it adds greatly to the probability that αγγελοι is the true reading of the Septuagint[48] : in the latter it shows us what a learned Jew, of that early age, understood by *Sons of God*. (*Eruvin*, 139.)

JOSEPHUS.—The passage in Josephus (*Ant.* I. iii. I) is known to all who have handled our subject. We give it in the words of Whiston's translation. "Many angels of God accompanied with women (πολλοι γαρ αγγελοι Θεου γυναιξι συμμιγεντες), and begat sons that proved unjust, and despisers of all that was good, on account of the confidence they had in their own strength. For, the tradition is, that these men did what resembled the acts of those whom the Grecians call giants (γιγαντων)." The original is quoted in full by Kurtz and Keil. Josephus adds, that "Noah was very uneasy at what they did: and being displeased at their conduct, persuaded them to change their dispositions, and their actions for the better. But, seeing they did not yield to him, but were slaves to their wicked pleasures, he was afraid they would kill him, together with his wife and children, and those they had married. So he departed out of that land."

It is maintained by the advocates of the Sethite hypothesis, as already observed, that Philo and Josephus, and indeed, all the ancients who receive the angel-story, have derived it, not from an analysis of the language of the sacred writer, but from the Book of Enoch. Dr. Kurtz points out the great improbability of such a supposition, in the case of Josephus, from the fact that not the least portion of his account is traceable to such a source, and that neither in the language nor in the matter can there be shown an allusion to the narratives of Enoch, the author having contented himself with representing, substantially, the facts as Moses has recorded them. It is worthy of remark, that Dr. Keil, while supposing the Jewish historian to have thus been indebted to the apocryphal book for his views on this subject, discovers, notwithstanding, a

striking resemblance between his representation of the Sethite mode of life (*Antiq.* I. ii. 3, and iii. I) and that which is found in some of the Oriental writers who rehearse the Sethite-story—a resemblance, he says, which renders very probable the opinion that Josephus was acquainted with that explanation of our passage, according to which the Bne-Elohim are pious descendants of Seth. There is something of inconsistency in these views of the learned German professor, who would thus make it appear that the Sethite-explanation was current as early as the time of Josephus. That the latter knew anything of that explanation, we cannot think, as the earliest traces of it do not appear until the close of the second or beginning of the third century.

With regard to Philo, Dr. Kurtz regards it as extremely doubtful, whether he, an Alexandrian Jew, had any acquaintance whatever with the Book of Enoch, published, as it was, in a country remote from his own, and hardly a hundred years before the time in which he lived, or, if Dr. Lawrence be right, perhaps not so many as thirty. He remarks on the entire want of correspondence between the observations of Philo on the subject, and the narrative of Pseudo-Enoch: and shows that Philo has himself expressly indicated the source, viz. Gen. vi. I, *sqq.*, from which were derived his views respecting the "Sons of God."

THE APOSTLES.—That two, at least, of the New Testament writers, SS. Peter and Jude, have made mention, not only of the sin, but also of the punishment of the *Bne-Elohim* of Gen. vi.: and that they believed these to be angels, we, in common with some others, entertain no doubt. The consideration of the two passages in which such reference to the sinning angels occurs, will occupy us presently. Meanwhile, a third may be briefly noticed here. In I Cor. xi. 10, St Paul, speaking of the impropriety of women appearing in religious assemblies with uncovered heads, says, "For this cause ought the woman to have ἐξουσια (the sign of power, *i.e.* of her subjection to the man, which the context shows to be a vail), on her head, *because of the angels.*" Whether, in these words, the Apostle intended an allusion to the Bne-Elohim and the angel-fall of Gen. vi., is perhaps doubtful—if on no other ground, at least on this, that there does not appear to be any sufficient reason, why such an injunction should be laid upon women, when present in assemblies held for religious purposes, more than on other occasions, unless, indeed, we suppose that angels are more frequently present in such assemblies. Alford (*Gr. Test in loc.*) having noted that some, by αγγελους here, understand *guardian angels*, and observed that, although such angels certainly do minister to the heirs of salvation, yet there does not appear to be any immediate allusion to them here, says,

Others, again, understand '*bad angels,*' who might *themselves* be lustfully excited: so Tertullian, de Virg. Vel. 7, 'propter angelos, scilicet quos legimus a Deo et Coelo excidisse ob concupiscentiam foeminarum.' See also contr. Marcion, v. 8.—or, might *tempt men so to be,*—Schöttgen, Mosh., al.,—or, might *injure the unveiled themselves*: so, after Rabbini-

cal notions, Wetst. But οἱ αγγελοι, *absol.* never means anything in the N. T. except the *holy angels of God.*

It is, however, by no means, certain that an allusion to the angel-fall of Gen. vi, was not intended by the Apostle. Others, since Tertullian's time, have been of his opinion. "This passage," says Dr. Nägelsbach, p. 386, "is an excellent commentary on Gen. vi. 2, *sqq.* as, conversely, the narrative in Genesis serves for an historical elucidation of the words of the Apostle." Dr. Kurtz, also, regards a reference to Gen. vi. as very probable. We have every reason to think, he says, that the reading of the Septuagint, in Gen. vi. 2, at the time when the Apostle wrote, was αγγελοι του Θεου, and that the greater number of those who might have read his epistle, and who had also read or heard of those αγγελοι του Θεου, seduced by female beauty, believed them to be verily and indeed *angels.* "This being so," he adds, "it appears inevitably necessary to admit, that the Apostle did intend, in this passage an allusion to Genesis vi. 2: because all his readers, acquainted with the ancient, and then commonly-received, explanation of that portion of the Mosaic narrative, would necessarily be reminded of it by his words."

The Syriac Version.—The ancient Syriac version of the Old Testament, known as the Peschitto, believed to have been made after the middle of the second century, and first printed in the Paris Polyglot, is claimed by Delitzsch, and by Kurtz, in opposition to the view of Dr. Keil (See Kurtz, Die Ehen, 45: and Keil in Zeit. 232), as supporting our interpretation, on the ground that its author, having left *Elohim*, in *Bne-ha-Elohim*, untranslated, clearly appears to have regarded the expression as a standing recognized term for designating angels, inasmuch as he has followed the same course in Job i. 6; ii. I, where, it must be admitted, only *angels* can be intended.

THE TESTAMENTS OF THE XII. PATRIARCHS.— This is the title of an apocryphal work written in Greek by a Hellenistic Jew, a convert to Christianity, as is generally believed, in the first or second century after Christ: though Dr. Grabe (see Maitland's *Eruvin*, 140), who published, it in his *Spicilegium SS. Patrum*, believes "that it was written by a Jew, before the Christian era, and afterwards interpolated by a Christian." It professes to contain the last words, as well as various particulars respecting the lives of the sons of Jacob, delivered by themselves to their children: but it has been regarded as spurious by all the moderns, except Whiston, the translator of Josephus, who, in his "Authentic Records belonging to the Old and New Testaments" (Lond. 1727), has published an English translation of it.

The angel-story is made use of, in this book, for the purpose of warning against fornication and meretricious adornment of the person. In the Testament of Reuben, the Patriarch, having spoken of divers sins into which mankind are liable to fall, and of the special sin which he had himself committed (Gen. xxxv. 22), is represented as saying to his sons:—

Do not you, therefore, look upon the beauty of women: neither muse you upon what they do: but walk with sin-

gleness of heart in the fear of the Lord: and busy yourselves at your work, and in learning, and about your flocks, until such time as the Lord shall give you such a yoke-fellow, as it seemeth good to Him. (*Sect.* 4.)

Avoid, therefore, fornication, my sons: and give it in charge to your wives and daughters, that they do not adorn their heads and their faces: for every woman that deceives men by such arts, is reserved for the punishment of the future world. For, so did they deceive the Egregori, before the Flood: when, by seeing those women continually, they desired one the other: and they conceived in their mind what they would do, and they were transformed into the figures of men; and when their husbands accompanied with them, they appeared to them at the same time: and these women, desiring their company, in their imaginations, bare giants: for, the Egregori appeared to them as reaching up to heaven.—*Sect.* 5. (*Whiston's Transl. Authentic Records.* Part I. pp. 294, &c.)

The observations made above, in the case of the Book of Enoch, respecting the value of apocryphal writings generally, are applicable here: and whatever may be the opinion entertained with regard to the contents of these Testaments, they serve, at all events, to shew how our passage was understood at the time when they were composed. Mr. Whiston, in his Dissertation on the Genuineness of the Book of Enoch, having alluded to the Jewish and heathen accounts of the great size of the old giants, says,

> To suppose that the bare intermarriages of the sons of Seth with the daughters of Cain, *i.e.* of the worshippers of the true God with idolators, should produce such enormous giants, is contrary to all fact and experience, which shews that such gigantic stature of children has no dependence on the virtues or vices of parents. But that unnatural or monstrous mixtures may produce an unnatural or monstrous offspring: and that what men weakly call the bare imagination of the mother, *not knowing*, in the meantime, *what they say, nor whereof they affirm*, may greatly affect the child, is very agreeable thereto. So that this account in Enoch, (I only mean as explained in the Testament of Reuben) gives us such a rational cause of this enormous stature of the old giants, as we otherwise are utterly at a loss for: and is therefore so far from rendering this book incredible, as is commonly supposed, that it is a strong attestation to its genuine truth and antiquity.—*Auth. Records*, pp. 273, &c.

Without adopting the views of this writer respecting the genuineness or the antiquity of these apocryphal books, we believe their authors have rightly understood the narrative in Gen. vi., and have, therefore, been able rightly to account for the peculiar characteristics of the antediluvian giants. We mention only one other apocryphal writing, referred to by some who handle our subject, as setting forth the same view of the nature of *the sons of God*. This book, which we have not seen, is known as the Liber Jubilaeorum, and is called by Greek writers Λεπτη Γενεσις, or the Little Genesis. It appears to have been known to some of the Fathers, and to the mediaeval historians, Syncellus and Cedrenus. It has been translated from the Ethiopia into German, by Dillmann (1859), and Rönsch has also published "Das Buch der Jubiläen oder die kleine Genesis erläutert und untersucht u.s.w." Leipzig, 1874.

Supporters of the angel-interpretation (the fathers, etc.)

Amongst those who have expressed an opinion respecting the meaning of the passage, Gen vi. 1–4, some of the Fathers of the Church occupy an important place. The early Fathers, generally, understood the expression "Sons of God," in accordance with the ancient interpretation, as designating angels: and although their views on the subject do not necessarily prove the correctness of the interpretation, yet they cannot be regarded as destitute of all weight: and even though the passages which we adduce from their writings, may contain what some may regard as visionary, or as savouring of heathenism, yet it cannot but be interesting to learn how the subject has been viewed by men, of whom it has been said that "the diversity of their individual value is as great as the range and variety of their writings: that nothing can be further from historical justice, than either the wholesale laudation or condemnation of these writers, as a body: but that, whatever stand we may take, we cannot but see that they are of the utmost moment"

JUSTIN MARTYR.—This Father, who died a.d. 167, says, in his Second Apology for the Christians, chap. v.—

God, when he had made the whole world, and subjected things earthly to man, and arranged the heavenly elements for the increase of fruits and rotation of the seasons, and appointed this divine law— for these things also He evidently made for man—committed the care of men and of all things under heaven to angels whom He appointed over them. But the angels transgressed this appointment, and were captivated by love of women, and begat children, who are those that are called demons, and besides, they afterwards subdued the human race to themselves, partly by magical writings, and partly by fears and the punishments they occasioned, and partly by teaching them to offer sacrifices, and incense and libations, of which things they stood in need after they were enslaved by lustful passions; and among men they sowed murders, wars, adulteries, intemperate deeds, and all wickedness. Whence also the poets and mythologists, not knowing that it was the angels and those demons who had been begotten by them that did these things to men, and women, and cities, and nations, which they related,

ascribed them to God Himself [*i.e.* Jupiter], and to those who were accounted to be His very offspring, and to the offspring of those who were called His brothers, Neptune and Pluto, and to the children again of these their offspring.

For whatever name each of the angels had given to himself and his children, by that name they called them.—*Writings of Justin Martyr and Athenagoras. Transl. Clark's Ante-Nic. Lib. Vol.* ii, pp. 75, 76.

ATHENAGORAS.—In the same century, another of the Greek Fathers, Athenagoras, in his *Legatio pro Christianis*, written about A.D. 177, having remarked that angels like men were created free agents, and that some of them continued in the state divinely appointed them, while others departed from it, says of some of the atter:

These fell into impure love of virgins, and were subjugated by the flesh, and he became negligent and wicked in the management of the things entrusted to him. Of these lovers of virgins, therefore, were begotten those who are called giants. And if something has been said by the poets, too, about the giants, be not surprised at this: [&c., &c. In the following chapter (xxv.) he continues:] These angels, then, who have fallen from heaven, and haunt the air, and the earth, and are no longer able to rise to heavenly things, and the souls of the giants, which are the demons who wander about the world, perform actions similar, the one (that is the demons) to the natures they have received, the other (that is the angels) to the appetites they have indulged.—*Writings of Justin Martyr and Athenagoras*, as above, pp. 406–7.

Julius Africanus.—It has been already remarked that Julius Africanus, in the third century, was unwilling absolutely to condemn the angel-explanation. Having given it as his opinion that by

Sons of God [the descendants of Seth are intended, he says:] But if it is thought that these refer to angels, we must take them to be those (scil. angels) who deal with magic and jugglery, who taught the women the motions of the stars, and the knowledge of things celestial, by whose power they conceived the giants as their children, by whom wickedness came to its height on the earth, until God decreed that the whole race of the living should perish in their impiety by the Deluge.—*Fragments of Africanus, &c.* as at p. 36.

Clementine Homilies.—We may offer here some extracts from the *Clementina*, or *Clementine Homilies*, not only because their author dwells at some length on the subject of the angels and giants, but also because he has adopted a singular mode of accounting for the commencement of the angel-intercourse—his narrative reminding the reader of Jupiter's transformation into a shower of gold, for the purpose of gaining access to the apartment of Danae. The Clementina are believed to have

been the work of an Alexandrine Jew of the *third* century, who, for the purpose of procuring them greater authority, ascribed them to the eminent Father Clemens Romanus (ob. cir. A.D. 100), who is represented as travelling with the Apostle Peter, and listening to his discourses, which he is supposed to have, in these Homilies, committed to writing. In Hom. Viii, the Apostle is made to address an assembly at Tripolis in Phoenicia, and some of his audience being "tormented with demons," he makes use of the opportunity, previously to healing them, to account for the power of demons over men, showing that all things having been created very good, and handed over to man as their lord, and that mankind having fallen and proved ungrateful to God, a certain just punishment came upon them.

For, of the spirits [he says, chap, xii.] who inhabit the heaven, the angels who dwell in the lowest region, being grieved at the ingratitude of men to God, asked that they might come into the life of men, that, really becoming men, by more intercourse they might convict those who had acted ungratefully towards Him, and might subject every one to adequate punishment. When, therefore, their petition was granted, they metamorphosed themselves into every nature; for being of a more godlike substance, they are able easily to assume any form. So they became precious stones, and goodly pearl, and the most beauteous purple, and choice gold, and all matter that is held in most esteem. And they fell into the hands of some, and into the bosoms of others, and suffered themselves to be stolen by them. They also changed themselves into beasts and reptiles, and fishes and birds, and into whatsoever they pleased. These things also the poets among yourselves, by reason of fearlessness, sing, as they befell, attributing to one the many and diverse doings of all.

Chapter XIII.

But when, having assumed these forms, they convicted as covetous those who stole them, and changed themselves into the nature of men, in order that, living holily, and showing the possibility of so living, they might subject the ungrateful to punishment, yet having become in all respects men, they also partook of human lust, and being brought under its subjection they fell into cohabitation with women, and being involved with them, and sunk in defilement, and altogether emptied of their first power, were unable to turn back to the first purity of their proper nature, their members turned away from their fiery substance, for the fire itself, being extinguished by the weight of lust, [and changed] into flesh, they trode the impious path downward. For they themselves, being fettered with the bonds of flesh, were constrained and strongly bound; wherefore, they have no more been able to ascend into the heavens.

The Apostle then (chap. xiv.) informs his hearers of that, which appears to have formed part of the original tradition, and which, although not having a foundation in the Biblical narrative—the mention of it, like that of the punishment of the angels, being not necessary for the purpose of the sacred writer—may, nevertheless, be true; namely, that the angels, wishing to please their mistresses, discovered to them the precious stones and metals[49] which lay hidden in the earth, instructing them, at the same time, in magic, astronomy, and the powers of roots, the melting of gold and silver, the use of dyes, "and all things, in short, which are for the adorament and delight of women." He next proceeds to the description of the giants:—

Chapter XV

But from their unhallowed intercourse spurious men sprang, much greater in stature than [ordinary] men, whom they afterwards called giants; not those dragon-footed giants who waged war against God, as those blasphemous myths of the Greeks do sing, but wild in manners, and greater than men in size, inasmuch as they were sprung of angels; yet less than angels, as they were born of women. Therefore God, knowing that they were barbarised to brutality, and that the world was not sufficient to satisfy them (for it was created according to the proportion of men and human use), that they might not through want of food turn, contrary to nature, to the eating of animals, and yet seem to be blameless, as having ventured upon this through necessity, the Almighty God rained manna upon them, suited to their various tastes; and they enjoyed all that they would. But they, on account of their bastard nature, not being pleased with purity of food, longed only after the taste of blood, wherefore, they first tasted flesh."[50]

St. Peter, having gone on, according to the author of the Clementines, to show how, from devouring flesh of beasts, the giants came to devour human flesh—and how, in consequence of the abounding wickedness, the deluge of water was sent, that thus the purified world might be handed over to him who was saved in the ark, in order to a second beginning of life—finally makes a practical application of the subject to the persons addressed, warning them especially against idolatry and partaking of sacrifices offered to demons—the sin against which St. Paul cautions the Corinthians, when he asks (I Cor. x.), "Are not they which eat of the sacrifices partakers of the altar?" and adds, "The things which the Gentiles sacrifice, they sacrifice to devils and not to God; and I would not that ye should have fellowship with devils."

LACTANTIUS.—The views of this Latin Father on the subject of the angels and their offspring, are set forth at some length in his Div. Institut., lib. II. c 15, an extract from which is given in Note L.

Lactantius (*ob.* 330) believed that there were two kinds of demons—a *genus coeleste* and a *genus terrenum*—the former consisting of the angels who, in the beginning were appointed by God to be guardians on earth of mankind[51], whom they preserved from the snares of the devil, but who being themselves seduced by that enemy, engaged in unlawful amours, and were, in consequence, consigned to perdition—the latter, the terrestrial demons are the beings (or rather the souls or spirits of these) sprung from the intercourse of those angels with the daughters of men, and possessing a nature partly angelic, partly human. These spirits, whom he describes as *unclean spirits*—"spiritus immundi tenues et incomprehensibiles—contaminati ac perditi"—he regards as the inventors of astrology and divination, as the authors of oracular responses—desirous of receiving worship—and, being permitted to wander about the earth, as finding a solace for their own perdition in causing divers evils to mankind.

These are substantially the views entertained by the heathen philosophers of Greece respecting demons—on which some remarks will be found in the next section. It may here be observed that Dr. Maitland, in his essay on False Worship, expresses an opinion that the *unclean* spirits cast out of men by our Saviour, were no other than the spirits of those beings whose origin is recorded in our passage. Having pointed out, in the section on Demoniacal Possession, the absurdity, and—as he properly terms it—blasphemy, of denying the reality of the possession of human beings by evil spirits, in the time of Christ, and having observed that these spirits, called in the New Testament *daemons*, however they may be subject to Satan, are not to be identified with him, he says:

> At the same time, whether more or less related to, connected with, or governed by, Satan, these daemons were '*evil spirits*.' Our Lord healed many of *evil* spirits, πνευματων πονηρων. (Luke vii. 21.) They were wicked spirits; and, it would seem, some wickeder than others. Our Lord represents the evil spirit as returning with others worse than himself, πονηροτερα εαυτου. (Matt. xii. 45, Luke xi. 26.) They were, as a class, 'evil'—this is plain—but why are they called 'unclean,' αχαθαρτα? 'Evil,' we may understand. We may, certainly, say, that it was wicked to invade the persons of mankind, and to make the victims of such invasion exceeding fierce, and terrible to their fellow-men; and it was wicked to throw a child into fire and water with the purpose of destruction. All this was, no doubt, sinful on the part of the aggressors; but I do not see anything in the history of those spirits, or of the persons possessed by them, which should lead to the use of the epithet 'unclean,' in any such sense as we should think of assigning to the word. If we could imagine the evil spirits or daemons thus represented as wandering on earth, to be the impure spirits who left their own habitations, we might perhaps suppose that they were characterized and described, not by the acts of their vagrant humiliation, but by the sin which had led to it. This, however, does not seem to be consistent with the idea of their custody; and I am more inclined to believe that the uncleanness, or impurity, relates to their mixed nature; not purely human or angelic. It is worthy of observation, that the word rendered 'unclean' is not used in the Gospels except as an epithet of these πνευματα. In the Acts only once in any other sense, and that is with reference to Peter's breaking through the distinction between Jew and Gentile (Acts x. 14, 28, xi. 8), and what is yet more observable, the Apostle Paul employs it in speaking of the offspring of mixed marriages, 'the unbelieving wife is sanctified by the husband, else were your children unclean; but now are they holy.' (i Cor. vii. 14.)

Those who may take the trouble to read this little book, will readily understand that we do not regard these views as by any means fanciful or groundless.

The extracts given above, together with those in Note L, show the views entertained by the early Fathers—as well those who adopted the new, as those who maintained the old explanation of our passage—respecting the nature of "the giants," and "the Sons of God." To those already named, may be added Irenaeus, Tatian, Clement of Alexandria, and Tertullian, in the second century. Bardesanes, in the same century, a native of Edessa in Mesopotamia, in his *Book of Fate*, written in Syriac, is mentioned by Delitzsch. In the third century, Cyprian and Methodius: and in the fourth, Ambrose, bishop of

Milan, and Sulpitius Severus. Eusebius of Caesarea is also included in the number of those early Christian writers, who believed the Sons of God to be angels: but, although, in quoting Gen. vi. 2, he reads αγγελοι του Θεου, he yet seems to be in doubt, whether the fathers of the giants should be regarded as *of a nature superior to that of mankind or not*— οἱ τῆς τουτων (sc. γιγαντων) γενεσεως αιτιοι, ειτε τινος κρειττονος μοιρας ἡ κατα θνητων φυσιν υπαρξαντες, κ. τ. λ.—*Ev. Praep.* vii. 8, ed. Gaisford, 1843, Vol. II., p. 147.

That the Church Fathers derived their views of the meaning of our passage from the Book of Enoch, as some assert, and not from the Scripture narrative, cannot be proved. There is no sufficient reason for supposing, that they might not have formed their opinions on the subject, as Prof. Kurtz says, from examination of the sacred text itself, especially if they read, in their copies of the Septuagint, not υἱοι, but αγγελοι, in Gen. vi. 2: and, still more, we may add, if they were aware, as some of them may have been, that the original term, translated "Sons of God" can only mean "angels" in the only other places, in the Old Testament, in which it is found. "The relation subsisting in the case," says the writer named, "was probably a reciprocal one. The fact of the Fathers understanding our passage, as they did, may have served as a credential to the Book of Enoch: while their belief in the authenticity of the latter, may have helped to confirm them in the view which they formed respecting the meaning of the Scriptural passage." With regard to the embellishments of the narrative, or the additions of whatever kind made to it, for which the Biblical narrative affords no ground—these, he admits, are derived from the apocryphal book: perhaps, we ought rather to say, from the general tradition relative to an unnatural intercourse of human and superhuman beings, and the remarkable offspring resulting from it. Of this tradition, it is to be observed, that it was not by any means confined to the Jews, but handed down, in some form, amongst Gentile tribes, both in the east and in the west: and whatever additions or adornment it may have received, in the course of ages, we cannot believe it to have been purely matter of invention. A tradition, widely spread, and presenting mainly the same form in the case of nations widely separated from each other, could not have been wholly without a foundation. It must preserve the remembrance of real events—a remembrance carried with them by the descendants of the sons of Noah, to the various regions into which they were dispersed.

MEDIAEVAL WRITERS.—The only writers in the middle ages who receive the angel-interpretation, are Jewish. From the fourth century, onwards, the true explanation of the passage was rejected by Christian theologians, as Dr. Keil and others show, and, for many centuries, does not appear, except in cabbalistic and other writings of the Jews. Amongst the latter may be reckoned the Targum of Jonathan and the Commentary of Raschi: for, these Jews, although apparently preferring the traditional explanation, so far as regards *Bne-Elohim*, were evidently not disposed to deny that our passage contains a reference to an angel-fall.

Whether it was, that they were reluctant to discard the Jewish explanation altogether, and hence adopted it to the extent of making *Bne-Elohim* mean "sons of great men;" or, that, believing the Nephilim to be superhuman beings, and perceiving the difficulty of identifying with them the *Bne-Elohim*, they were induced to retain the Jewish interpretation of the latter term—we know not: but, certain it is that Raschi, having first interpreted *Bne-ha-Elohim* (Gen. vi. 2), "of princes and judges," adds as another explanation, "These were the שרים [used Dan. x. 13; comp. Rev. xii. 7] who went on His [i.e. Elohim's] mission:" and that Jonathan translates, or rather explains, the first clause of Gen. vi. 4, "Schamchazai and Uzziel fell from heaven, and were on earth in those days," while the former, in his note on הכפילים, Num. xiii. 33, makes use of terms nearly the same [52].—*Vide sup.* p. 99. Whether the angel names were borrowed by these writers from the Book of Enoch or not, they seem to have believed that Gen. vi. 4 speaks of the fall of some of the angels, and of their dwelling on the earth.

Dr. Keil, whose historical notice of the interpretation of Gen. vi. 1–4, has supplied some materials for ours, and who has referred to the passages from Jonathan and Raschi, just quoted, mentions also some others of the later Rabbinical writings, in which the angel-legend appears. Amongst these are the *Pirke* of Rabbi Eliezer, written at the earliest in the eighth century: the *Bereschith Rabba* of the eleventh century: the famous Cabbalistic book, *Sohar*, attempted to be fathered on R. Simeon Ben Jochai, but really compiled in the thirteenth century: and some others, less known, of the eleventh and thirteenth centuries, one of which contains a large extract from the Book of Enoch, relative to the watchers, the heavens, and mysteries revealed to Noah. (See Zeit. p. 227.) Of all these Dr. Keil says, their views on the subject were derived from the Book of Enoch, but this is an arbitrary assumption. We may, with as much reason, in their case as in that of the Fathers, believe that they were led to adopt such views, by an examination of the Scriptural passage—rather, indeed, with greater reason, inasmuch as the Fathers, in general, had but little acquaintance with Hebrew, while the others, masters of the language, may have come to the conclusion that those who "chose wives of the fair daughters of men," were no others than angels, from the fullest conviction that the Hebrew term *Bne-Elohim* cannot admit of any other signification.

THE MODERNS.—In addition to the mediaeval Jewish writers mentioned, as above, by Dr. Keil, as upholding the angel legend, he names two others of modem date, Rabbi Menasseh Ben Israel, and Rabbi Jacob Ben Isaac, two German Jews of the seventeenth century, who are also to be included in the number of its supporters. Not until the last century, however, did our interpretation again come into favour with Christian divines. The causes of its restoration, to some extent, to its former place, have been already adverted to. Amongst writers on the Continent, now or recently living, by whom it has been defended, are Engelhardt, Hofmann, Delitzsch, Drechsler, Nägelsbach, Richers, Von

Zezschwitz, quoted in the preceding pages. Dr. Richers mentions F. C. Oetinger, adding in a note that he adopts the view of "the cohabitation of demons with daughters of men."

The following also are named by Dr. Kurtz, viz. Köppen (The Bible, a Work of Divine Wisdom, I. 104): Baumgarten (Comm. on Pent.): Stier (Ep. of Jude): Dietlein (on 2 Pet.): Dillmann, (B. of Enoch): Fr. V. Meyer (Blätter für höh. Wahrh. xi. 61): Twesten (Dogmatics, II. i, p. 332): Nitzsch (System, p. 234): Huther (Comm. on Eps. Pet. and Jude). Dr. Keil, indeed, says that the four last named are improperly claimed by Kurtz, as supporting his view: but, from the words of Huther which he quotes (*Zeit.* 240, *note*), it appears that he, at least, does not decide either for or against that view: while Meyer, we think, may fairly be reckoned amongst its adherents, inasmuch as he regards the Bne-Elohim, if not as heavenly angels, at least as unearthly beings of some sort—demons—*daemones incubi*, as D. Keil himself suggests.

In these countries, the angel-interpretation has been adopted only by a few. Of English writers who have accepted it, Whiston, who died 1752, appears to be amongst the first In his explanation of the passage, however, the angel and Sethite views may be said to be combined. In his Dissertation on the Book of Enoch, already quoted, he says,

The account Moses gives us of the angels of God conversing with the daughters of men (for so the text was by all Jews and Christians read and understood in the first, and by almost all of them in several following centuries), with its consequence, the procreation of the antediluvian giants, seems little more than an epitome of the larger original account of the same thing in the Book of Enoch. [Having placed the two accounts in parallel columns, for the purpose of comparison, he continues,] We may here observe that the Alexandrian copy distinguishes the *angels of God*, Gen. vi. 2, which had to do with the wicked *daughters of Cain*, before the children of Seth had been perverted, from the *Sons of God* or the *children of Seth*, ver. 4, with whose wives, of the *posterity of Cain*, those angels of God had also to do, after their perversion. Which copy exactly agrees with all our accounts of these two sets of gigantic offspring before the Flood, ch. vi. 4. And this distinction in Moses, between the *angels of God*, and the *Sons of God*, seems to me to be just, and to give the greatest light to the present matter, of the descent of the Egregori, and the origin of the several sorts of antediluvian giants from them.—*Auth. Rec.* I. 271.

Dean Alford, from his remarks on a passage in the Epistle of Jude, must be regarded as favouring the angel-interpretation of Gen. vi. 2. Having observed that the rebel angels constitute the second example of Divine vengeance adduced by St Jude, he says, "The fact alluded to is probably that which is obscurely indicated in Gen. vi. 2," and compares with the *bonds* and *darkness* of the apostle, the Hesiodic passage, ἔνθα θεοι Τιτηνες υπο ζοφο, κ.τ.λ. (Theog. 729), where, in the words of the English translator—

> —The Titanic gods, in murkiest gloom
> Lie hidden, such the cloud-assembler's will.
> There, in a place of darkness where vast Earth
> Has end. (*Elton's Transl.* 970)

In the Prolegomena to the Epistle Alford says, "In the notes on these verses (Jude 6, 7) I have mentioned the probability, in my view, that the narrative in Gen. vi. 2 is alluded to." He adds that this impression has been much strengthened by the reading of, what he justly terms, a very able polemical tract [*Die Ehen, &c.*] by Dr. Kurtz: and that he thinks the latter has gone far to decide the interpretation as against any reference of Gen. vi. 2 to the Sethites, or of Jude 6, 7 to the fall of the devil and his angels.

Dr. Maitland's views have been frequently referred to: those of the Rev. G. V. Garland have also been noticed. We may add the name of the Rev. T. Campbell of Lurgan, in Ireland, who advocated this view in letters which appeared in the *Irish Eccl. Gazette* (1867), as mentioned at p. 95.

Lord Byron (Heaven and Earth) and Coleridge, who speaks (Kubla Khan, Sybilline Leaves) of—

> A savage place, as holy and enchanted
> As e'er beneath a waning moon was haunted

> By woman wailing for her demon lover!—

may have believed in, at least, the possibility of such an occurrence as that, which we feel assured has been recorded by Moses in Gen. vi. 2.

Demons

That Justin Martyr and others of the Fathers named in last section, have rightly understood our passage, so far as relates to the reality of an unnatural intercourse between angels and human beings, some will agree with us in thinking: although they may reasonably refuse to subscribe to all that these writers have said on the subject. The views of some of the Church Fathers, in the second, third, and fourth centuries, on theological matters, were largely influenced by their predilection for the Eclectic or Neo-Platonic philosophy, which did much evil to Christianity, by mixing up with its truths various Pagan notions. With regard to the opinion entertained by Lactantius, Athenagoras, and others, that *the spirits of the giants are demons*, permitted for a time to wander about this world, and to exercise in various ways a pernicious influence on mankind and human affairs, it seems desirable to say something. To many, no doubt, such opinions will appear to be strange and groundless. For our part, having regard to the peculiar origin, nature, and character, which we believe to have belonged to the *Nephilim*, we are so far from viewing them in that light, that we rather look upon them as neither improbable, nor wholly without foundation, although, of course, to assert anything positively on the subject, is to profess to be wise beyond what is written.

The Platonic philosophy, and, perhaps, still more, the Pythagorean, contributed largely to the development of the doctrine of demons. "The Divinity," says F. A. Ukert, in his treatise, *Ueber Dämonen, Heroen, und Genien*[53], "according to these philosophers, is a soul diffused throughout the universe: human souls are portions of it: they pass from one body to another. Souls floating in the air they called demons and heroes" He quotes a passage from Plutarch (*Is. et Osir.* 25) to the effect that "Pythagoras, Plato, Xenocrates, and Chrysippus, following the old theologians, had taught that demons were much stronger than men, and possessed a more powerful nature—that they partook of the Divine nature, but not without mixture"—and, in a note, he refers to Ocellus Lucanus, a Pythagorean, who lived before the time of Plato, as having taught that "the gods are in heaven, men on earth, and the demons in the space between."

It was taught in the Italic School, [says the author of an English abridgment of Brucker's great work on the History of Philosophy,] that, subordinate to the Deity, there are three orders of Intelligent beings, gods, demons, heroes, who are distinguished by their respective degrees of excellence and dignity, and by the nature of the homage which is due to them—gods being to be preferred in honour to demigods or demons, and demons to heroes or men. These three orders, in the Pythagorean system, were emanations at different degrees of proximity from the Supreme Intelligence, the particles of subtle ether assuming a grosser clothing, the farther they receded from the fountain. The third order, or heroes, were supposed to be invested with a subtle material clothing. Hierocles defines a hero to be a rational mind united with a luminous body…

The region of the air was supposed by the Pythagoreans to be full of spirits, demons, or heroes, who cause sickness or health to man or beast, and communicate, at their pleasure, by means of dreams, and other instruments of divination, the knowledge of future events.—*Enfields Hist. of Philosophy*, Vol. I. p. 420.

The views of the Platonists, generally, relative to the nature and the agency of demons, are these:—Demons are middle intelligences between God and men, stronger and more powerful than the latter, but endowed, like them, with passions and affections: they are immortal: great in number: and possessed of a subtile, spiritual body, of a substance similar to flame. They inhabit the region between earth and heaven, but occupy themselves everywhere, over the face of the earth, in the affairs of the world. With reference to the actions attributed to them, demons are good or evil—the former, protectors of men and beasts, regulators of the seasons, dispensers of earthly good, watchers and overseers of human affairs, presenting to the gods the prayers and offerings of men. Evil demons, on the contrary, are the authors of those disasters which befal men and beasts: they cause earth-quakes, inundations, famines, pestilence, excite bad passions and desires in men, and lead men unawares to worship them. They delight in sacrifices, and in bloody and dismal rites: they deal in divination and incantations, and make prophetic and oracular announce-ments. Demons may be provoked and con-ciliated, and they have occasionally appeared to men. (*See* Ukert, *ueber Däemonen, u.s.w.* pp. 157, 160, etc.)

That these were the opinions of heathen philosophers, is true: and that the Fathers referred to derived their notions on this sub-ject, in great measure, from heathen sources, may be admitted: but, after all, if we exclude the doctrine of *emanation*, great part of what the Pythagoreans and Platonists have said of demons, appears to be true of angels. We gather from Holy Scripture that these, holy and fallen, execute various purposes of God, and perform many of those offices and acts, which the heathen philosophy ascribed to demons. The holy angels are "ministering spirits sent forth to minister to them that are heirs of salvation:" and "the Angel of the Lord encamps round about them that fear Him, and delivereth them." (Gen. xxiv. 7—xxxii. I: I Kings xix. 5: 2 Kings vi. 16, 17, *cp.* Ps. Ixviii. 17: Ps. xxxiv. 7—xci. 11, 12: Dan. Vi. 22—ix. 21: Zech. i. 8–11: Luke xxii. 43: Acts xii. 7: Heb. i 14.) Both good and evil angels are employed by God, in punishing the wicked, or in chastening the righteous: they are either

commissioned or permitted by Him to cause death, pestilence, famine, war, and other things hurtful to mankind.

(Gen. xix. I: Judges ix. 23: I Sam. Xvi. 14: 2 Sam. xxiv. 16: 2 Kings xix. 35: Job i. 12—ii. 7: Ps. Lxxviii. 49: 2 Cor. xii. 7, *cp.* Luke xiii. 16: Jude 9: and the cases of demon pos-session in the Gospels.) Evil angels are per-mitted to tempt men to sin, to suggest evil thoughts, and excite evil passions, (I Chr. xxi. I: 2 Chr. xviii. 20, 21: John xiii. 2, 27, *cp.* vi 70.) How spirits communicate with our spirits, we know not, and are unable to form any but useless conjectures: but that they may convey thoughts into our minds, as well as understand those which arise in them, is an opinion which not only does not contravene any analogy or any evidence, but has ample foundation in the Divine Word. That fallen spirits actually received the idolatrous worship of the heathen, and, in some way, partook of the heathen sacrifices, is a point that appears to be established, and one to which we will presently revert: and that they have co-oper-ated with mankind in such practices as those of magic, divination, sorcery, and delivering of oracular responses, we cannot doubt, when we look into such passages as Ex. vii. 11, 12: Deut. xviii. 10, 11, 12: I Sam. xxviii. 7: Acts xvi. 16.

In this variety of acts and ministrations are included many of those which the Platonics and Pythagoreans attributed to their demons. Some of the views, indeed, entertained by these philosophers on the subject, as that demons act the part of mediators between men and the Supreme Being, and that we may, with propriety, invoke their intercession and aid—we, as believers in the New Testament, of course, reject "There is One Mediator between God and men." But, probably, the pagan theology, so far as it deals with intermediate beings, is not a whit more erroneous, than the doctrine of the lapsed and heretical Church of Rome, on the subject of angels and canonized men.

An opinion appears to have been widely entertained by heathen, Jews, and Christians, in ancient times, that the abode of demons was placed in the air or atmosphere which surrounds the earth, where they were supposed, at least by some, to be reserved to the judgment-day, when they will be cast into the abyss (Luke viii. 31); and in accordance with this view, they understand the question (Mat viii. 29), "Art thou come to torment us before the time?" Dr. Bloomfield (Gr. Test.) in a note on the words, "according to the prince of the power of the air" (Eph. ii. 2), says, "Mede, Whitby, and Wetstein have shewn at large, that both the Jews and the Gentiles (especially of the Pythagorean sect) believed the air to be peopled with genii or spirits, under the governance of a chief, who there held his seat of empire." Both he and Whitby quote the words of Diogenes Laertius, in his life of Pythagoras (viii. 32), that "all the air is full of souls" (ψυχων), and refer to the Rabbinical *Pirke Aboth* (a treatise of the Talmud), fol. 83, p. 2, as showing that the Jews also maintained the belief, that the whole air is filled with such beings, arranged in troops, and under regular subordination (*a terra usque ad firmamentum omnia esse plena turmis et praefectis.*) The phi-

losopher Democritus, Maximus Tyrius, Varro, Plotinus, (*see Ukert, ueber Dämonen*, pp. 151, 162, &c.), Philo Judaeus, and others, are mentioned as having held the same opinion. That this view was largely shared in by the Fathers, appears from the remark of Jerome on Eph. Vi. 12—"Haec autem omnium Doctorum opinio est, quòd aër iste, qui coelum et terram medius dividens, inane appellatur, plenus sit contrariis potestatibus." Dr. Bloomfield (Gr. Test), rejecting this notion of demons dwelling in the air, says, that we are not, on the one hand, to ascribe to St. Paul all the dreams of the Rabbins: nor on the other, to suppose that he disbelieved this notion, and yet countenanced it for a temporary purpose.

A learned Professor of the present day. Dr. Eadie, having noticed, in his commentary on the Ephesians, the various modes of explaining the words, της εξουσιας του αερος, "the power of the air" (Eph. ii. 2), adopted by some of the Fathers, and by ancient and modern commentators, viz. that they denote those powerful fallen spirits who inhabit the air, and that the Apostle has borrowed the notion from the Pythagorean or Gnostic demonology, or employed the language of the rabbinical schools: or else, that they are to be taken figuratively, either as denoting that the power of those evil spirits resembles that of the atmosphere, swift, mighty, invisible, or that *power of the air* is equivalent to *power of darkness* (Col. i. 13), says:

In none of these various opinions can we fully acquiesce. That the physical atmosphere is, in any sense, the abode of demons, or is in any way allied to their essential nature, appears to us to be a strange statement. [In a note to this he says, 'But see Cudworth's Intellectual System, vol. ii. p. 664, ed. Lond. 1845.'] When fiends move from place to place, they need not make the atmosphere the chief medium of transition, for the subtler fluids of nature are not restricted to such a conductor, but they penetrate the harder forms of matter as an ordinary pathway. There is certainly no Scriptural hint that demons are either compelled to confinement in the air, as a prison, or that they have chosen it as a congenial abode, either in harmony with their own nature, or as a spot adapted to ambush and attack upon men, into whose spirit they may creep with as much secrecy and subtlety as a poisonous miasma steals into their lungs, during their necessary and unguarded respiration. (*Eadie. Comm.* on Eph. 1854, p. 114, &c.)

Dr. Eadie's own explanation is, substantially, that the words ἀήρ and κόσμος in this passage correspond in relation—that the κόσμος of the New Testament is a spiritual world, the region of sinful desires, the sphere in which the ungodly live and move, an ideal sphere, comprehending all that is sinful in thought and pursuit, a region on the actual physical globe, but without geographical boundary—in short, all that moral territory that lies out of the living Church of Christ: and that, as there is an atmosphere surrounding the physical globe, so likewise an ἀήρ envelops this. All that animates the world of the ungodly, all that gives it community of sentiment, and contributes to sustain its life in death, and enables it to breathe and be, may be termed its atmosphere: and such an air or atmosphere, belting a death-world, whose inhabitants are νεκροι τοις παραπτωμασι και ταις αμαρτιαις, is really Satan's seat. We cannot, while admiring the learning and ability of this writer, help regarding his explanation in this instance as laboured and far-fetched. We prefer, at all events, taking ἀήρ in its natural and primary signification: and it seems to us that, understanding it so, the words in question, especially when viewed in connection with such passages as Eph. vi. 13, Matt. xii. 43, and Job i. 7, afford some ground for the opinion—albeit that of heathen philosophers also—that the region of the air, enveloping the material world, is really the abode of demons, whose time to be cast into the deep (εις την αβυσσον), the place reserved for the devil and his angels, has not yet come, and who, until that time, may be permitted to range, through the physical atmosphere, over the face of our globe. With regard to the expression εν τοις επουρανιοις, in Eph. vi. 12, the common interpretation is that it designates the abode of fallen spirits in the aerial regions, and Dr. Eadie himself says that such a view is maintained by no less names than Jerome, Ambrosiaster, Luther, Calvin, Beza, Bullinger, Bucer, Estius, Grotius, Bengel, Hyperius, Koppe, Hammond, Meier, Holzhausen, Meyer, Olshausen, Harless, Von Gerlach, De Wette, Whitby, Barnes, Bloomfield, and Macknight.

In last section reference was made to the

view of Dr. Maitland, that the spirits of the giants of Gen. vi. 4, may probably be the unclean spirits (πνευματα ακαθαρτα and οαιμονια ακαθαρτα) of the New Testament.

We have alluded above to the opinion, that the gods of the heathen actually participated, in some manner, in the sacrifices offered by the Gentiles, and, consequently, that these gods were not imaginary, but real beings. To the consideration of the latter point, Dr. Kurtz has devoted some pages of his History of the Old Covenant (Vol. II., pp. 211–217, Eng. Transl.), in a few extracts from which his views on the subject will best be presented to the reader.

The whole of the ancient Church, [says this writer,] was most fully convinced of the *reality of the heathen gods*. Idolatry in its esteem was devil-worship in the strict sense of the term. The Fathers of the Church had no more doubt than the heathen themselves, who still adhered without the least misgiving, to the religion they had inherited from their fathers, that the gods and goddesses of mythology were real beings, and had a personal existence, and that the worship with which they were honoured was not only subjectively directed, in the minds of the worshippers, to certain supernatural beings, but actually reached such beings and was accepted by them. The Fathers of the Church undoubtedly lived in an age, when the original power of heathenism was broken; but even this shattered heathenism, the *dis-jecta membra poetae*, still produced upon their minds the powerful and indelible impression, that there was something more in all this than the empty fancies or foolish speculations of idle brains; that there were actually supernatural powers at work, who possessed a fearfully serious reality. The impression thus produced upon their minds, by their own observation of the tendency of heathen idolatry, was confirmed by their reading of both the Old and New Testaments; and the greater the confidence with which they looked upon the salvation they had experienced in Christ, as something real and personal, the less doubt did they feel, as to the reality of the powers of evil by which it was opposed in heathenism. In a word, the gods and goddesses of heathenism were in their estimation the destructive powers of darkness, the fallen spirits, the principalities and powers that rule in the air, of whom the Scriptures speak. It is not to be denied, that in this they went farther than the Bible authorised them to go. But it must be maintained, on the other hand, that they laid hold of the substantial truth contained in the Bible; whilst their error was merely formal, and confined exclusively to their doctrinal exposition of that truth. But modern theology, both believing and sceptical, by denying all objective reality to the heathen deities, and pronouncing them nothing but creations of the imagination, has departed altogether from the truth, and rendered it impossible to understand either heathenism itself, or the conflict which is carried on by the kingdom of God, against the powers of heathenism.

Having referred to Hengstenberg as following this false track, and on the other hand to some theologians of the present day, or recently living, who have again arrived at the true solution of the problem, he says:—

What impartial expositor can possibly deny that such passages as Exodus xii. 12, xv. 11; Num. xxxiii. 4; Deut. x. 17; Ps. lxxxvi. 8, xcv. 3, xcvi. 4, xcvii. 9, cxxxv. 5, cxxxvi. 2, *sqq.*, &c., attribute to heathen deities not merely a 'sphere of existence,' but a 'sphere of action' also? In Exodus xii. 12, Jehovah promises, 'I will pass through the land of Egypt this night…and against all the gods of Egypt I will execute judgment, I Jehovah.' In his song of praise (Exodus xv. 11), Moses sings: 'Who is like unto Thee, O Lord, among the gods?' In Exodus xviii. 11, Jethro confesses: 'Now know I that Jehovah is greater than all gods!' Even on the gods whom Israel served in the desert Jehovah executed judgment. (Num. xxxiii. 4.) In Deut. x. 17, Moses declares to the people: 'Jehovah, your God, is the God of gods and the Lord of lords.' The Psalmists describe Jehovah as highly exalted above all gods (Ps. xcvii. 9, cxxxv. 5), as a great King above all gods (Ps. xcv. 3), as to be feared above all gods (Ps. xcvi. 4), whilst there is none like Him among

the gods. (Ps. lxxxvi. 8.) In the Prophets, the judgments of God on heathen powers are spoken of, as a victory on the part of God over the heathen deities, and a judgment inflicted on them.

Now who would suppose the theocratic law-giver, the poets, or the prophets, capable of such absurdity, as to think that the best way of convincing the people of the absolute power and supremacy of Jehovah, was to demonstrate continually that He was stronger than *nothing*, more exalted than a mere fancy, greater than what had no existence at all, victorious over something which had no sphere of operation or of life, ruler over that which was not, and judge of that which had never been? *Cervantes* makes the Knight of La-Mancha fight against windmills: but the prophets would have done something worse than this, if they had made their Jehovah attack, conquer, and execute judgment upon something, of which they were convinced that it never existed at all.

The following passage exhibits very clearly the relation subsisting between the mythological world of deities, and the demon-world:—

The Scriptures do not anywhere affirm, that the mythological world of heathen deities exactly corresponds to the objective world of daemons, that is to say, that every individual god in the heathen worship is to be personally identified with an individual daemon, or, vice versâ, that each particular daemon is represented by some heathen deity, so that we can say that Osiris and Isis, or Jupiter, Mars, Venus and others, are all representatives of particular personal daemons, and that the same name always denotes the same daemon. On the contrary, they merely affirm that the worship of the heathen has respect to real objects; that all the homage paid to a heathen deity reaches some existing, personal, supernatural power, and is accepted by that power; and that as the heathen devotes himself to some such power by the worship which he presents, so does that power come near to him, and enter into living fellowship with him. 'The things which the heathen sacrifice,' says Paul, 'they sacrifice to daemons'—they think they are offered to a god, but they only reach a daemon, a being opposed to God, and not God; and he who sacrifices entets thereby into fellowship with daemons, as the Christian, when he comes to the table of the Lord, enters into fellowship with Christ.

Views substantially the same with those of Kurtz are expressed by Dr. Nägelsbach (127, 129), who, contrary to the opinion of Maitland, that false worship was first introduced by the fallen angels of Gen. vi., maintains that idolatry would have arisen, though demons had never come into actual communication with mankind, the source of it existing already in the corruption and weakness of human nature: so that although the historical continuity of idolatry was interrupted by the Deluge, yet not the continuity of the motives which led to it, human nature remaining the same. He shows that St. Paul, who, in I Cor. viii. and x, refers idolatry, objectively to the demons, exhibits in Rom. i. its subjective origin in the "*vain imaginations* and *darkness*" of the human heart. It was not devil worship, but the deification of the objects and phenomena of nature, that formed, he thinks, the beginning of false worship. At the same time, he admits, that the appearance in the world of demons must have contributed largely to the support and the increase of the evil. They lent to the ideal abstractions the solid support of historical personality. They substituted themselves in the consciousness of men, for the God-idea which floats in the mind—and this in a manner so complete, that the vision of the man, originally directed upwards to the One Supreme, sank downwards, and became divided amongst many small divinities.

Both these writers point out, that from the use of the word δαιμονια, by the LXX. translators, as the rendering of שׂרים, Deut. xxxii. 17: Ps. cvi. 37, and אלילים Ps. xcvi. 5, we may gather that the opinions of later Jews respecting the heathen deities were similar to those which have now been indicated, viz. that these deities were representatives of demon powers—a view which, they add, has been fully sanctioned by the New Testament, as appears from the description of the spirit by which the girl at Philippi was possessed (Acts xvi. 16), as a πνευμα Πύθωνος: and from the words of St. Paul in I Cor. x. 20, "The things which the Gentiles sacrifice, they sacrifice to demons (δαιμονιοις), and not to God: and I would not that ye should have fellowship with demons (κοινωνοι των δαιμονιων).

S. Peter and S. Jude

The passages in the writings of these apostles, in which allusion is made, as many believe, to the narrative in Gen. vi. 1–4, are as follows:—

2 Peter ii. 4, 5, 6.—For if God spared not the angels that sinned, but cast them down to hell, and delivered them into chains of darkness, to be reserved unto judgment; and spared not the old world, but saved Noah the eighth person, a preacher of righteousness, bringing in the flood upon the world of the ungodly; and turning the cities of Sodom and Gomorrha into ashes condemned them with an overthrow, making them, an ensample unto those that after should live ungodly.

Jude 6, 7.—And the angels which kept not their first estate, but left their own habitation, he hath reserved in everlasting chains under darkness unto the judgment of the great day. Even as Sodom and Gomorrha, and the cities about them in like manner, giving themselves over to fornication, and going after strange flesh, are set forth for an example, suffering the vengeance of eternal fire.

The resemblance between these passages is so striking, that, to use the words of Alford, it precludes all idea of entire independence. The Dean accounts (*Proleg. 2 Peter*) for the resemblances existing between portions of these Epistles, by supposing that St. Peter had in his thoughts, and made use of, the text of the other, contracting or omitting, expanding or inserting, as suited his purpose.

It will be admitted that these passages relate to one and the same apostasy of angels. But the question for us is, Do they relate to the fall of Satan and his angels, anterior to the creation of man? Or, do they speak of some other angel-fall, and, if the latter, do the passages themselves afford ground for identifying these angels with the "Sons of God" of Genesis vi?

To the minds of those who have not bestowed special attention on any of these passages, it has probably never occurred to think of any other fallen angels than those who are often brought before us in the New Testament, viz. Satan and his angels: while some who have made our passage a subject of investigation, but who find in the "Sons of God" only pious Sethites, are obliged to identify the sinning angels of Peter and Jude with the wicked spirits just referred to: because, if the passage, Gen. vi. 2, has no reference to angels, there is no intimation in the Bible, that any fall of angels has taken place, excepting that of Satan and those who fell with him.

Before presenting what we regard as the weightiest argument against the opinion that Satan and his angels are here referred to, we notice two others advanced by Prof. Kurtz. One is founded on the use, by New Testament writers, of the term αγγελοι.

I believe, [he says,] I must here advert to a point which has not hitherto been observed. Both apostles designate those who are punished, simply as αγγελοι: and if we examine the Biblical usage of the Greek, we discover that this word, when used by itself, is never employed to denote those spirits who fell εν άρχή. These are always spoken of as δαιμονες, and their head as διαβολος or σατανας.

Dr. Kurtz says, he is well aware of such passages as Matt. XXV. 41, 2 Cor. xii. 7, Rev. ix. 11, xii. 7, 9, and observes that, in these, Satan's angels either appear as in opposition to God or to holy angels, or else the term αγγελοι is joined with words which limit and define its meaning. He admits that 1 Cor. vi. 3, "Know ye not that we shall judge angels (αγγελους)," appears to be opposed to his view: but even in this instance, he remarks, that if Satan and his angels are included, so likewise are those who continued holy after his fall. He, hence, concludes that αγγελοι, alone, is not used to designate the former, at least to the exclusion of the latter: and that as the apostles have employed the naked term, neither they themselves intended, nor would their first readers have been likely to perceive, an allusion to the fall of Satan and his angels.

An argument, however, [Dr. Kurtz continues,] of greater weight is furnished in the fact, that Satan himself is not mentioned. Wherever else allusion is made to the Tempter and those who were associated with him in his fall, mention is expressly made of *him*, and, for the most part, of him only [54]. That it should be otherwise, in the passages under consideration, is the more remarkable, as it was manifestly the aim of both Apostles to show, that God, when He judges, does not spare even the most eminent in rank: and had they intended a reference to the Satan-fall, they would undoubtedly have named the most distinguished of those apostate spirits, the chief and leader of the rest. (*Die Ehen*, &c., 21, 22.)

An argument stronger than either of these, against the opinion that these apostles refer to the fall of Satan and his angels, is derived from a consideration of the present condition of the angels "who kept not their first estate," as compared with that of "the devil and his angels." With regard to the former, St. Peter says that they have been "cast down to hell (Tartarus), and delivered into chains of darkness, to be reserved to judgment"—Jude, that they are "reserved in everlasting chains under darkness, to the judgment of the great day." This is surely not the state in which Satan and his angels are, or have been, since their fall. From both the Old and New Testaments we learn that they are yet permitted to move throughout this world, to approach mankind for the purpose of tempting them, and to overcome those who are not arrayed in the armour of God. Satan "goes to and fro upon the earth"—Job i. 7. He tempted Eve in the garden: he tempted Cain, David, and Judas. "We wrestle not with flesh and blood, but with principalities and powers." The same apostle who describes the "sinning angels" as having been "delivered into chains of darkness, to be reserved to judgment," tells us (I Pet. v. 8) that "the devil, as a roaring lion, walketh about, seeking whom he may devour."

In short, [it is well observed by Dr. Maitland,] as if to preclude all mistake, and to certify us that Satan is not one of those beings already delivered into chains, to await the judgment, it is declared (Rev. xx.) that he *shall hereafter* be chained: and it is thereby implied (whatever may be the precise meaning of the term) that he is not already in chains.—*Eruvin.* 113.

It is difficult, therefore, to conceive how those angels, who are reserved in chains and darkness, to the judgment day, can be regarded as identical with those other angels, who evidently are still permitted to roam about. Nor is it a very satisfactory solution of the difficulty, to say. with Dr. Keil and others, that the punishment of the angels, described by these apostles, does not involve such a state of existence, as absolutely to exclude all influence on the world of men—that the expressions, "chains of darkness," and being "reserved in everlasting chains under darkness," are not to be understood in the literal and material sense, as may be inferred from Wisdom xvii. 2, 17, but may mean the chains of sin, of spiritual darkness, of a guilty conscience, and the restraints put upon wicked angels in their attempts to frustrate the Divine purpose. The words, μτ τηρησαντας την εαυτων αρχην αλλα απολιποντας κ. τ. λ., "may be very well

interpreted," Dr. Keil says, "as they were by the earlier Christian theologians, as relating to the fall of Satan and his angels, to whom all that is said concerning their punishment fully applies." We cannot concur in this view, or in the further opinion expressed by the writer, that even the verb ταρταρωσας, used by St Peter, does not necessarily mean removal to a region, whence an influence can no more be exercised in this world, but may denote merely the condition of beings fallen from their holy state, shut out from communion with God and holy creatures, and destitute of hope of redemption. "Ταρταροω," he says, "may indeed mean '*to cast into Tartarus*,' or '*to make one an inhabitant of Tartarus*;' but it may also mean '*to reduce to the condition of those in Tartarus*.'" Holy Scripture, he adds, while it speaks of heaven and hell as places, also uses these terms in a figurative sense, the one, to denote the sphere of divine life and holiness, the other, the state of unholiness and damnation. In short, it is thought that, when these apostles tell us that the angels are kept in hell (Tartarus) under bonds and in darkness, there to remain to the judgment day, we should understand them not as describing a prison, in which they are fast bound, and debarred from all intercourse and connexion with our world[55], but only as expressing, in a figurative way, the estrangement of these angels from God, their enmity to Him, and the controlling power which He exercises over them.—(See Keil's *Der Fall der Engel*, in *Zeitschrift für die luth.* Theol., 1856: and his *Comm. on Pent.* p. 132, n. 1.)

Dean Alford takes, no doubt, a more correct view, when he says, "There is apparently a difference which we cannot explain, between the description of the rebel angels here (Jude 6.) and in 2 Peter, and that in the rest of the New Testament, where the devil and his angels are said to be powers of the air, and to go about tempting men. But perhaps we are wrong in absolutely identifying the two sets of evil spirits."

On the grounds now set forth, we think it lawful to conclude that by the term αγγελους, in these passages in the epistles of SS. Peter and Jude, Satan and his hosts could not have been intended. We are further led, by such examination of the passages as we have been able to make, to the belief, that the angels whose present condition they describe, are no others than those who are designated in Gen. vi., as the "Sons of God."

Firstly, the argument of St. Peter appears to be strikingly defective, unless we connect the angels with the bringing on of the Deluge. Dr. Maitland, having quoted at length the words of the Apostle, observes that his object was, to warn against false teachers, to declare the certainty of the judgment which awaited such apostates, and at the same time to give assurance of the safety of those who should continue stedfast in the faith.

With this view, [says Maitland,] he reminds them, that on other occasions, when His wrath had been revealed against sinners to their destruction, God had manifested His power and fidelity in the preservation of His servants. Thus, when He cast down the angels, and over-whelmed the world of the ungodly in a flood. He saved Noah and his family: when He destroyed Sodom and Gomorrha, He preserved Lot. The argument is plain: but unless there was some connection between the fallen angels and the Flood, why are they mentioned? If, indeed, the Apostle had said,—'For if God spared not those angels who sinned [but preserved those who had not sinned, in the judgments which fell upon the guilty]—if He spared not the old world, but saved Noah—if He spared not Sodom, but preserved Lot—It is manifest, that He knoweth how to deliver the godly out of temptation, and to reserve the unjust unto the day of judgment to be punished:'—if the Apostle had said this, the argument would have been plain, and the consequence would have followed rightly: but the case of the angels, as it is commonly understood, is so far from illustrating the doctrine which the Apostle is maintaining, that it is, in reality, one of unmixed severity.

The writer justly remarks, that as the passage stands, there is evidently something wanted to complete its meaning, unless we connect verse 4 with the following verse: but that, if we suppose these angels were the instruments of bringing on that flood of vengeance, in which Noah and his family were wonderfully preserved, the sense is obvious, and the case is precisely suited to the Apostle's argument.

An examination of the passage in St. Jude,

also, will incline us the more to believe, that the angels intended by these Apostles are identical with "the Sons of God" of Gen. vi. The design of St. Jude's epistle was, to guard believers against the corrupt principles and the licentious practices of certain persons, whom he describes as "turning the grace of God into lasciviousness:" and his discourse (see vv. 4, 7, 8) as well as St. Peter's (vv. 6, 7, 8, 10, 14, 18) is "pointedly and especially directed against that particular sin. He therefore reminds them of the recorded instances in which that sin had brought down the divine judgment. First, in the case of Israel[56]—then, in that of the angels—and then, in that of the inhabitants of Sodom and Gomorrha and the cities about them, in like manner, giving themselves over to fornication, and going after strange flesh."—(*Eruvin*, 155.) The expression, "in like manner," or, as it ought to have been translated, "in like manner to these" (τον όμοιον τουτοις τροπον) must be specially noted. To what does the τουτοις refer?—to the *ungodly men* of whom the Apostle speaks, or to the *angels*, or to *Sodom and Gomorrha*? Some suppose the latter, and understand St. Jude to say, that the circumjacent cities of Admah, Zeboim, and Zoar, in like manner to Sodom and Gomorrha, committed fornication—the difficulty presented by the *masculine* τουτοις being met by regarding it as referring to the *inhabitants* of those cities.

Dr. Keil quotes a passage from Calvin to this effect:—"When he (Jude) says that the neighbouring cities committed fornication in like manner *to these*, I refer the latter term, not to the Israelites, or to the angels, but to

Sodom and Gomorrha. The circumstance of the pronoun τουτοις being masculine, is not an obstacle, as Jude had regard to *the inhabitants*, rather than to the places."

Dean Alford remarks that it is fatal to this view, that thus we should have αί περι αυτας πολεις as the main subject of the sentence, and Sodom and Gomorrha only mentioned by the way. The reference, by Bengel and Rosenmüller to the *ungodly men* who are being treated of, he regards as still less likely, seeing that they come in verse 8, evidently after a series of examples, in which they have not been mentioned, with όμοιως μεντοι και ουτοι. Alford himself understands τουτοις as referring to the angels. "*In like manner to these* (τουτοις), the angels above mentioned. The manner was similar, because the angels committed fornication with another race than themselves, thus also απελθοντες οπισω σαρκος έτερας." (*Gr. Test. in loc.*) He names, as taking this view, Ludovicus Capellus, Herder, Augusti, Schneckenberger, Jachmann, De Wette, Arnaud, Stier, Huther. We might add Delitszch, Kurtz, Richers, Maitland, and others.

We cannot, in view of all this, avoid the conclusion, that St. Jude, in using the words τον όμοιον τουτοις τροπον, has drawn a comparison between the sin of Sodom, and the sin of the angels—in each case, *a going after strange flesh*. Dr. Keil, indeed, thinks that:

the reference of τουτοις to the angels, is altogether precluded by the clause και απελθοντες οπισω σαρκος έτερας, which follows the word εκπορνευσασαι. For fornication on the part of the angels could only consist in their going after flesh, or, as Hofmann expresses it, 'having to do with flesh, for which they were not created,' but not in their going after *other*, or foreign flesh. There would be no sense in the word ἑτέρας unless those who were ἐκπορνεύσασαι were themselves possessed of σαρξ; so that this is the only alternative, either we must attribute to the angels a σαρξ or fleshly body, or the idea of referring τούτοις to the angels must be given up.

On the subject of the acquisition of fleshly bodies by the angels we have already dwelt (XIII.), so that, even though the ἑτέρα σαρξ should necessarily presuppose an ἰδία σαρξ, the difficulty would not be insurmountable: but, apart from this, it seems to us that, in this objection, undue stress is laid on the expression ἑτέρα σαρξ, and that the idea intended to be conveyed by the Apostle is nothing more than this, that the Sodomites resembled the angels, in that, like the latter, they departed from the appointed course of nature, and sought the gratification of lawless and unnatural desires.

That the ἀγγελοι of St Jude, can be no others than those mentioned in the Book of Enoch, and, consequently, "the Sons of God" of Gen. vi., can hardly be doubted, if we bear in mind, that not only was the Apostle himself, but also his first readers, acquainted, if not with the Book of Enoch, at least with the traditional matter of which it is the depository: and, as he has introduced, in his epistle, ideas and expressions, relative to the angel-fall and its punishment, similar to those employed by Pseudo-Enoch (see Kurtz, *Die Ehen*, 27, and De Zezschwitz, *De Christi Descensu*, 60), these readers would, as a matter of course, suppose that he alluded to the narrative in Gen. vi., with the traditional explanation of which they were familiar.

It is well observed by Dean Alford (*Prolegom. to Jude*) that the fact that the particulars related, by St. Peter and St. Jude, of the fallen angels, are found also in the Book of Enoch, is not a proof that the Apostles took them from that book. The apocryphal writer, on the contrary, may have borrowed from the Apostles; or, the source, in each case, may have been ancient tradition. The Apostles accepted the tradition so far as it agreed with Holy Scripture and with the facts of the case: and written down by them, under the inspiration of the Holy Spirit, the tradition became an authentic record, and a part of the Word of God.

We close this last section of our essay with an humble expression of thankfulness to Him, who has granted the opportunities favourable to its being written, and vouchsafed, as we believe, the Divine guidance, which alone can bring men to the knowledge of the truth.

Notes

NOTE A

GIANTS, TITANS, γιγαντες, Τιτανες, Τιτηνες—
See Hesiod, Theog., vv. 125 sqq. for the origin of the Titans (Hyperion, Japetus, etc.) sons of Coelus or Uranus and Terra: and (vv. 154–186) of the μεγαλοι γιγαντες. Also, V. 820, of Typhon, sprung from Tartarus and Terra.

It may be remarked that, while Hesiod represents the giants as sprung from earth impregnated with the blood which fell from *Coelus*, when wounded by his son Saturn, another mythologist, Hyginus, makes them to be sons of Tartarus and Terra. Is there in these traditions, which thus respectively ascribe the origin of the giants to Heaven and Tartarus, any reference to the original condition and subsequent fall of the real progenitors of these beings—the Bne-Elohim of Gen. vi.?

HEROES, DEMIGODS.—In the Op. et D. I., 155, sqq., Hesiod speaks of the άνόρων ήρωων θειον γενος οι καλεονται ήμιθεοι "the divine race of heroes called demigods" (Hesiod's fourth race): and Homer (II. xii. 23.) of the ήμιθεων γενος ανόρων, "the race of semi-divine men." See Virgil, *Georg.* I., 276: Ovid, *Met.* I., 151, etc. See also Nägelsbach, 40, III—Delitzsch, p. 193—Ukert, *ueber Dämonen, Heroen, und Genien,*—Leipzig. 1850. pp. 176, etc.

We quote, for the English reader, Hesiod's account of the origin of the giants, from Elton's Metrical Version:—

—Vast heaven came down from high,
And with him brought the gloominess of
  night
On all beneath: with ardour of embrace
Hovering o'er Earth, in his immensity
He lay diffused around. The wily son
From secret ambush then his weaker
  hand
Put forth: his right the sickle grasped,
  with teeth
Horrent, and huge, and long: and from
  his sire
He swift the source of generative life
Cut sheer: then cast behind him far away
The bloody ruin. But not so in vain
Escaped it from his hold: the gory drops
Earth, as they gushed, received. When
  years rolled round.
Thence teemed she with the fierce
  Eumenides,
And giants huge in stature, all in mail
Radiant, and wielding long-protended
  spears:
And Nymphs, wide worshipped o'er the
  boundless earth
By Dryad name.—(*Theog.* vv. 241–58)

Hesiod describes, in the following, his
third and fourth races, in which Dr. Nägelsbach recognises the races of the Cainites and
Sethites.—

The Sire of earth and heaven created
  then
A race, the third, of many-languaged
  men:

Unlike the silver they: of brazen mould,
Strong with the ashen spear, and fiercely
  bold:
Their thoughts were bent on violence
  alone,
The deeds of battle, and the dying groan:
Bloody their feasts, by wheaten food
  unblest:
Of adamant was each unyielding breast.
Huge, nerved with strength, each hardy
  giant stands.
And mocks approach with unresisted
  hands:
Their mansions, implements, and
  armour shine
In brass—dark iron slept within the
  mine.
They by each other's hands inglorious
  fell.
In horrid darkness plunged, the house of
  hell:
Fierce though they were, their mortal
  course was run,
Death gloomy seized, and snatch'd them
  from the sun.
Them, when th' abyss had cover'd from
  the skies,
Lo! the fourth age on nurturing earth
  arise:
Jove formed the race a better, juster line,
A race of heroes and of stamp divine:
Lights of the age that rose before our own.
As demigods o'er earth's wide regions
  known.
Yet these dread battle hurried to their
  end:

Some, where the seven-fold gates of The-
bes ascend:
The Cadmian realm: where they with
fatal might
Strove for the flocks of Oedipus in fight:
Some war in navies led to Troy's far shore,
O'er the great space of sea their course
they bore,
For sake of Helen with the beauteous
hair,
And death, for Helen's sake, o'erwhelm'd
them there.
Them on earth's utmost verge the god
assign'd
A life, a seat, distinct from human kind:
Beside the deep'ning whirlpools of the
main,
In those blest isles where Saturn holds his
reign, &c. (*Works and Days*, I., 189,
&c)

The latter portion of the Theogony of Hesiod is occupied with the legends of the war of
the gods and Titans, and the combat of Jupiter
and Typhoeus, the offspring of Tartarus and
Earth. (See Works of Hesiod, &c., prose and
metrical versions, in Bohn's Classical Library.)

NOTE B

The Targums of Onkelos and Jonathan Ben
Uzziel (Gen. vi. 1–4), from the Chaldee. By
J. W. Etheridge, M.A., Translator of the New
Testament from the Pescbito Syriac.—Lon-
don. 1862.

TARGUM OF ONKELOS

And Noach was a son of five hundred
years, and Noach begat Shem, Cham,
and Japheth. And it was when the sons
of men had begun to multiply upon the
earth, and daughters were born to them,
that the sons of the mighty saw the
daughters of men that they were beautiful, and took to them wives of all whom
they pleased. And the Lord said, This
evil generation shall not stand before me
for ever, because they are flesh, and their
works are evil. A term (or length) will I
give them, an hundred and twenty years,
if they may be converted. Giants were in
the earth in those days: and also when,
after that the sons of the mighty had
gone in unto the daughters of men, there
were born from them giants who from of
old were men of name.

TARGUM OF JONATHAN

And it was when the sons of men began
to multiply upon the face of the earth,
and fair daughters were born to them;
and the sons of the great saw that the
daughters of men were beautiful, and
painted, and curled, walking with revelation of the flesh, and with imaginations
of wickedness: that they took them wives
of all who pleased them. And the Lord
said by his Word, All the generations of
the wicked which are to arise shall not
be purged after the order of the judgments of the generation of the Deluge,

which shall be destroyed and exterminated from the midst of the world. Have I not imparted my Holy Spirit to them (or, placed my Holy Spirit in them), that they may work good works? and behold their works are wicked. Behold, I will give them a prolongment of a hundred and twenty years, that they may work repentance, and not perish.

Schamchazai and Uzziel, who fell from heaven, were on the earth in those days: and also, after the sons of the great had gone in with the daughters of men, they bare to them: and these are they who are called men who are of the world (*Gibreen demëalma*) men of names.

NOTE C

A few extracts from the Commentary of M. M. Kalisch, Ph.D., will show the light in which the narrative in Gen. vi. 1–4 is regarded by Rationalist writers. Having alluded to the interest which attaches to the record of events in the Noachian age, Dr. Kalisch says:

The very commencement of the narrative contains a notion, which cannot be explained from the Bible, but which is indisputably borrowed from foreign and heathen sources. The 'Sons of God' descended to the beautiful 'daughters of man.' They deserted their pure and ethereal nature, and abandoned themselves to despicable depravities: they left the heaven, in order to corrupt the earth

and themselves: and it is but natural that their wicked sons, excluded from the abodes in heaven which their fathers had enjoyed, should attempt to force access to it by a desperate and flagitious assault. This is the story of the Titans storming the heavens: it is a tradition which recurs, in many modified forms, among most of the ancient nations.

Having referred to the Hindu and Chinese mythology, and to the legends of the north and west, and having shewn, in a brief notice of the angel-story, as it appears in the Book of Enoch, how the notions respecting the 'Sons of God' became gradually more and more amplified, from various heathen sources, or from the fictions of the imagination, he asks:—

Who recognizes in these fables the spirit of the Old Testament? and yet, they develop only the statement concerning the Sons of God, who took the beautiful daughters of men to wives, and begat the giants (ver. 4). Do they not rather remind us of the Persian myths, which relate that Ahriman and his evil spirits entered the creation, mixed with it, and corrupted its purity: that they defiled nature, deformed its beauty, and debased its morality, till the whole earth was filled with black crime, and venomous reptiles? Greek mythology, also, sings of the loves between the gods and the beautiful daughters of the earth: and the Hindus mention marriages between nymphs and

Divine heroes. But why has this heathen element been retained in the Mosaic narrative?

In answering his question, the writer appears to regard the Scriptural account of the "Sons of God" as merely a heathen allegory, made use of by Moses to shew that, henceforth, man can no more plead the seduction of superior beings to palliate his own misdeeds—that the "Sons of God," *if they ever existed*, having now been extirpated, with all their infamous progeny, there is no other evil demon but man's own passion—that his heart may be weak, but temptation proceeds only from himself, for the whole race of heavenly seducers is destroyed. "Thus," he concludes, "the Hebrew historian admits, for one moment, the existence of a superstition, in order for ever to subvert and to eradicate it."

The *Philological Remarks* on verse 2 contain the following:—

בכי אלהים are 'Sons of God' opposed to בכות האדם as is clearly evident from Job i. 6; ii. r. But they are here not the בכי אלים of Psalm xxix. I, who glorify God before the throne of His majesty; they are not traceable in the Old Testament: they belong to the general circle of the eastern legends, and are introduced only in order to be annihilated. They are the δαιμονες, who were considered as the θεων ταιδες (Plato): not the αγγελοι του Θεου (Sept. *Joseph.*): they may be the 'fallen angels' of mythology (Bonfrerius): but they are by no means the descendants of Seth, calling themselves after Elohim (iv. 26), or called 'Sons of God' on account of their piety (Deut xiv. 1; Ps. lxxiii. 15: *Ephraem Syrus, Clericus, Dathe*, etc): nor the descendants of Cain, arrogantly assuming that proud name, in consequence of their prosperous commercial enterprises (*Paulus*, Memorab. vii 131): nor 'a race of pre-Adamites:' nor the mighty or influential men who insulted the low-born 'daughters of men' (*Symmach. Saad.*: for אדם) has never, in itself, the meaning of a 'poor or common man:' comp. Ps. lxxxii. 7; xlix. 3: *Maimonides*, Mor. Neb. i. 14): nor are they ordinary men, who were called Sons of God, because they bear His image (*Schumann*).

It is, therefore, out of the question to suppose that our text alludes to intermarriages between the pious Sethites and the wicked Cainites, and that it intends to brand such unions as unholy. But we may add, that, according to the belief of the Persians, the holy Djemshid married the sister of a *dev*, and their offspring were monsters, black and impious men: and that, in the laws of the Hindus, the children of illegitimate marriages are declared to be invariably false and wicked. (*Manu* iii. 41, 42)—*Comm. on the O. T. with Transl. by M. M, Kalisch*, 1858, pp. 170–5.

An American writer. Dr. William T. Hamilton, author of "The Pentateuch and its Assailants" (T. and T. Clark, 1852, 8vo.), referring, in Lecture viii., to the notion that the narrative

131

in Gen. vi. 1–4 was borrowed from the Oriental mythologies, remarks that "the ancient *Indian* mythology cannot be traced, with certainty, beyond an era very long posterior to that of Moses. If there be borrowing in the case, the Gentoos must have borrowed from the Hebrews. As it respects Egyptian mythology, it was, *toto coelo*, different from the teachings of the Mosaic legends." He refers, for proof, in the latter case, to his Lecture, in the same volume, on the character of Moses as a statesman, and also to Pritchard's Egyptian Mythol. It should be added that Dr. Hamilton himself adopts the view (erroneous, as we believe) that the Sons of God were pious men.

NOTE D

Whether Lamech's wives were of the family of Cain, or of Seth, does not appear from the narrative. Gesenius says, the name Adah (עדה) signifies *ornament, beauty. Zillah,* he says, means *shadow,* and seems to be the feminine form of צל, shadow, which is used, as the English word is, in the several senses of *image, shelter,* or of something *transient* and *fleeting.* The name Naamah (*Heb.* and *Chal.* כעמה *LXX.* Νοεμα, *Vulg.* Noema), means *pleasant* or *lovely.* So Gesenius, Parkhurst, Newman, in their Hebrew Lexicons. "The names of the women," says Dr. Keil, "are indicative of sensual attractions," while he adds that the inventions of Lamech's sons "show how the mind and efforts of the Cainites were directed towards the beautifying and perfecting of the earthly life." Of Naamah he writes, "The allu-

sion to the sister of Tubal-Cain is evidently to be attributed to her name, Naamah, the lovely, or graceful, since it reflects the worldly mind of the Cainites." Kurtz appears (*Old Cov.,* I., 89) to take a like view, as do many others; but whether the circumstances really furnish ground for the inferences drawn from them may be questioned.

"The sister of Tubal-Cain was Naamah."

This, [Dr. Kitto writes,] is all we hear of her. It is remarkable that her name should be found at all in a record in which the names of so few women are preserved; and it is still more remarkable, that it is given without any circumstances to indicate the cause of its insertion. The name means *fair* or *beautiful.* Was her beauty her distinction? Did that beauty produce effects by which great families were united or broken? Beauty has, within the compass of historical time, moved the world. Did it in her person shake the old world also? Her brothers were the great fathers of social arts. Was her fame of the same sort as theirs? Some ascribe to her the invention of spinning and weaving; and others, who find in her brother the Vulcan of the Greeks, recognise in her Minerva, who had among her names that of Nemanoun. (*Plutarch de Iside et Osiride,*) But all this is bald conjecture. Her name was Naamah; her father was Lamech; her mother Zillah; her brother Tubal-Cain; she lived; she died. This is all we know of her.

To what she owed her fame—a fame

of five thousand years—must remain inscrutable. As one finds among the ruins of time, some old gray monument, too important and distinguished to have been constructed for a person of mean note, but discovers thereon only a Name, which the rust of ages has left unconsumed—so it is with Lamech's illustrious daughter.—*Daily Bib. Ill—Antediluv.*, p. 107.

That the Tubal-Cain and Naamah of Moses appear in the heathen mythology, as Vulcan and Venus, is highly probable. The author of "*De Prima Mundi Aetate,*" referring to Tubal-Cain's inventions in metallurgy, says,

Quam utramque (scil. artes aerarias et ferrarias) Tubalcainus invenit, cui adjungitur soror ipsius Nahama, tanquam laboris socia. Hujus veritatis vestigia manifestissima extant apud ipsos ethnicos. Haec enim sunt verba Platonis, in Politico—Πύρ μέν παρα Προμηθεως, τεχναι δέ παρ' Ἡφαίστου καὶ τῆς συντέχνου, 'Ignis quidem à Prometheo: artes autem à Vulcano, ipsiusque conjuge, ejusdem artis socia.' Quid magis consentiens dici potest? Nam quis dubitat quin Ἡφαίστος Graecorum, id est, Vulcanus ille vetustissimus Latinorum (plures enim fuerunt ut docet Tullius, lib. 3, de nat. Deor., et Arnobius, lib. 4, contra gentes), sit Tubalcainus Mosis, quùm si mutetur T in V (quarum literarum facilis est in sese migratio) nomen ipsum et vox *Tubal-cainus* sit Vulcanus? Praetereà, quis nescit *Nahama* significare

pulchram seu Venerem, quae quùm ab ipsis ethnicis dicatur, uti et Vulcanus, filia Jovis, certè soror est Vulcani: eadem verd ab iis ipsis ethnicis dicitur uxor quòque Vulcani, ut planè illi cum Mose in eo concordent.—p. 218.

The change of Tubal-Cain into Vulcan is better accounted for by Kitto, by supposing *Tu*, which was likely to be regarded as a prefix, to have been omitted, and the exceedingly femiliar change to have been made of *b* into *v*.

The old writer above quoted, Lambertus Danaeus, alluding to the fact that Moses, in recording the genealogy of the Sethites, has not given the name of any female, while in that of the Cainites he records the name of Naamah, conjectures that mention has been made of the latter, either because of her having been associated with her brother in the invention of some arts, or else on account of the mischief which her beauty caused in the world: "*Ob formam, cujus abusu postea nocuit mundo innotuisse videtur.*" Ainsworth (Comment. Gen. iv. 22) says, "The Hebrew Doctors (in Midrash Ruth, and Zohar) say of this Naamah, that *all the world wandered (in love) after her, yea, even the Sons of God, as in Gen, vi. 2: and that of her there were born evil spirits into the world.*" It may be remarked that Naamah, as sixth in descent from Cain, whose birth took place many years before that of Seth, would have been in the world, while Jared, Enoch, and Methuselah, were all living: that is, in other words, about the time at which we suppose the angels to have formed alliances with the daughters of men.

NOTE E

When we attribute bodies or corporeal forms to angels, we mean bodies of a kind very different from the human.

The angels, [says Kurtz,] possess nothing of a character other than spiritual: their corporeality also is of a spiritual nature, and even their bodily constitution bespeaks the spirit. The corporeality of man, on the other hand, partakes not of a spiritual but of a fleshly character: the dualism of flesh and spirit has not yet in his case been done away with, by his fleshly body having been glorified and transformed into a spiritual body.

Again, observing that the circumstance of angels having appeared on earth in human form, is far from justifying us in the immediate inference, that their form is properly and necessarily one similar to the human; he says, it is more than probable that they only assumed that form for the time, in order that they might conveniently hold intercourse with men[57].

Amongst the Fathers who ascribed corporeality to angels, are Origen, Clement of Alexandria, Caesarius, Tertullian, and others. Caesarius (4th cent.) says, *"Angels are incorporeal, as compared with us: they have, however, bodies suited to their nature, of a substance resembling wind, flame, smoke, air—subtle bodies, not formed of such gross matter as ours."*—(*Dial. I., Interrog.* 48.) Methodius Patarensis (3rd cent.), in his book *On the Resurrection of the Body,*[58] against Origen, remarks that the latter maintained that the resurrection body, which he called a spiritual one, will consist of an ethereal, or fire-like substance, like to that of the bodies of angels.

The Egyptian Macarius (4th cent.) in *Hom. IV., p.* 47, and Theognostus of Alexandria (3rd cent.), a friend of Origen, and of whose works an abstract has been preserved by Photius (*Biblioth. Cod., CVI., p.* 280) ascribe bodies to angels, but bodies of refined substance—σωματα λεττα, *corpora tenuia.* Tertullian's view of the subject will be found above, at page 93. Gregory Nazianzen and Augustine appear to be undecided in opinion on this question; the former saying that the angel is *"incorporeal, or as nearly so as possible"*—Orat, xxxiv., p. 560—while Augustine, on the words, *Qui facit ministros suos ignem ardentem,* says, *"It is doubtful whether we should understand by this a reference to the bodies of angels, or merely that the ministers of God should burn with Divine love."*—De Civ. Dei., XV., 23.

Dr. Kurtz, whose words we have quoted above, has discussed the subject of the Corporeality of Angels in his "Bible and Astronomy," translated from the German by Simonton. (Philadelphia, 1861.) To that work we refer the reader, contenting ourselves with a notice of one argument advanced in support of the opinion, that angels possess corporeal forms, and which is, in our judgment, sufficient to establish such a view. The translator has judiciously introduced, in a note, remarks by Isaac Taylor (*Physical Theory of Another Life*) coinciding with those of his author, both writers arguing that the idea of an absolutely incorporeal being, is irreconcilable with the idea of a finite creature.

A creature without any bodily form, [says Kurtz,] is wholly inconceivable, since that which is created, as the created, can only work and subsist within the limits of time and space, and since corporeality alone confines the creature to time and space. God alone is an infinite, an absolute Spirit: He only exists above and beyond time and space. A created spirit without a corporeal form to confine it to time and space, to bound its being, and give it a species of form, must either be like God, infinite, omnipresent, and eternal—be God Himself: or, since that would be irreconcilable with the idea of its having been created, be dissipated into nothing, and utterly lost.

The writers maintain that, only in combining itself with matter, can mind bring itself into alliance with the various properties of the external world: only thus can it find or be found, be known or employed, be detained or set at large—that Body is necessary for bringing Mind into relationship with space and extension, and so, of giving it—Place: and that an unembodied spirit, or sheer mind, is nowhere.

We might as well say, [writes Taylor,] of a pure spirit, that it is hard, heavy, or red, or that it is a cubic foot in dimensions, as say that it is here or there, or that it has come and is gone. It is only in a popular and improper sense that any such affirmation is made of the Infinite Spirit, or that we speak of God as everywhere present God is in every place in a sense altogether incomprehensible by finite minds, inasmuch as His relation to space and extension is peculiar to infinitude. Using the terms as we use them of ourselves, God is not here or there, any more than He exists now and then. Although, therefore, the idea may not readily be seized by every one, we must nevertheless grant it to be true that, when we talk of absolute immateriality, and wish to withdraw mind altogether from matter, we must no longer allow ourselves to imagine that it is, or that it can be, in any place, or that it has any kind of relationship to the visible and extended universe.

In short, they conclude, and, as we venture to think, with reason, that an embodied state is indispensable to a finite mind, before its faculties can come into play, or be productive of effects: and that none but the Infinite Spirit can be more than a latent essence, or inert power, until compacted by some sort of restraint.

Perhaps it may not be unworthy of note, that some of the Greek writers who deny the corporeality of angels, yet say that they are περιγραπτοι, or that they are *in loco*. "*The Divine nature alone*," says Theodoret, "*is uncircumscribed,… Wherefore, although we confess that the nature of angels is incorporeal, yet we say that their substance is circumscribed*."—Quaest III. in Gen.

"*Angels,*" says Athanasius, "*are in place: where they are sent, there they are: God alone is without bound.*"—Cat. in Job c. II., p. 26. "*Angels are* περιγραπτοι," says John Damascene, "*for when they are in heaven, they are not on earth: and when sent by God to earth, they do not remain in heaven.*"—Lib. 11., Orth. Fid. Cap. iii, p. 69.[59]

NOTE F

Subsequently to the writing of Section xiii., we discovered that the idea of the possession of human bodies by demons, for the purpose there supposed, had long ago been conceived (though not with special reference to the angels of Gen. vi. 2) by the author of the Clementine Homilies. In Hom. IX., St. Peter is made to account, as follows, for demon possession of bodies.

> The reason why the demons delight in entering into men's bodies is this. Being spirits, and having desires after meats and drinks, and sexual pleasures, but not being able to partake of these by reason of their being spirits, and wanting organs fitted for their enjoyment, they enter into the bodies of men, in order that, getting organs to minister to them, they may obtain the things that they wish, whether it be meat, by means of men's teeth, or sexual pleasure, by means of men's members, &c.—*Clementine Hom. Transl. Clark's Ante-N. Library.*

The Rev. G. V. Garland has referred in his Notes on Genesis (vi. 2, 4) to the New Testament accounts of demon possession, as serving to render credible the story of the bodily presence on earth of angels in the time of Noah. On the expression *Bne-Elohim* he says,

> In the Old Testament only in Job i. 6; xxxviii. 7, where it refers clearly to angels… The description in Job, and the allusion to the presence of the fallen angels (כפלים or 'giants' of A. V., LXX., and Vulg. verse 4), upon earth in these days, appears to support their supernatural character. They are termed 'angels, sons of heaven' in the apoc. Book of Enoch, cap. Vii.,, where their names are also added, and a similar account of their intermarriage with the daughters of man is given… Does not this theory receive support from the New Testament account of demoniacal possession, *cf,* πνευμα ακαθαρτον, Mark i. 23, with the use of ἁκαθαρσία, in Eph. v. 3; Col. iii. 5, etc.? [Having noticed the etymology and some of the renderings of כפילים, he writes:] It is difficult to conceive why so many theories should have been started to confute the doctrine of the bodily presence of the fallen angels in days when miracles were of common occurrence. No greater difficulty presents itself in this case, than in that of the appearance of the devils in the demoniacs of the New Testament.

It seems, however, from the following remark, that Mr. Garland supposes the angels of the antediluvian time to have acquired bodies in some other way, than by occupying the bodies of living men—"From the assumption of the human form (he says) they were called אכשים, *men*, as in the case of the angels, *cf.* xviii. 2; xix. 16, etc."—*Genesis with notes* (Rivingtons.)

NOTE G

INCUBES.—Nom que les Payens ont donné à certains demi-dieux, appellez autrement Faunes et Satyres. Ce nom vient d' *incubo*, coucher: parce que l' on feignoit, qu' ils desiroient fort la compagnie des femmes, et qu' ils venoient quelque fois coucher avec elles la nuit.—*Moreri. Le Grand Dictionaire Historique.* 1798. 2 Vols. fol.

The following is from Augustine's *City of God:*—

In eâdem Scripturâ ubi dicti sunt dilexisse filias hominum filii Dei iidem dicti sunt etiam angeli Dei: unde illos multi putant non homines fuisse sed angelos. Quam quaestionem nos, transeuntèr commemoratam in tertio hujus operis libro, reliquimus insolutam, utrùm possint angeli, cùm spiritus sint, corporaliter coire cum foeminis… Apparuisse tamen hominibus angelos in talibus corporibus, ut non solùm videri, verùm etiam tangi possent, eadem verissima Scriptura testatur. Et

quoniam creberrima fama est (multique se expertos, vel ab iis, qui experti essent, de quorum fide dubitandum non est, audisse confirmant), Sylvanos et Faunos quos vulgò Incubos vocant, improbos saepè extitisse mulieribus, ct earum appetisse ac peregisse concubitum: et quosdam daemones, quos *Dusios* nuncupant Galli, hanc assiduè immunditiam et tentare et efficere, plures talesque asseverant, ut hoc negare impudentiae videatur: non hinc audeo aliquid temerè definire, utrùm aliqui spiritus elemento aëreo corporati, (nam hoc elementum, etiam cùm agitatur flabello, sensu corporis tactuque sentitur) possint etiam hanc pati libidinem, ut quomodo possunt, sentientibus foeminis misceantur.—*August. (Ce Civ. Dei.)*—*Venetiis*, 1470, *lib.* 15, *c.* 23.

The belief, common amongst the early Church Fathers, of the carnal intercourse of spirits with women, exhibited itself in the middle ages also, when, however, the subject of our passage, instead of being turned to profitable account, as a warning against the unlawful desires of the flesh, appears to have only furnished ground for the opinions entertained, by Jews and Christians, concerning the *daemones incubi* and *succubi*—opinions followed by practical consequences of a terrible kind, when witchcraft came to be treated as heresy. In the middle ages, the belief in the reality of witchcraft was general: and readers know that, at least from 1484, when Innocent the VIII. issued a bull, charging inquisitors to put to death all practisers of diabolic art, prosecutions for the supposed crime became frequent, forming one of the most deplorable episodes in human history. By numbers of the unfortunate creatures accused, confessions of guilt were made, in some instances voluntarily, but oftener in consequence of the application of torture. Occupying a prominent place in these confessions, appear the *Incubus* and the *Succubus*—the former the visitant of females, the latter of males. The writer of the article Witchcraft in the Penny Cyclopaedia, says that, in a curious book published at Leyden, in 1656, entitled "Magica de Spectris et apparitionibus Spirituum"—it is given at page 262, as a characteristic of the confession of a female—"Ex eo tempore Deo et religioni renunciasse, et ilium [diabolum] sic concubuisse secum, ut viri cum foeminis solent," &c. Reference, the writer adds, may be made to the Appendix to Pitcairn's "Criminal Trials"—p. 610, and to a pamphlet called "History of the Witches of Renfrewshire."

NOTE H

Genesis vi. 3.

This verse has been variously interpreted. Some regard it as breaking the connexion between verses 2 and 4, and would remove it from its present position: while others believe it to be fitly placed, conceiving that they find in it a special reference to the sin of the Bne-Elohim, who had just been named. We have not thought it necessary to enter, in the course of our essay, on an examination of verse 3, as it does not directly throw much light on the nature, either of the Sons of God, or of the giants: but as it forms a portion of our passage, and has intimate connexion with the subject of it, it is desirable that its meaning should here be inquired into.

Dr. Nägelsbach has dealt with this verse (133 sqq.) and has noticed some of the interpretations which have been proposed. All of them, we think, may be reduced to two classes, according as they take רוח to mean (1) the Holy Spirit, or (2) the principle of the animal life, the vital principle in man and beast.

(*a*) Amongst those who have understood it in the latter sense, may be reckoned the authors of the Septuagint, Vulgate, Syriac, Arabic (Saadias): also Onkelos, and, amongst the moderns, Calmet, Le Clerc, Ilgen, Böttcher, Gesenius, Schumann, Hofmann, Kurtz, Keil, and Delitzsch. These, however, are not agreed on the rendering of ירון. By the ancient versions above named it is rendered in the sense of *continuing, remaining in*. According to their authors, God, in the words ירון לא simply pronounces sentence of death on the wicked race—"The breath of life which I have implanted in man, shall not always continue in him"—he must die when 120 years shall have expired. Some of the moderns also explain it similarly, as Gesenius, who says (Lex. רון,) that the ancient versions have well rendered the words *according to the sense*, and that there is no occasion for supposing them to have had a different reading, such as ידום shall continue, or ירון shall dwell. Delitzsch and Nägelsbach, on the contrary, maintain that the interpretation "dwell" or "remain" depends on the exchange of ירון for ידור and that such exchange is not warrantable.

Delitzsch, taking the verb in the significa-tion of *rule* (Germ. *Walten*), translates, "My Spirit shall not always rule in man."

It is not the Holy Spirit, in His charac-ter of Reprover, who is here meant… the resolve of God to deprive of the Spirit, means the extinction of the physical life: and hence, the life-breath which animates (Gen. ii. 7) man is called, on account of its Divine origin,—its God-allied nature—or even on account of its being a Divine gift—His Spirit (רוחי): and this life-breath rules in man, inasmuch as it animates and governs the material part of his nature This spirit God will take back, so that man will fall, a lifeless form, to the dust from which he was taken, and the history of the race come to a close.

So, likewise, Kurtz, Hofmann, and Keil interpret the words. The last-named writer says, "רוח is the divine spirit of life bestowed upon man, the principle of physical and ethi-cal, natural and spiritual life. This, His Spirit, God will withdraw from man, and thereby put an end to their life and conduct."

Of those who thus understand רוח to mean the principle of life breathed into man, or the created spirit, some regard the rendering of ידון by rule or dwell as unsuitable, and pre-fer the signification of being *depressed, hum-bled, desecrated.* "My Spirit, or my life-breath, shall not always be humbled (desecrated) in man," says Tiele, as quoted by Nägelsbach—

an explanation of which Gesenius, Tuch, Ewald, Baumgarten, and others, are men-tioned as approving. Gesenius, who at first understood ידון as Delitzsch does, in the sig-nification of rule, subsequently adopted the following—"My Spirit, *i.e.*, my superior and divine nature[60], shall not be always humbled in men: *i.e.*, shall not dwell in a mortal body, descending from heaven, and having to do with earth"—an interpretation with regard to which the translator of the Lexicon (Dr. Tre-gelles) asks, with reason, "What can anyone make of this theology?"

(*b*) The other class of interpreters includes those who take רוח to mean the Holy Spirit, the Third Person of the Trinity. The autho-rised English version has—"My Spirit shall not always strive with man"—the common explanation of which is, that the Divine Spirit had been, through the ministry of Enoch, Noah, and perhaps others, as well as through men's own consciences, reproving the wicked race, and calling to repentance: that now, pro-voked by the obstinate disregard, on the part of that race, of the Divine warning, the Lord declares, probably by the mouth of Noah, that He will not much longer strive thus to bring men to repentance: and that, unless before the close of 120 years, the race on earth should have come to a better mind, He would destroy them from the face of the earth.

This yields a good sense, and is in accor-dance with such passages as I Pet. iii. 20: 2 Pet. ii. 5: Heb. xi. 7. To *strive, contend with,* is one of the meanings of the verb—see the Lexicons of Gesenius, Parkhurst, Newman—accordingly, this explanation of the words has found many supporters. Amongst these are Jonathan, in his Targum, and the author of the Jerusalem Targum. Augustine may also be named, (see Civ. Dei., xv. 23), and the Samaritan version of the Pentateuch, which has "My servant," *i.e.*, Noah, instead of "My Spirit" Nägelsbach adduces several translations (some, indeed, rather paraphrases or explanations) of the clause, and remarks that the authors of them take some one or more of the words in a sense decidedly opposed to the usage of the language. We may mention that of the number are Vatablus, Castalio, Drusiuis, Rosenmüller, Sebastian Münster, and J. D. Michaelis, all of whom understand the sentence in nearly, or precisely, the same sense as does the English version.

To these may be added Lambert De Daneau, the Commentators Ainsworth, Patrick, Gill, Henry and Scott, Garland (Notes, &c.), Dr. Wordsworth, Bishop of Lincoln, R. S. Candlish, D.D., and Dr. Murphy: also Joan. Morinus, who first edited the Samaritan Pentateuch[61], Parkhurst (Heb. Lex.), and Dr. Tregelles, translator of the Lexicon Manuale of Gesenius.

It appears to us that Dr. Nägelsbach's own explanation of the words is not very different from that of our authorised version. The spirit spoken of in verse 3 must, he thinks, be necessarily regarded as *the living principle of the religious and moral life*—that this is, objectively, the Holy Spirit: subjectively, the created spirit in man—and that, here, we are to conceive of these, not separately, but as in union. In other words, as we understand him, רוחי, in verse 3, denotes the soul of man, influ-

enced, or operated on, by the Holy Spirit. The signification of ירון he determines (with Delitzsch) to be that of "rule, lord, or be master, over": and interpreting לֹא...לְעוֹלָם, *not... for ever, i.e.*, absolutely never—he translates, "My Spirit shall not, to eternity, become lord or ruler over man," *i.e.*, shall never become so—God thus declaring, as he conceives, that the natural element in mankind had become so entirely predominant over the spiritual—that the race had become so utterly carnal and ungovernable, that it was not to be subdued in any of the ways in which God ordinarily works, or pervaded by the influences of His Spirit. This is, substantially, our view, the words of our Authorized Version expressing the Divine resolution, consequent on such a state of things.

It ought to be added that some, who understand, by רוחי the Third Person of the Trinity, take ירון in the signification of judging. Amongst the renderings or explanations, above mentioned, as given by Nägelsbach, is that of Symmachus—Ου κρινει το πνευμα μου τους ανθρωπους αιωνεως, of which Jerome's interpretation is (*see* Der Gottm. p, 407), "Non eos ad aeternos *servabo* cruciatus, sed hic illis *restituam* quod merentur"—the Deity being thus represented as pronouncing judgment on the antediluvians, and determining that their punishment should be in this world, not in the next. From a passage in his essay on the Fallen Angels (Eruv. 152) it appears that Dr. Maitland did not disapprove of this view. Referring to ver. 6 of the Epistle of S. Jude, he writes in a note—"My Spirit shall not always strive [or, judge eternally] with man [or, as it regards the human race], for that also [or, truly] is flesh. So Jerome has translated: he says, 'In Hebraeo scriptum est, Non judicabit Spiritus meus homines istos in sempiternum, quoniam caro sunt.' Quaest. in Gen., vol. iii., 71 D. Is there in this any reference to the eternal judgment of those who were *not* flesh?"

This notion appears to have been commonly entertained by the Jews, as may be inferred from the following passage from the Talmud, quoted by Whitby (Comment, i Pet. iii. 19)—"The generation of the old world have no portion in the world to come, neither shall they stand up in judgment; for it is said. My Spirit shall not always judge with man." It is true that one of the significations of רון is *to judge*: but we cannot, notwithstanding, avoid looking on this interpretation as a forced one. The Divine determination, we conceive, has reference, not to the eternal state of these sinners, but to their then impenitent condition, and its result, the ceasing of the Holy Spirit's striving with them.

"For that he also is flesh"—The ground of the Divine determination is briefly stated in this sentence. The oldest interpretation of the words, we believe, agrees with the rendering of our Authorized Version, as it has been generally understood, viz., "for that (or because) he (man as a race) is flesh"—*i.e.*, Jehovah resolves to destroy men, unless they repent, in consequence of their having become wholly carnal in their affections and inclinations, walking after their own lusts, and no longer led by the Spirit of God. The term בשגם is, thus, taken to be a particle-group, compounded of

ב, שׁ for אשר, and גם also—the whole equivalent to "*because also*," "*for that*, or *in that also*:" but this is objected to on the grounds that גם introduces an incongruous emphasis (because *also* he is flesh) into the clause—that גם *also*, is everywhere pointed with *Patach* not *Kametz*,—that שׁ for אשר is not used in the Pentateuch—and that the words, thus translated, serve to break the connection of the preceding verses with verse 4.

Accordingly, some, taking בשגם to be the Inf. of שׁגג to err, with suffix ם and ב prefixed, translate "In their erring (*i.e.*, the erring of the angels, or of men themselves) he (man, as a genus) is become flesh." So Keil, Kurtz, Nägelsbach, Hofmann, Gesenius, Rev. G. V. Garland, C. H. H. Wright. Even Delitzsch, though he prefers the old rendering, says that, if the word is properly pointed it must be the Inf. of שגג, the particle גם being everywhere written with Patach. He admits also, that the harshness appearing in the change of number (ם, *their*, הוא, *he*) would not be a sufficient objection to such translation, as many instances of a like kind might be adduced.

Writers who adopt this rendering of the sentence, are not agreed on the question of the application of ם, *their*—whether to the angels, or to mankind. Kurtz, who follows Hofmann (*Schriftbeweis*), and Keil prefer the latter. "In their erring (*i.e.*, the erring of individuals) he (man, the human race) has become flesh." "The sin of individuals led to the ruin of the race. Verse 3 teaches that the sin of the daughters of men, who, contrary to nature and the Divine allotment, joined themselves in carnal union with the Sons of

God, was the means of introducing into that organism, which we call the human race, a principle at variance with the ordination of God, and one which affected not merely the individuals who introduced it, but even those who had no immediate or direct participation in the sin."—*Kurtz*, 70.

On the other hand, Nägelsbach refers ם to the Bne-Elohim. He believes that, otherwise, verse 3 is out of place; while, interpreted as he suggests, it is seen to fee closely connected with that which precedes, "Sever this one link," he says, "and I do not see how the verse is suitably placed. I cannot, therefore, agree with those who refer בשגם to ארם, especially as the latter is subsequently marked, in a striking way, as singular, namely, by the use of ימיו,"—the suffix to which denotes *his*, not *their*. That the sin of the angels was the cause which led to the extraordinary development of "*the flesh*" in mankind: and that, but for the presence and influence of these spirits, in the world, the evil could not have become so incurable, or so widely diffused, is, he thinks, implied in the sacred narrative.

It must be observed, with respect to the remarkable expression, "*he is flesh*" הוא כשר, that the German theologians, to whom we have been referring, or most of them, are of opinion that it signifies something more than what we generally understand, when it is said of men, that they have become carnal in their disposition and affections, slaves to fleshly lusts. The words "indicate something more than sensual disposition. Does not *the flesh*, even in the case of the Christian, often overcome the spirit, without our being able, for

that reason, to say, that the person has become flesh—that his nature and essence have been wholly carnalized?"—*Kurtz*, 72. The writer appears, from what he further says on the subject, to think, that the expression in question is used to denote the vitiated condition of the race, in consequence of the foreign and impure element introduced into its constitution, by the unnatural intermixture of the angelic and human orders.

Dr. Nägelsbach's view is worthy of notice. Admitting that הוא may point either to ארם or to רוח—"for that he (man) is flesh," or "it (the spirit) is flesh"—he gives the preference to the latter. Although there is not (he says) any essential difference between them, the carnalization of the man consisting in the fact that the spirit becomes fleshy yet the assertion, that "the spirit is become flesh," appears to go more deeply into the subject. (134). He says:—

In point of essence, the spirit can no more, at any time, become body, than the body can become spirit. But there are certain imperceptible media or links between both, which partake of the nature of both, inasmuch as they adjust to the spirit its corporeal tenement, and to the latter its higher animating principle. These physical organs of the spirit, as I may call them, may certainly become, through the preponderating influence from beneath, so grossly material, that the spirit wades in them, as in a slough, and thereby becomes incapable of fulfilling its higher office, as a religious principle in the personal organism. I might, in illustration of these remarks, refer to the observations that have been made on the brain of debauchees. Not that the brain alone represents all these connecting media: but it is one of them—a link in the chain—and one of the last of such links observable by us.

In accordance with this view, our author believes that, when it is said in the sacred text, אוה בשר, a process is meant, which stands in the relation of direct contrary to the *spiritualization* or *glorification* of the human body, after the resurrection. As, in the latter case, the spirit will, as it were, penetrate through the bodily organs, and shine in them with increasing lustre[62], all the while that these will not cease to retain their corporeal nature; so, in the process of *carnalization*, the reverse may be the case. Here, not only may the gross material element, generally, be developed in the highest degree, but especially may those medial-organs, those connecting links between body and spirit, be so much affected, and come to a materialism so gross, that the spirit becomes shackled as with a weight of lead, and unable to discharge its proper functions. It moves, in such case, *only* in the service of the body: and, instead of the latter being obliged to serve and obey it, it becomes itself merely the organ and slave of the body. Hence, he concludes there is expressed in the words הוא בשר, the idea of the complete and hopeless *slavery* of the spiritual part of the individual to the material.

The rendering of בשגם "in their erring," with reference either to the Bne-Elohim, or to ארם

and especially to the former, does, undoubtedly, exhibit the connexion between the preceding and following verses, more clearly than that of the English and some other versions. Yet, it may be doubted whether this was the meaning of Moses. Had it been, he would probably have employed, not בשגם which is, to say the least, capable of another interpretation, but some fuller form of expression, or one respecting the meaning of which there would not be any uncertainty.

Dr. Delitzsch, having adverted to the grounds on which the rendering, "in their erring" is defended, says, nevertheless, that בשגם with הוא, not היה, leaves on one's mind the impression, that the meaning attached to it by the writer was that of *quoniam*—introductory of the reason assigned for the Divine resolve—and that this is what we would naturally expect.

We may add that a comparison with the clauses in Gen. xxxix. 9, 23, in which באשר, below referred to, is found, will help to deepen the impression. Dr. Delitzsch further observes that, in the Soncino edition of the Hebrew Bible[63], printed 1488, some other early editions, and one old codex, the word is punctuated, not בְשגם, but בְשגם, a form in which the difficulty arising from גם with Kametz disappears, and also that, according to the punctuation-system of the Babylonian schools, שׁ and אשר are the forms usual, instead of שׁ and אשר, On the latter ground, the בְשגם of the Soncino Bible may be regarded as equivalent to בשגם the punctuation of which appears to be the proper one, if the word be composed of בְ, שׁ = אשר, and גם. If, then, we take בשׁ as equivalent to באשר, Gen. xxxix. 9, 23, and גם in its intensitive signification, or as merely indicating emphasis yea, just, indeed—a sense in which it is sometimes used—we may translate the whole clause—"My Spirit shall not always strive with man, yea (or, even) because that he is flesh"—or, "inasmuch, indeed, as he is flesh." The incongruous emphasis introduced into the clause, when גם is rendered *also*, to which some justly object, is thus avoided.

Such translation of בשכם הוא בשר has the support of the Septuagint, Vulgate, Arabic of Saadias, Syriac, and Samaritan Versions: of Onkelos and the Jerusalem Targum. That of Jonathan differs so entirely from the original, that it is impossible to say how he understood בשכם. It is favoured by Jerome (*quoniam*—Quaest. in Gen.), by Junius and Tremellius, Sebastian Munster, Parkhurst and Newman in their Hebrew Lexicons, by Calmet, and by the commentators Patrick, Ainsworth. Gill, Henry and Scott, by Dr. Wordsworth, Bishop of Lincoln, Dr. Harold Browne, in the Speaker's Commentary, and Dr. Murphy. Delitzsch observes that it has also the support of the Jewish interpreters, who are in no way embarrassed by the circumstance, that the punctuation of the word, as it appears in the greater number of MSS., is not in accordance with this rendering of it.

"His days shall be an hundred and twenty years."—The Bishop of Ely, in the Speaker's Commentary, says these words "are supposed to allude to the shortening of the term of human life by Josephus, and by Tuch, Ewald, Hävemick, Baumgarten, Knobel, Hupfield, Davidson, Colenso, &c. [we may add Kalisch]; but as a respite or time of repentance, by Saadias, all the Targums, by Luther's Version, Rosenmüller, Hengstenberg, Ranke, Hofmann, Kurtz, Delitzsch, &c." The latter is evidently the meaning of the words, inasmuch as, for several generations after the Deluge, the term of man's life considerably exceeded 120 years. "Non sic accipiendum est (says Augustine) quasi praenuntiatum sit posthac homines 120 annos vivendo non transgredi, quùm et post diluvium 500 excessisse annos inveniamus." To those already named, as taking this view, may be added Raschi, Tremellius and Junius, Dr. Gill, Henry, Shuckford, Dr. Wordsworth, Bishop of Lincoln, Dr. Kitto, Dr. Murphy, and others.

With regard to the time occupied in the construction of the ark, some have supposed it to have been 100 years, from the fact that Noah is said (Gen. v. 32), immediately before the first mention of the ark, to have been 500 years old. Others think that, from comparison of i Peter iii. 20 and Heb. xi. 7 with Gen. vi. 3, we may infer that the work was commenced 120 years before the Deluge, and was in preparation during the whole period of the Divine forbearance. Chrysostom, Augustine, and Jerome, are said (Calmet, Diet. *Ark*) to have been of this opinion. Mohammedan writers say the building of the ark occupied two years: the Rabbins, 52: but for neither of these does there appear to be any ground, although the former might not be far from the truth.

The state of the case appears to be, that the first intimation of the coming Deluge was long prior to the command to build the ark.

Genesis vi. 3 either records the secret purpose of God—"Resolved with Himself"—is the comment of Bishop Patrick and of Dr. Gill; the latter adding that the words were not spoken to Noah, as in verse 13, for that, as yet, he is not addressed: or else, from the circumstance of a certain space of time being fixed for repentance, we may suppose it to contain the first announcement made to Noah of the intended judgment, from the date of which announcement he began to warn the wicked: while, in verse 13, we find a second intimation made to him, that "the end of all flesh was come before God"—this second announcement being accompanied by the Divine command to build the ark. So Lambert De Daneau.

If this be admitted, then, as Noah's three sons were born less than 100 years before the Deluge—as they were married at the time when he received the command (vi. 14) to build the ark—the natural conclusion is, that only a few years before the irruption of the Deluge was the work of constructing the ark begun.

NOTE I

"וגם אחרי כן אשר יבאו וגו'"—There are three ways in which these words might be translated:—

1. Taking וגם = "*and also*;" and אחרי כן אשר = "posteà quùm," "*afterwards when*;" connecting the whole, not with the preceding, but with the following part of the verse. "The Nephilim were in the earth in those days; and also, afterwards, when the Sons of God came in, &c."—*Auth, Vers. Dr. Keil, &c.*

2. Taking these Hebrew words in a like signification, or אשר = "*because*" (Gen. xxx. 18:1 Kings viii. 33.) and connecting with the sentence which precedes. "In those days and also afterwards the Nephilim were on earth, when (*i.e.*, whenever, as often as) the Sons of God came, &c."—Drechsler, etc, "Erantque super terram gigantes in illis diebus, et post illos: quia filii Elohim ingressi sunt ad filias Cain, &c."—*Arab. Saad.*

3. Taking וגם = "*even,*" "*yea,*" and כן אשר אחרי = "*postquam.*" "*after-that,*" introductory of what follows. "The Nephilim were on earth in those days, even (= *i.e.*) after-that the Sons of God had come in, &c."—*Vulg., Kurtz.*

כן אשר אחרי occurs only in Gen. vi. 4, but אחרי without אשר is often found, and almost always as an adverb of time, *posteà, afterwards*, (Gen. xv. 14; xxiii. 19; Ex. iii. 20, etc.)

That גם and וגם are, perhaps most commonly used to indicate *accession*, may be admitted: and as אשר sometimes means *when*, quùm, ετó, (Deut. xi. 6; I Kmgs viii. 9; 2 Chron. xxxv. 20, where we find זאת אשר אחרי בל), it appears that the rendering, No. I above, accords with the usage of the language. It implies, however, as Dr. Keil and others rightly maintain, the existence of the Nephilim previously to, and independently of, the intercourse of the Bne-Elohim and the daughters of men; and believing this to be contrary to fact, we prefer even a harsh or unusual translation, not involving such a difficulty.

No. 2 (Drechsler, Saad.) meets the requirements (according to our view) of the case. It must, however, be admitted that, in other passages in which אחרי כן occurs, its immediate connection is, not with the words which precede, but with the sentence which follows, and of which it forms the introduction. The passage, to be rendered as it is by Drechsler and the Arabic translator, would rather, perhaps, have been written, "In those days *and after them*, (ואחריו or ובאחרוכם—see Josh. x. 14: I Kings xvii. 13) the Nephilim were on earth," &c.

No. 3, (Kurtz), which makes the Hebrew words signify "*even after-that*," the opposers of the angel-hypothesis declare to be inadmissible, on the grounds that it ignores וגם, or gives it an insupportable meaning: that it is opposed to the accentuation: and that it takes יבאו in the sense of באו. But אחרי כן without אשר, having, as has been observed, the signification of *posteà, afterwards after it was so*—the addition of אשר must alter the meaning to that of *after it was so that*, or, briefly, *after that, postquàm*. Of this we can have little doubt, when we find such forms as אחרי אשר omitting כן (Josh. ix. 16; xxiii. I; Deut. xxiv. 4.) and אחרי כאשר (Josh. ii. 7.), a form almost identical with that in our passage—both of these having no other meaning than that of *postquàm*. In 2 Sam. xxiv. 10, אחרי כן without אשר has the signification of *postquàm, after-that*—on which Dr. Kurtz remarks that the

אשר is manifestly elided, and that we have, in fact, the same expression as in Gen. vi. 4, only in curtailed form.

A more serious obstacle, in the way of this interpretation, is presented by וגם. Dr. Keil quotes the confession of Dietlein (on 2 Pet) that we cannot, in consequence of the presence of וגם, "make use of verse 4, for the purpose of proving that the Sons of God are angels."

The particle גם is properly a substantive, denoting *addition, accumulation*, and is used, alone or in combination with ו to introduce something additional to what had been mentioned, in which case it is rightly translated "*also*," or "*and also*." Gen. iii. 6, 22; vii. 3; xix. 35. It has, however, another signification, and is often employed to render a sentence or word emphatic, as in Judges v. 4; I Sam. xxiv. 12; and in Gen. xxix. 30, cited by Kurtz, where this particle serves only to emphasize the name of the favourite Rachel, and should have been left untranslated in English. With regard to ו, Gesenius observes that, to the widely-extended use of this particle, is to be ascribed a looseness of expression in Hebrew: and Buxtorf (*Thesaurus*), having referred to it as a copulative, adds, "Ea tamen etiam, pro ratione et commoditate sententiae, aliter explicari solet." He notes a passage in which it is plainly redundant, and is accordingly omitted in a parallel passage—Gen. xxxvi. 24 ("both ו Aiah and Anah") compared with I Chron. L 40. In I Sam. xxviii. 3, ו is merely emphatic: and for מגן (*LXX.* γέ) in Eccles. ix. 3, "*yea, even*" would be, perhaps, a better rendering than the "*yea, also*" of the English version. See also Gen. xlii. 22.

To the objection urged by Keil against Kurtz's rendering of the passage, viz., that it takes the imperfect יבאו in the sense of the perfect באו in other words, that it makes the Hebrew verb signify "had come in" instead of "came in"—the latter replies at length, in his *Die Ehen*, &c., pp. 76, 77, and argues the question on grammatical grounds. To us it seems that, if his rendering of וגם אחרי כן אשר be allowed, the tense of the Hebrew verb can but little affect the question. "Owing to the poverty of the Hebrew language (says Gesenius) in the means of expressing the absolute and relative circumstances of time, we might naturally expect variety in the uses of the same form;" and so Buxtorf says, "Quod autem quôque loco exprimi debeat, ex tenore sententiae facilè intelligitur." Hence, a translator will employ the tense which, according to the usage of his own language, best expresses what he believes to be the meaning of the Hebrew. Construction analogous to that in Gen. vi. 4, viz., an imperfect preceded by a conjunction, is met with in Gen. xxiv. 45,—אבלה מרם "before that I had made an end," where the verb is properly translated by the English pluperfect.

Taking these considerations into account, it may, perhaps, be thought allowable to translate, with Kurtz, "The Nephilim were in the earth in those days, even after that the Sons of God had come in to the daughters of men," &c.

NOTE J

Dr. Maitland, referring, in a following section (17) of his book, to the connexion or identity which he had assumed of the Rephaim with the Giants, adduces in support of that view passages from a sermon of Mede on Prov xxi. 16, in which the latter shows Scriptural ground for the opinion that the Sacred Writers sometimes meant, by *Rephaim*, the antediluvian giants. The reader is referred to *False Worship*, pp. 244–7, or to the passage in Mede's Works, as there noted. (*Book* I., *Disc.* vii., *p.* 32.) The subject is likewise noticed in Smith's Dictionary of the Bible, art. *Giants*. For those who may not have access to these works, we add here that the passages, in which the Greek translators have taken *Rephaim* to mean the antediluvian giants in a state of misery in the other world, are—Job xxvi. 5, where we would translate "The giants (Heb. *Rephaim*) writhe, *or*, are in pain יחוללו—*Pilel of* חול) beneath the waters," &c. *Vulg.* Gigantes gemunt sub aquis. Prov. ii 18, where it is said of the strange woman, that "her paths incline to the dead" (Heb. *Rephaim*. LXX. γηγαιεις.) Prov. ix. 18. Prov. xxi. 16, "The man that wandereth out of the way of understanding shall remain in the congregation of the dead." (Heb. *Rephaim*. LXX. γιγαντες. Symm. θεομαχοι.) Isa. xiv. 9, "Hell (*sheol*) from beneath is moved for thee, to meet thee at thy coming: it stirreth up the dead (Heb. *Rephaim*) for thee, even all the chief ones of the earth," &c.—where the LXX. and Vulgate have "all the giants, the leaders of the earth, have arisen to thee." Mede mentions also the xxxii. of Ezek., where גבורים occurs. See ver. 21, and especially ver. 27, where is the noteworthy conjunction of גבורים כפלים.

NOTE K

Dr. John Richers, in his work on the *Creation, Paradise*, and *Deluge*, infers from the words in Gen. vi. 12, "*All* flesh had corrupted his way on the earth," that the unnatural intercourse of different kinds of creatures, in the antediluvian period, was not confined to angels and human beings, but took place in the brute creation also (forbidden, Lev. xix. 19)—a view which has the support of Jewish tradition, and which, he thinks, can be established on the ground of the revelations of Palaeontology. He refers especially to the evidence afforded by the remains in the Kirkdale Cave, described by Buckland, in his *Reliquiae Diluvianae*, and to the light thrown on the subject by anatomical investigations. We transcribe the passage in Richers for those who may care to read it:—

Verse 12. *Da sah Elohim die Erde,* Jetzt wendet auch Elohim Seinen Blick der Erde zu. והכה, *und siehe,* Er sieht sie durchaus *verderbt. Denn es verderbete* alles *Fleisch seinen Weg auf Erden,* wozu in dem Buche Zennorenna jüdischer Tradition ausdrücklich bemerkt wird, dass selbst das Vieh in widernatürlicher Begattung gelebt habe, eine Thatsache, die Geologie, und besonders die Pälaon-

tologie unserer Tage schon hundertmal würde bestätigt haben, wenn sie anders nur Ohren hätte zu hören, was der Geist der Berge und Erdschichten vor ihr spricht. Unter dem Trotz der Sünde, der Frechheit des Bösen, hatte sich greuliche Unzucht und Unnatur über alle Kreatur ergossen, verbunden mit blutdurstiger Wurg- und Mordgier, die zur höchsten Höhe gelangt war. Dies bestätigen, wie schon angedeutet, die thierischen Reste des Diluviums hinreichend, besonders die Hyanenhöhlen, deren eine zu Kirkdale bei York W. Buckland in seinen *Reliquiae Diluvianae* beschnehen hat. Schon manchem sinnigen Betrachter sind die thierischen Raubhöhlen der Diluvialbildung aufgefallen, und schon manche Stimme hat sich über die Schänderei, die in ihnen einst geherrscht haben muss, vernehmen lassen.[64] Denn selbst Spuren von Knochenfrass und Venerie will der Anatom Weber an den Gebeinen der Sündfluththiere entdeckt haben.—*Die Schöpfungs- Paradieses- und Sündfluthgeschichte, u. s. w.,* p. 402.

NOTE L

Extracts, from the writings of some of the Fathers and Mediæval Historians, on the subject of Gen. vi. 1–4. Latin versions are used in the case of Cyril, Syncelius, Cedrenus, and Eutychius:—

TERTULLIAN.—This Father, having said (*De Velandis Virginibus*, c. 7), that the angels, alluded to by S. Paul in I Cor. xi. 10, are those, "quos legimus à Deo et coelo excidisse ob concupiscentiam foeminarum:" says also that as Moses has spoken, in Gen. vi., of the daughters of men, whom the angels took for *wives* (γυναιπας), "manifestè virgines portendit, quae adhuc apud parentes deputarentur."

In the *Liber De Idololat*, c. 9, he refers to the angels as "desertores Dei, amatores foeminarum, proditores etiam hujus curiositatis, propterea quoque damnatos à Deo:" and in *De Hab, Muliebri*, c. 2, he recounts the various arts in which the angels instructed the women;—

Nam cùm et materias quasdam benè occultas, et artes plerasque non benè revelatas, saeculo multo magis imperito prodidissent (siquidem et metallorum opera nudaverant, et herbarum ingenia traduxerant, et incantationum vires promulgaverant, et omnem curiositatem, usque ad stellarum interpretationem, designaverant) propriè et quasi peculiariter foeminis instrumentum istud muliebris gloriae contulerunt: lumina lapillorum, quibus monilia variantur: et circulos ex auro, quibus brachia artantur: et medicamenta ex fuco, quibus genae colorantur: et ilium ipsum nigrum pulverem, quo oculorum exordia producuntur… Hi sunt nempe angeli quos judicaturi sumus: hi sunt angeli quibus in lavacro renunciamus: haec sunt utique, per quae ab homine judicari meruerunt.—*Tertitlliani Opera ed. Semler. Halae*, 1770.

LACTANTIUS.—The fall of the angels is related in Book ii., chap. 15, of the *Divin. Institut.* in these words:—

Cùm ergo numerus hominum coepisset increscere, providens Deus ne fraudibus suis diabolus, cui ab initio terrae dederat potestatem,[65] vel corrumperet homines, vel disperderet, quod in exordio fecerat, misit angelos ad tutclam cultumque generis humani: quibus quia liberum arbitrium erat datum, praecepit ante omnia, ne terrae contagione maculati, substantiae coelestis amitterent dignitatem…Itaque illos cum hominibus commorantes dominator ille fallacissimus consuetudine ipsa panllatim ad vitia pellexit, et mulierum congressibus inquinavit. Tum in coelum ob peccata, quibus se immerserant, non recepti, ceciderunt in terram. Sic eos diabolus ex angelis Dei suos fecit satellites ac ministros. Qui autem sunt ex his procreati, quia neque angeli, neque homines fuerunt, sed mediam quamdam naturam gerentes, non sunt ad inferos recepti, sicut in coelum parentes eorum. Ita duo genera daemonum facta sunt, unum coeleste, &c. (*Vide sup.*, p. 152.)

SULPITIUS SEVERUS.—After brief notice of the Creation and Fall, and of the antediluvian patriarchs to the time of Noah, he says:—

Quâ tempestate [*sc.* Noachicâ] cùm jam humanum genus abundaret angeli,[66] quibus coelum sedes erat, speciosarum forma virginum capti, illicitas cupiditates appetierunt: ac naturae suae originisque degeneres, relictis superioribus, quorum incolae erant, matrimoniis se mortalibus miscuerunt. Hi paulatim mores noxios conserentes, humanam corrupere progeniem, ex quorum coitu Gigantes editi esse dicuntur, cùm diversae inter se naturae permixtio monstra gigneret. Quibus rebus offensus Deus, maximèque malitia hominum, quae ultra modum processerat, delere penitùs humanum genus decreverat.—*Sacra Hist.*, I., 3.

The following maintain the Sethite-explanation of the passage:—

Augustine.—Having made allusion in his City of God (xv. 23) to the opinions entertained respecting the *daemones incubi* (See Note G), he says:—

Dei tamen angelos sanctos nullo modo isto tempore sic labi potuisse crediderim, nec de his dixisse apostolum Petrum, 'Si enim Deus angelis peccantibus non pepercit, sed carceribus caliginis inferi retnidens, tradidit in judicio puniendos reservari'—sed pottiùs de illis qui primùm apostantes à Deo cum diabolo principe suo ceciderunt, &c.

Further on, he writes:—

Potuerunt igitur gigantes nasci et priusquiàm filii Dei, qui et angeli Dei dicti sunt, filiabus hominum, hoc est, secundùm homines viventium misceren-

tur, filii scilicet Seth filiabus Caym. Nam et canonica Scriptura sic loquitur, in quo libro haec legimus, cujus verba ista sunt:—'*Et factum est, postquam coeperunt homines multi fieri-super terram, et filiae natae sunt illis: videntes angeli Dei filias hominum quia bonae sunt, sumpserunt sibi uxores ex omnibus quas elegerant. Et dixit Dominus Deus, Non permanebit Spiritus metis in hominibus his in aeternum, propter quod caro sunt. Erunt autem dies eorum centum viginti anni. Gigantes autem erant super terram in diebus illis. Et post illud cum, intrarent filii Dei ad filias hominum, et generareni sibi, illi erant gigantes a saeculo homines nominati.'* Haec libri verba divini satis indicant jam illis diebus fuisse gigantes super tenrram, quando filii Dei acceperunt uxores filias hominum... Sed et postquàm hoc factum est nati sunt gigantes. Sic enim ait, Gigantes autem erant super terram in diebus illis: et post illud, cùm intrarent filii Dei ad filias hominum. Ergo et antè in illis diebus, et post illud... Non autem illos (*sc.* filios Dei) ita fuisse angelos Dei, ut homines non essent, sicut putant quidam, sed homines proculdubio fuisse, Scriptura ipsa sine ulla ambiguitate declarat. Cùm enim praemissum esset quòd videntes *angeli* Dei filias hominum quia bonae sunt, sumpserunt sibi uxores ex omnibus quás elegerant: mox adjunctum est, Et dixit Dominus Deus, Non permanebit Spiritus mens in hominibus his in aeternum, propter quòd caro sunt, &c.—(*Augustinus, De Civ.*

Die.—Venetiis, per Joan. et Vindelinum de Spira. 1470.)

CYRIL OF ALEXANDRIA.—The Emperor Julian having asserted, in his work against Christianity, that the υἱοὶ τοῦ Θεοῦ of Gen. vi. are angels, that the *giants* there mentioned sprang from the intercourse of mortal with immortal, and that Moses has thus made mention of certain inferior deities, while he has not made any explicit mention of the Only-begotten Son, whom Christians hold to be God—Cyril, in his confutation of Julian's work, says in his ninth book:—

Caeterùm quoniam angelorum quoque meminit praestantissimus ille Julianus, et eò intemperantiae provectos asserit, ut muliercularum forma nescio quomodo capti fuerint, et corporeis libidinibus graviter iiretiti, in voluptates à natura sua abhorrentes incurrerint: agedum et in hoc ostendamus illum ab omni scopo longius aberrare… Qaòd igitur eorum, quae scripta sunt, sensum ignorarit, nullo negotio demonstrabimus. Scripsit quippe nobis divinus Moses. '*Et factum est, postquàm coeperunt homines multi fieri super terram, et filiae natae sunt eis: videntes autem filii Dei filias hominum, quia pulchrae sunt, acctperunt sibi uxores ex omnibus quas elegerant. Et genuerunt,* inquit, *Gigantes,*' Tamen Julianus extrinsecus additum asseruit angeli Dei (οι αγγελοι του Θεου), licet Scriptura verior, et quae in manibus est, habeaty (οἱ υἱοι του Θεου).

Having said that Enos, on account of his virtue and piety, received from his contemporaries the appellation of Θεος, he continues:—

Ejus autem prosapia ad Noe tempora propagata est, qui Justus erat. Placuit enim Deo, sicuti de illo scriptum est. Itaque Caini genus, quùm sequeretur avi mores, impiam ac nefariam vitam instituit. Enos autem cognomento Dei posteri, avitae probitatis vestigiis ad usque Noe tempus insistentes, boni ac justi omnique virtute praediti cemebantur. Porrò genus illi son miscebant, et à profanis puri sejungebantur, vocabanturque *Filii Dei* Noe temporibus. *Filii Dei,* hoc est, Enos posteri, *videntes filias hominum quod essent pulchrae, acceperunt sibi uxores.* Igitur, quùm prosapiae inter se mistae essent, et implexu mali bonum deletum esset, quùm justitia et integritas vitae non esset ampliùs apud terrae incolas, eluvionem immisit universi Deus, unam in omnes ex aequo mortem statuens.

Of the giants he writes:—

Erant autem Gigantes illi vasti forsan ac robostissmi, sed multa deformitate laborantes… Non enim nos, Graecos poetas sequuti, immani mole praeditos fuisse illos dicimus, ac tam altis corporibus, ut insulas è medio mari arreptas in coelum projicerent: sed vultu quidem defonnes et monstrosos, ac praeferoces, non tamen ultra humanam mensuram in tantum elatos, quantum Graecorum principibus placuit ementiri.

Absit, igitur [he adds], ut sanctos angclos incusemus aut carpamus, et eis voluptates impuras affingamus.— (*Fuliani Imp. Op, et S. Cyrilli Alex. Cont. Ful, libri X.—ed. Spanheim; cum vers. Lat. N. Borbosii et Auberti. Lipsiae, 1696—pp. 295–7.*)

SYNCELLUS.—Of Seth he says:—

Pietate in Deum, ac summa corporis venustate, excellebat: et ex eo cuncti progeniti, pii quoque ac corpore elegantes, visi sunt. Isti ex Adami mandate terram superiorem Edem, è regione Paradisi, angelicam ducentes vitam, ad millesimum usque mundi annum, habitavere… Millesimo vero mundi conditi anno, Jared quadragesimo, ipsius Seth septingentesimo septuagesimo, ducenti ex ejus stirpe Egregori seducti descenderunt, et ex filiabus hominum sibi delegerunt uxores, nominatissimosque illos, de quibus Scriptura loquitur, procrearunt Gigantes. At cùm in adversa opinione nonnulli sint, pauca quaedam de his, turn ex Enoch primo, turn ex ipsius Moysis, ac denique ex Coryphaei apostolorum Petri libris delibare decrevi.

Syncellus then relates, from the Book of Enoch, the story of the Egregori, of whom he gives the number and the names, and says:—

Isti caeterique cuncti acceperunt sibi uxores anno mundi millesimo centesimo septuagesimo, et ad diluvium usque in eas insanierunt: ex eis verò nati in tria genera sunt divisi, quorum primum Gigantes, homines proceri. Gigantes autem Naphelim procreaverunt: ex Naphelim porrò Eliudaei orti sunt.

Having referred to Gen. vi. 1–4, and 2 Pet ii. 4, and offered some other fragments from the Book of Enoch, he finally expresses his opinion of the contents of the apocryphal book—

Et haec quidem ex primo libro Enoch, de Egregoris: quibus sane apocryphis animo simpliciores certam fidem addere non decet: supervacanea quippe et ab ecclesiastica traditione aliena continent, et à Judaeis ac Haereticis adulterata constat.—(*Georgii, Monachi et S. P. N. Tarasii Patriarchae, CP. quondam Syncelli, Chronographia, &c. Paris,* 1652, *pp.* 10–27.)

CEDRENUS.—His account of the Egregori and Giants is as follows:—

Anno ab origine mundi millesimo ducentesimo, qui fuit Jaredo vitae annus quadragesimus, Setho septingentesimus septuagesimus, Egregores, Sethi progenies, errore ducti descenderunt, ac sibi mulieres de filiabus hominum sive Caini desumpserunt, atque Gigantes illos celebres generaverunt. Gigantes hi propter justum Sethum fuerunt robusti, ac vastissimis corporibus, monstrosique ob id et abominandi, unde et nomen iis impositum. Propter impium verò Cainum validi, fortissimi, et firmissimo robore, vita homicidiis et impietati ac lasciviae deditissima… Horum multos coeliths Deus igneis globis sive fulminibus ictos absumpsit: cùm autem reliqui nullo poenae sensu moverentur, neque quicquam de flagitiosa vita descisserent, posteà diluvio universes sustulit. Hi in montem Hermonim conjuraverunt, se uxores ex filiabus hominum seu progenie Caini sibi delecturos: montique id nomen indidere, quòd in eo conjurassent, seque diris mutuò obstrinxissent. Hi suas uxores veneficia et incantationes docuerunt: primusque Azaelus, decimus ipsorum princeps (nam eorum qui descenderunt principes ducenti erant) docuit eos gladios ac thoraces fabricari, omniaque instrumenta bellica: turn ex visceribus terrae aurum, argentum, et reliqua metalla eruêre. Similiter quivis principum aliquid docuit: alius corporis exomationem, alius pretiosos lapides et tincturas, alius radices herbarum, alius sapientiam, et ea quae incantationes inefficaces redderent: alius astronomiam et siderum, observationem, alius astrologiam, alius aeris considerationem, alius terrae signa, alius solis et lunae.—(*Georgii Cedreni Annales ab exordio Mundi ad Isaacum Comnenum usque &c. Basil. 1566—pp. 7, 8.*)

EUTYCHIUS.—Having spoken of the Creation, of Adam and Eve, Cain and Abel, and of the birth of Seth, he says:—

Setho, cùm ducentorum et qninque annorum esset, natus est Enosh. Post mortem autem Adami subduxit se familia Sethi à familia Kaini maledicti. Seth, ergo, assumptis secum filio primogenito Enosho, et Kainano Enoshi filio, et Mahlaliele Kainani, unà cum uxoribus et liberis ipsorum, traduxit in montis fastigium, ubi sepultus est Adam: Kain, verò, omnesque ipsius filii, infra substiterunt in valle ubi occisus est Abel.

Coluerunt autem filii Sethi in isto monte puritatem et sanctimoniam, vocem angelorum, à quibus prope aberant, audientes, unàque cum ipsis Deum laudantes et celebrantes: appellatiquè sunt ipsi cum uxoribus et liberis suis *Filii Dei*. Cùmque jam appropinquaret Sethi mors, filios suos per Abelis sanguinem adjuravit, neminem ex ipsis de monte isto sancto descensurum, nec permissuros se ut quispiam è liberis suis ad Kaino maledicto prognatos migraret… Quod ad posteros autem Kaini homicidae, adhinniebant viri mulieribus instar equorum; eodemque modo absque pudore viris foeminae scortantes; aliique cum aliis turpia patrantes, palamque congredientes: eâdem cum foeminâ viris duobos aut tribus rem habentibus: erantque vetulae juvenibus salaciores: patres cum filiabus, juyenes cum matribus suis venere promiscuâ utebantur, adeò ut nec liberi patres suos, nec patres liberos dignoscerent. Omnibus interim instrumentis musicis utebantur, adeò ut clamoris et lusûs ipsorum sonus ad fastigium montis sancti ascenderet: quem cùm audivissent Sethi posteri, convenerunt ex ipsis centum viri, ut è monte ad posteros Kaini maledicti descenderent, quos juramento per sanguinem Abelis obstrinxerat Jared, ne de monte sancto descenderent. Ipsi, tamen, dictum ejus nihil morati, descenderunt: cùmque descendissent, filias Kaini maledicti specie pulchras, et sine pudore nudas, conspicientes, cupidine exarserunt Eos similiter conspicientes Kaini filiae, viros specie pulchrâ, staturâ giganteâ, ipsos ferarum instar insilientes corpora eorum inquinârunt, atque ita cum filiabus Kaini scortando perierunt filii Sethi. Pepererunt autem filiae Kaini maledicti, filiis Sethi, gigantes. In Lege siquidem ait, '*filios Dei* (Bani Elohim appellatos), *cùm conspexissent filias Kaini pulchras, ad ipsas descendisse, atque ex ipsis prognatos Gigantes.*' Qui autem errant, neque sciunt quid dicant, aiunt angelos descendisse ad filias hominum, cùm intelligendi sint filii Sethi qui à monte sancto ad filias Kaini maledicti descenderunt. Sethiadae enim, ob sanctitatem suam, et quòd montem sanctum incolerent, appellati sunt *Bani Elohim, i.e., filii Dei*. Errant ergo qui dicunt angelos descendisse ad filias hominum, cùm substantia angelorum substantia simplex sit, nec competat naturae ipsorum *Veneris*

usus. Homo autem substantiae compositae sit, cujus naturae ejus usus competat, paritèrque omnia animantia. Quòd si angeli cum mulieribus congrederentur, nullam uspiam è filiabus hominum virgin em, incorruptam reliquissent. Cùm autem vellent filii Sethi, qui è monte ad filias Kaini maledicti descenderant, in montem sanctum ascendere, facti sunt lapides montis ignis, ita ut nullo modo pateret ipsis in montem reditus. Deinde coeperunt alii post alios de monte sancto descendere ad Kaini maledicti filias,— (*Contextio Gemmarum, sive Eutychii Patriarchae Alexandrini Annales. Arab. et Lat. Interp. E. Pocock. Oxon., Vol. I, pp. 19–27.*)

NOTE M

The chronological differences which exist between the Hebrew original, the Septuagint, and the Samaritan text, are known to Biblical scholars, and need not be specified here. They are of such a nature, that it is generally admitted they cannot be ascribed to the mistakes of translators or transcribers. The divergences of the Samaritan and Septuagint texts from the Hebrew, are, by the greater number, supposed to be intentional changes, made for the purpose of meeting the views of their authors, as, for example, in the case of the Alexandrine version, to reconcile the chronology of the Bible with that which was current in Egypt Modern theologians and chronologers, therefore, for the most part, receive the statements of the Hebrew, text, as alone authentic. It has been remarked, however, by Bayle (*see Penny Cyclop*. Chronology) that those who hold a contrary opinion, although the least numerous, have been, generally, *des savans d'elite*, inquirers of a superior order: and the Rev. C. Crosthwaite expresses the opinion, that, although the facts and arguments brought forward in support of the longer and shorter systems, by their respective advocates, are of such weight and importance as to make it difficult to decide between them, the longer system will finally establish itself. Shuckford (*Sac. and Prof. Hist.*) says that the whole Christian Church, eastern and western, followed the Greek account, until some Roman writers, from a regard to the decree of the Council of Trent about the vulgar Latin, adopted the Hebrew computations, not because they were the Hebrew, but because they agreed with those of the Vulgate. He adds that, amongst the moderns, Beza was the first who had any doubts about the Greek chronology, although he never absolutely rejected it.

Isaac Voss, and, we may add, Bp. Horsley, have preferred the Septuagint account. The chronological system of Dr. Hales, formerly Rector of Killeshandra, in Cavan, was founded on that of Josephus and of the Septuagint. A recent writer, Dr. Hamilton (*The Pentateuch and its Assailants*), says that every year serves to increase the probability that the chronology of the latter is the true one: and Dr. Kitto, though feeling bound, as he says in his Bib. Illust., to follow the chronology in general use, believes that of the Septuagint to be the more correct.

On the other hand, Dr. Kurtz feels assured that the Septuagint computation would have been as readily discarded as that of the Samaritan, had it not been for the use made of the Greek version by New Testament writers. Perhaps we may add, with respect to the Samaritan account, that it was adopted, so far as relates to the antediluvian period, in preference to all others, by the learned compilers of the *Universal History*, an elaborate work in many volumes, published in the last century; also, that Mr. Whiston, translator of Josephus, believed that the genuine chronology of the Jewish historian agreed very nearly with that of the Samaritan Pentateuch, especially as it stood in the copy used by Jerome: and that his original numbers (afterwards corrupted) exhibited the true chronology of the period extending from Adam to Moses.

Endnotes

1. "Die Ehen der Kinder Gottes mit den Töchtern der Menschen," u, s. w.

2. As Noah is the grand figure in the mythology of Bryant, so with Huetius, all the heathen deities are Moses—the various acts and words of the Hebrew law-giver, the events of his life, and the characters which he sustained, being ascribed to a number of deities called by different names. "Priscos illos gentium Deos et Heroas quicunque per universum feré orbem culti sunt: earumdem etiam conditores plerosque ac legum latores, totamque Ethnicorum theologiam, ex Mose ipso, Mosisve actis, aut scriptionibus, manâsse demonstrabimus."—*Dem. Ev.* Prop. 4, c. 3, *Ed. Stia, Paris*, 1690. Again, he says (Cap. 10, *Summary of Contents*):—"Fabulares omnes Dii unus idemque sunt nempe Moses,—Fabulares omnes Deæ una eademque Dea sunt, atque hæc Sephora est Mosis uxor. Fabularium quoque Dearum pleræque Mariam Mosis sororem referunt. Fabularis historiæ Græcorum bona pars ex Mosis libris et doctrina, atque ipsis etiam verbis profluxit."

3. See Bryant's *Analysis*, vol. 3, pp. 15, 560, &c., 2nd Ed., 1775.—Faber's *Pag. Idol.*, vol. 3, pp. 16, 604, 610, &c.—Lond., 1816.—Huet. *Dem. Ev.*, Prop. 4. Bochart, *Phaleg.*, I., i, 2, and II., 13. *Canaan*, I., 18, &c.—Cadomi, 1651. Vossius, *De Orig.*, &c., lib. I., cc. 5, 15–18, 25, 26, &c.—Amst. 1641.

4. See Keightley's *Mythology of Greece and Italy*, Lond. 1838, pp. 11–13.

5. In Note B will be found Etheridge's English version of the Targums of Onkelos and Jonathan on Gen. vi. 1–4. It has not been thought necessary to insert at length the original passage, the Greek of the Septuagint, or the Chaldee of the Targums, as the important terms in each

are noticed in the course of the exposition: and any who may wish further to examine the Hebrew or these versions will either be possessed of copies, or can have access to them.

6. *Daily Bible Illustrations.* By John Kitto, D.D. Antediluvians
   and Patriarchs. Tenth Edition, 1866, p. 136.

7. When Adam converses with Raphael (*Par, Lost.*, B. VIII.), and speaks of his meeting with Eve,
   and of himself as—"only weak against the charm of Beauty's powerful glance," he adds:—

> Or Nature failed in me, and left some part
> Not proof enough such object to sustain;
> Or, from my side subducting, took perhaps
> More than enough: at least on her bestowed
> Too much of ornament, in outward show
> Elaborate, of inward less exact.
> For well I understand in the prime end
> Of nature her the inferiour, in the mind
> And inward faculties, which most excel:
> In outward also her resembling less
> His image who made both, and less expressing
> The character of that dominion given
> O'er other creatures: yet when I approach
> Her loveliness, so absolute she seems
> And in herself complete, so well to know
> Her own, that what she wills to do or say.
> Seems wisest, virtuousest, discreetest, best.

8. The poets have given expression to this idea. Moore, in his "Loves of of the
   Angels," represents one as recalling to the recollection of his companions the effect
   which the sight of the newly-created woman had produced upon them—

> When, 'mid the worship and surprise
> Of circling angels, woman's eyes
> First open'd upon heaven and earth:
> And from their lids a thrill was sent,
> That through each living spirit went,
> Like first light through the firmament!
> Can you forget how gradual stole
> The fresh awaken'd breath of soul

Throughout her perfect form—which seem'd
To grow transparent, as there beam'd
That dawn of mind within—?

And then he describes one in whom there was
A union, which the hand
Of Nature kept for her alone,
Of everything most playful, bland,
Voluptuous, spiritual, grand,
In angel-natures and her own—
Oh! this it was that drew me nigh
One who seem'd kin to heaven as I,
My bright twin-sister of the sky—

Another angel—
One morn, on earthly mission sent,
And midway choosing where to light,
I saw from the blue element—
Oh beautiful but fatal sight!—
One of earth's fairest womankind,
Half veil'd from view, or rather shrined
In the clear crystal of a brook:
Which, while it hid no single gleam
Of her young beauties, made them look
More spirit-like, as they might seem
Through the dim shadowing of a dream.
Pausing in wonder, I look'd on,
While, playfully around her breaking
The waters, that like diamonds shone,
She moved in light of her own making.

In a note on this passage, the poet says, "This is given on the authority, or rather according
to the fancy, of some of the Fathers, who suppose that the women of earth were first
seen by the angels in this situation; and St. Basil has even made it the serious foundation
of rather a rigorous rule for the toilet of his fair disciples." But what, if St. Paul has said
that "because of the angels ought the woman to have a covering on her head"?
In Lord Byron's "Heaven and Earth," the archangel Raphael warns the

sinning angels, and, reminding them of the fall of Satan, he says—

Yet undestroy'd, be warned! eternity
With him, or with his God, is in your choice:
He hath not tempted you: he cannot tempt
The angels, from his further snares exempt:
But man hath listened to his voice,
And ye to woman's—beautiful she is,
The serpent's voice less subtle than her kiss.
The snake but vanquish'd dust: but she will draw
A second host from heaven, to break heaven's law.

We only add words (partly quoted in the text) to which Milton makes the fallen archangel give utterance, when he first beheld the human pair in the garden—

What do mine eyes with grief behold!
Into our room of bliss thus high advanced.
Creatures of other mould, earth-born perhaps,
Not spirits, yet to heavenly spirits bright
Little inferiour: whom my thoughts pursue
With wonder, and could love; so lively shines
In them divine resemblance, and such grace
The hand that form'd them on their shape hath pour'd.—*Par. Lost.*, B. IV.

9. We employ these terms, not perhaps the best that might be found, but the best that present themselves, to define that great class or circle of beings, in which we regard angels and men as included. The term *intelligent*, often used for the purpose, appears to us unsuitable, as we think it must be held to be comprehensive of other beings besides these. We reject, with abhorrence, all theories which connect the human species, as to its origin, with pre-existing and inferior forms of animal existence, whether on the principle of progressive development, or any other: and we recognize at once the vast difference, *in Degree*, between human and animal intelligence: but we doubt whether a distinction, *in kind*, between these can properly be made, and whether, therefore, we are right in excluding "the beast of the field" from the order of intelligent beings, and maintaining that the lowest in the series is man. That there exists "a great gulf" between him and the most highly endowed of what are usually termed the irrational creatures, is evident—he was made "in the image of God," and ordained to have dominion over them. That his future destination is different from theirs (for we are not disposed to deny the immortality of the brutes) is also to be

maintained. But who will show that reason is the property, exclusively, of man? Are all the actions of the lower animals directed by instinct? Or, are there not instances on record of an intelligence displayed by some of them, in no respect, apparently, differing from what we term reason—at least so closely resembling reason, as not "to be distinguished from it, but by the microscopal powers of metaphysics, or through the partial medium of human pride"?

 To those for whom the subjects of Animal Intelligence and Animal Futurity possess an interest—who think it possible that other ends, besides that of ministering, for the present, to the wants or the pleasures of mankind, were intended in the creation of the inferior creatures—and who, in view of the treatment to which they are sometimes subjected, compassionate those inoffensive beings, who have not the power or disposition to defend themselves—we heartily recommend the perusal of "Animal Futurity: a Plea for the Immortality of the Brutes," by J. Hamilton, 1877—a little volume, ably written, in a thoroughly Christian spirit, and with fullest reverence for the authority of the Word of God,—one that will yield gratification to those with whom the hypothesis of a future life being in reserve for those beings is not a subject for ridicule.

10. Swainson's *Natural History* (in Lardner's *Cabinet Cyclopœdia*). See section on the Station of Man in the Creation, p. 11.

11. Kurtz, 98, and Hist Old Cav. I. 100.

12. Pentateuchus, cum Targg. et comm. Raschi, Aben Ezra, etc.—Berolini, 1705.

13. *Paradise Lost*, XI.—In *Paradise Regained*, however, the angel story appears. The Bishop of Lincoln (*Holy Bible, with notes*) refers to the passage in Book II. (we quote it at length) where, after the failure of Satan's first temptation of our Lord, the infernal council is assembled:—

> When from amidst them rose
> Belial, the dissolutest spirit that fell,
> The sensuallest, and, after Asmodai,
> The fleshliest incubus: and thus advised.
> Set women in his eye, and in his walk,
> Among daughters of men the fairest found:
> Many are in each region passing fair
> As the noon-sky: more like to goddesses
> Than mortal creatures, gracefiil and discreet.
> Expert in amorous arts, enchanting tongues
> Persuasive, virgin majesty with mild
> And sweet allay'd, yet terrible to approach,
> Skill'd to retire, and, in retiring, draw
> Hearts after them, tangled in amorous nets.

Such object hath the power to soften and tame
Severest temper, smooth the rugged'st brow,
Enerve, and with voluptuous hope dissolve,
Draw out with credulous desire, and lead
At will the manliest, resolutest breast.
As the magnetic hardest iron draws.
Women, when nothing else, beguil'd the heart
Of wisest Solomon, and made him build.
And made him bow, to the gods of his wives.
To whom quick answer Satan thus return'd:
Belial, in much uneven scale thou weigh'st
All others by thyself: because of old
Thou thyself doatedst on womankind, admiring
Their shape, their colour, and attractive grace,
None are, thou think'st, but taken with such toys.
Before the flood, thou with thy lusty crew,
False titled sons of God, roaming the earth.
Cast wanton eyes on the daughters of men.
And coupled with them, and begot a race.
Have we not seen, or by relation heard,
In courts and regal chambers how thou lurk'st.
In wood or grove, by mossy fountain side.
In valley or green meadow, to way-lay
Some beauty rare, Calisto, Clymene,
Daphne, or Semele, Antiopa,
Or Amymone, Syrinx, many more,
Too long, then lay'st thy scapes on names adored,
Apollo, Neptune, Jupiter, or Pan,
Satyr, or Faun, or Sylvan?'—

Even in the *Paradise Lost*, Book V., where Milton describes the beauty of Eve, as she entertains
Raphael in the garden, he says;—

If ever, then,
Then had the sons of God excuse to have been
Enamoured at that sight.—

14. This book having been for some time out of print, the present writer
    was kindly accommodated by its author with the use of his own
    copy, an obligation which he desires to acknowledge here.

15. The original Greek of these passages will be found in Suicer's *Thesaurus*, s.v. αγγελος. It is
    given in Kurtz's Treatise also. We have preferred Suicer's Latin, as more generally intelligible.

16. See Maitland's *Eruvin*, pp.132–4.

17. For instances of the use of κατεναντι, see in the Sept., Exod. xix. 2: xxxii.
    5: I Chr. v. 11: Zech. xiv. 4: and, in the New Testament, Mark xi.

2: xii–41: xiii. 3: Luke xix. 30.

18. *Filii Dei—filii piorum, sive profitentes veram religionem, qui FILII DEI saepe vocantur
    in V. et N. Test. Quales erant filii sanctorum Patriarcharum, maximè qui orti erant ex
    Setho et Enoscho, qui se vocabant de nomine Iehovæ, ut habetur in fine capitis quarti,
    quò nimirùm hic respicit Moses*—Ita Piscator, Lyra, Estius, Menochius, Tirinus,
    Ainsworth, Cornelius a Lapide, Bonfrerius, Vatablus, etc. (Poli Synop. in loc.)

19. Raschi (*comm. in loc.*) explains the words—"Then was it begun to call the names
    of men and the names of images after that of the Holy and Blessed One—to make
    idols, and to call them gods."—*Pent. with Rasch's Comm. Amsterd.* 1721.

20. We cannot forbear noticing the singular view of the meaning of this passage taken
    by Cardinal Bellarmine (*De Monachis*, c. 5,), who, following the Vulgate translation,
    supposes that we read here of the institution, by Enos, of monkery! Adam, Abel,
    and Seth, he says, before the time of Enos, called upon God: the latter, therefore,
    must have invoked the Deity after a different manner, and hence may be concluded
    to have established "peculiarem aliquem cultum et sublimiorem quàm esset religio
    vulgi."—Disputationes R. Bellarmini, Paris, 1608, tom. II., p. 351, col. I.

21. See Kurtz, Die Ehen, &a, p. 57.

22. See Horne, Introduction, Vol. IV., part I., ch. iii. I. London: 1825; and Hales, Analysis of
    Chronology, as there referred to—also Gray's Key to the Old Test., 7th ed., 1817, pp. 241, *sqq.*

23. In Bythner's *Lyra Prophetica*, London, 1664, we read, Psalm xxix.—בכי אלהים, *filii
    fortium*, vel *filii deorum*, i.e., potentum. Targ. בתי מלאכיא, *coetus angelorum*.

24. Bp. Pearson says, "As the angels are termed 'the Sons of God,' it sufficiently denoteth that
    they are from Him, not of themselves: all filiation inferring some kind of production, and
    seeing God hath but one proper and only-begotten Son, whose propriety and singularity
    consisteth in this, that He is of the same increated essence with the Father, all other offspring
    must be made, and consequently even the angels, created sons."—*Exposition of Creed, Art I.*

25. See Ex. iv. 22, 23; 2 Sam. vii. 14; I Chr. xvii. 13, xxviii. 6; Jer. xxxi. 9.
    In the New Testament, Matt. v. 9; John i. 12; Rom. viii. 14, 19; and
    Rom. ix. 26, where the expression in Ilosca is translated literally.

26. See Judges XX. 1–12.

27. Antiq. I., 3, I, Whiston's Transl.—See also the extracts from the Book of Enoch and the Clementine Homilies, in sections 18, 19.

28. We insert the following, one of the annotations to the Douay Bible, not only as being curious in itself, but as exhibiting the views of the Doctors of the College of Douay on this question:—

Gen. vi. 4. And Giants were upon the earth in those dayes. For after the sonnes of God did companie with the daughters of men, and they brought forth children, these be the mightie of the old world, famous men.
Some have thought that these giants were not men, nor begotten by men, but that either divels, which fel at first from heaven, or other Angels allured with concupiscence begat them of the daughters of Cain. Philo Judeus, in his booke *de Gigantibus* writeth, that those whom Moyses here called Angels, the Philosophers called Genios, which are living creatures with ayrie bodies. Josephus saith that Angels begat these giants. Tertullian also holdeth the same erroure, and divers more otherwise good Authours. But S. Ciril of Alexandria, S. Chrisostom, and other most principal Doctours teach it to be untrue, yea unpossible, that these giants should have been begotten by any other creatures then by men. For that angels and divels are mere spirits without al natural bodies. And if they had ayrie bodies (as they have not) yet they could not have such generation. For the power or force to engender belongeth to the vegetative soule, whose proper operations are to turne nutriment into the substance of the subject wherein it is, and to engender new issue or offspring from the same, as Aristotle sheweth. And in what bodies soever there is vegetative soule, it must needs be, that the same was engendered, and must sometimes decay and die, and so divels should be mortal. Moreover, if they could have generation together with mankind, then such issue should be a distinct species both of man and divel, as a mule differeth both from horse and asse. Againe, if spirits had abused women in assumpted bodies, and shape of men, yet they did not take them to wives, as the Scriptures saith they did who begat these giants. Finally, the Holy Scripture here expressly calleth the giants men. These be the mightie ones, famous men; the modestie of Scripture terming them famous, whom our common phrase would cal infamous, being more monstrous in wickednes of mind, then in hugenes of bodie. For they were most insolent, lascivious, covetous, cruel, and in al kind of vices most impious.—The Douay Bibley Edition of 1635.

29. Dr. Delitzsch remarks (Comm. on Gen. 18), that Josephus, Philo, the Talmud, and most of the Fathers, believe the eating, on the part of the angels, to have been only in appearance—

an opinion, however, in which he and others do not concur. Keil (Pent. 228) says, "The eating of material food on the part of these heavenly beings was not in appearance only, but was really eating: an act which may be attributed to the corporeality assumed, and is to be regarded as analogous to the eating on the part of the risen and glorified Christ (Luke xxiv. 41 *sqq.*), although the miracle still remains physiologically incomprehensible." At page 132 of the same volume, he writes (note I), "We cannot admit that there is any force in Hofmann's argument in his *Schriftbeweis*, I., p. 426, that 'the begetting of children on the part of angels is not more irreconcilable with a nature that is not organized like that of man, on the basis of sexual distinctions, than partaking of food is, with a nature that is altogether spiritual: and yet food was eaten by the angels who visited Abraham.' For, in the first place, the eating in this case was a miracle wrought through the condescending grace of the omnipotent God, and furnishes no standard for judging what angels can do by their own power in rebellion against God. And, in the second place, there is a considerable difference between the act of eating on the part of the angels of God who appeared in human shape, and the taking of wives and begetting of children on the part of sinning angels." There is much weight in these observations. It is not to be supposed that the Divine Being exerted miraculous power, in order to assist the angels of Gen. vi. in the accomplishment of their object, or in any manner co-operated with them in their acts. Hence, we attach the less importance to the argument drawn from the fact of angels' partaking of human food, and prefer supporting our interpretation on other grounds. We will endeavour presently to shew that cooperation, in this case, on the part of the Creator (with reverence be it spoken) was not necessary: and that even fallen angels, if not restrained by the power of the Most High, had, inherent in themselves, the power requisite to effect their purposes.

30. Of course, this view can be entertained at all, only on the ground that angels are possessed, in their original constitution, of a certain corporeality. Otherwise, the idea of the development of sexual distinctions, or procreative powers, must be wholly abandoned, for only in a corporeal constitution of some sort, could the germ of these exist. That there is much ground, however, for believing in the possession of corporeal forms by angels, we feel assured, and indeed regard the opposite opinion as untenable.—See Note E. Readers of the Paradise Lost may remember the passage in Book I., where the poet names the chiefs of the fallen angelic host after the idols of the Canaanites and others. Of some he says, they bore the general names—

Of Baalim and Ashtaroth, those male,
These feminine: for spirits, when they please.
Can either, sex assume, or both; so soft
And uncompounded is their essence pure:

Not tied or manacled with joint or limb,
Nor founded on the brittle strength of bones,
Like cumbrous flesh: but, in what shape they choose,
Dilated or condensed, bright or obscure.
Can execute their aery purposes.
And works of love or enmity fulfil.

31. Some remarks on this subject will be found In Note E.

32. Cardinal Bellarmine says—"In Scripturis, qui videbant et tangebant assumpta ab Angelis corpora, Gen. xviii. et xix., non fallebantur, cùm se corpus videre et tangere credebant: sed fallebantur, tamen, cùm se corpus humanum tangere et videre existimabant." This very learned Romish theologian makes this remark, not in the course of an inquiry into the nature of angels, but to illustrate his argument in support of the monstrous and impious doctrine of the apostate Church, known as that of Transubstantiation"—*De Sacramento Euchar. lib I., c, 14.*

33. It may be worth remarking, that the tradition preserved in the Book of Enoch represents the angels as instructing mankind in various arts, and communicating to them a knowledge of some of the mysteries of nature.—See Lawrence's Translation, chaps, vii., viii., ix., and ixiv.

34. *The Bible and Astronomy.* By J. H. Kurtz, D.D., translated by Simonton, 1861, p. 203.

35. Eminently worthy of attention are the remarks of Nägelsbach, in Sections 107–113, where he traces and explains the connection between the Cainite and Sethite races, and the legends preserved by Hesiod and others—especially Sections 109, 110, 111, in which he shows how exactly Hesiod's description of his third and fourth races corresponds with the Biblical representation of the Cainites and Sethites respectively. Sec Note A.

36. Thomas Malvenda, a learned Romanist, (ob. 1628) writes, in opposition to those who maintain the existence of the Nephilim before the coming of the sons of God to the daughters of men—"Satis hoc versu (4) innuit Moses eos anteà non fuisse, nam ut rem novam eorum originen exponit."—*Pol. Synopsis.*

37. See Note I.

38. We may remark that, in the story of the Egregori, given by Syncellus, from the Book of Enoch, it is said that those descended from the angels were of three kinds—the *giants*, sons of the angels—*Nephilim*, sons of the giants—and the *Eliudaei*, sons of the Nephilim.—*Syncelli Chronograph*, Paris, 1652, p. II.

39. It is said in Dr. Keil's Comm. on Pent., I., p. 138, note, that Kurtz has tried *three* different explanations of ver. 4, but this appears to be a mistake, as the interpretation proposed in his History of the Old Covenant, is identical with that given above.

40. See article *Giants* in the following:—Calmet, *Dict. of the Bible*; Chambers' *Encyclopædia*: Penny *Cyclopædia*; *Bible Cyclopædia*, London, 1841, 2 vols.; Smith's *Dict. of the Bible*, and the classical and other writers referred to in the section.

41. The writer of the article OG, in the Bible Cyclopædia (London, 1841) says—"In reference to Og's bedstead Maimonides (*Moreh Nevochim* ii. 47) observes that we are to understand the bedstead to have been one-third longer than the man for whose use it was destined. This proportion brings down his stature to little more than 9 feet. The correctness of this estimate is supported by the fact, that this was also just the stature of Goliath, whose height was 6 cubits (9 feet) and a span—a stature that no one will call incredible or unlikely, who calls to mind the numerous and well-authenticated instances that might be produced of such stature in comparatively modern times."

42. The Jewish cubit and span were longer than we usually reckon them—the former being 1 foot 9.894 inches, English measure, and the span 10.944, or nearly 11 inches. It should be remarked, on the other hand, that while the Hebrew and Vulgate say *six* cubits, the LXX. and Josephus read four.

43. See Kurtz, pp. 69, 70, where he shows why it might have been necessary that, not alone the female portion of humanity, who had offended with the angels, but also the male, should be destroyed. He suggests in addition to the reason specified above, p. 106, that the fathers and brothers of the erring women, may have countenanced or promoted their doings, and so participated in their sin: and we may add that, if the sin which at a later date caused the overthrow of Sodom, were prevalent in those times, as tradition declares it to have been, we have a further reason for the necessity of the general destruction of the race.

44. To the remembrance of some reader may present itself the passage in Lord Byron's *Heaven and Earth*, in which Noah is represented as meeting the angels, Azaziel and Samiasa, with the Cainite women:—

NOAH. These are they, then,
Who leave the throne of God, to take them wives
From out the race of Cain: the sons of heaven,
Who seek earth's daughters for their beauty?
AZAZ. Patriarch! Thou hast said it.
NOAH. Woe, woe, woe, to such communion!
Has not God made a barrier between earth
And heaven, and limited each, kind to kind?
SAM. Was not man made in high Jehovah's image?
Did God not love what He had made? And what
Do we but imitate and emulate
His love unto created love?
NOAH. I am
But man, and was not made to judge mankind,

Far less the sons of God: but as our God
Has deigned to commune with me, and reveal
His judgments, I reply, that the descent
Of seraphs from their everlasting seat
Unto a perishable and perishing,
Even on the very *eve of perishing* world.
Cannot be good.

45. The Ethiopic version, with various readings, was published by Dr. A. Dillmann, Leipsic, 1851. A German taanslation, with commentary, by the same, in 1853. For this and some other books referred to in these pages, see Hodges, Foster, and Figgis' (Dublin) Catalogues of Foreign Theology, and of Greek and Latin Writers; 1878.

46. As the *taking of wives* by the angels, and the *devouring*, on the part of their monstrous sons, are prominent features in the above legend, it will be admitted, perhaps even by those who regard the angel-story as fabulous or absurd, to be a somewhat remarkable circumstance, that the only matters of which our Lord has made special mention, when referring to the social condition of the world before the Flood, are that of *eating and drinking*, and that of *marrying and giving in marriage*—things which, if not in some way abused, are not only lawful and in accordance with the ordination of the Creator, but even essential to the existence and perpetuation of the race. Dr. Maitland has adverted to this in his essay on False Worship, p. 24. Quoting the words of Christ, as recorded by St. Matthew (xxiv. 38), "They were eating and drinking, marrying and giving in marriage, until the day that Noe entered into the ark"—he says, "I lay no stress on it, but would suggest that there may be a significancy in our Lord's words which has not been commonly observed. It seems natural that the eating and drinking should form a feature in the character of the gigantic sons of violence and sin: and that it should be followed by every species of outrage: but perhaps we should hardly have expected the mention of marrying. At all events, it is more easily understood if we consider it as relating to marriages essentially unlawful, and of such a character as to have called for the impending visitation." We admit that the Saviour's words, as commonly explained, were intended to shew the state of careless security, and utter worldly-mindedness, into which the antediluvians had fallen, and their total disregard of the Divine warning conveyed through Noah—a state of things somewhat similar to that which will exist at the time of the Second Advent—but that they have, as observed, a further significancy, we do not doubt, taking them in connexion with our passage, interpreted in accordance with the usage of the Hebrew language, and the voice of ancient tradition.

47. With the last two extracts the reader may compare the opimons of Lactantius, and of Dr. Maitland, at p. 152, *sqq., infra*. It may be thought by some, that the description of the "spirits of the giants,' given in the apocryphal book, and by some of the Fathers,

corresponds in a considerable degree, with what we read of the "unclean spirits" or "demons" cast out by our Saviour. Compare verses 8 and 9, above quoted, with Mark ix. 17–26, and Luke ix. 39. Is it worthy of remark that the term *bruising* which occurs in this passage of St. Luke's Gospel, is used of the spirits of the giants in Enoch xv. 9? It is not likely that the evangelist borrowed the language of the apocryphal book, and less likely that our Saviour did so in the case referred to in the preceding note.

48. The following may be read in Pfeiffer's edition of Philo, as part of a note on the first of the passages above mentioned:—"Codex Alexandrinus habet αγγελοι; atque ita Philouem in suo codice legisse nullus dubito, adeòque ista lectio vel à primis interpretibus est profecta, vel certè est evangeliis antiquior: ita ut sententia ilia de angelis foeminas vitiantibus, Judaeos non Christianos habuerit auctores, et fortè ex hac ipsa Graeci textus lectione originem duxerit."

49. Tubal-Cain lived about the time in which tradition has placed the descent of the angels.

50. "The Clementine Homilies and Apostolical Constitutions." Translated in Clark's Ante-Nicene Christian Library, Vol. xvii. 1870—pp. 142–46.

51. So Lord Byron (*Heaven and Earth*) makes Azaziel say to Japheth:—

Knowest thou not, or forget'st thou, that a part
Of our great function is to guard thine earth?

And again, when Raphael addresses the erring angels—

RAPH. Spirits!
Whose seat is near the throne.
What do ye here?
Is thus a seraph's duty to be shown.
Now that the hour is near
When earth must be alone?
Return!
Adore and bum
In glorious homage with the elected "seven."
Your place is heaven.
SAMIASA. Raphael!
The first and fairest of the sons of God,
How long hath this been law.
That earth by angels must be left untrod?
Earth! which oft saw
Jehovah's footsteps not disdain her sod!

The world He loved, and made
For love: and oft have we obey'd
His frequent mission with delighted pinions:
Adoring Him in His least works display'd:
Watching this youngest star of His dominions:
And, as the latest birth of His great Word,
Eager to keep it worthy of our Lord.

52. Heb. Pent with Raschi's Comm., &c. Amsterd. 1721.

53. Published in the *Abhandl. d. Kön. Sächs. Gesellschaft d. Wissenschaften*, Leipzig, 1850—p. 150.

54. See Matt xxv. 41; John viii. 44; 1 John iii 8; Rev. xii. 9, &c.

55. Whitby (2 Pet. ii. 4) cites authorities to show that by *Tartarus* was sometimes understood the region of the air between earth and heaven, where not only heathen and Jews, but also Church Fathers, placed the abode of Demons: but this is again to confound the angels of SS. Peter and Jude, with the δαιμονες and "the prince of the power of the air."

56. See Kurtz, *Die Ehen*, &c., p. 30.

57. The author of "Meet for Heaven" (Edinb. 1866) takes a different view. "So far," he says, p. 99, "as I can learn from the Bible, *the human form is the type and symbol, almost universally, of spiritual beings.* Wherever mention is made of angels appearing to men upon earth, they do so in *human form.*" He is aware, he says, that some interpreters of Scripture put this construction upon all the Bible passages in which these visits of angels are described—that angels, on these occasions, merely *assumed* the *human form* for the time, divesting themselves of it when their part on the occasion of their appearance was acted. "In reply," he writes, "to such a view as this of these appearances of angels, I have to say that it is merely the *supposition* of these interpreters of the Bible: the sacred writers themselves never even hint that angels, on these occasions, were playing any such part, but were making their visits in their own peculiar *form* and *appearance.*" This opinion, he thinks, derives confirmation from the fact, that the highest Being in the universe, the Second Person of the Trinity, has *assumed*, not for a time, but for ever, the *human form*, and thus put the *stamp of divinity* upon it. But does not Hebrews ii. 14–17 seem to be opposed to the writer's views?

58. Edited, with the works of Amphilochius and Andreas Cretensis, by Francis Combefis, Paris, 1644, fol.—see p. 326.

59. The original passages from Damascene and some other Greek writers, referred in this note, will be found in Suicer's Thesaurus, s.v. αγγελος.

60. That Gesenius did not, by this definition, mean the Holy Ghost, the Third Person of the Trinity, appears from his having elsewhere (See Lex. רוח, 4)—defined רוח יהוה to be "the Divine power, which, like the wind and the breath, cannot be perceived, and by which animated beings live, Job xxvii. 3, &c. Compare Gen. vi. 3," &c., &c.

61. Both the Hebrew-Samaritan text and the Samaritan version were edited by Morinus in the Paris Polyglott. As the latter is, for the most part, an exact rendering (see Havernick and Prideaux) of the original, Morinus made one Latin translation serve for both. There are, however, some variations: and hence, while the Latin of Morinus has "*spiritus meus*" the Samaritan has עוכרי *servus meus*.

62. The author of "Heaven our Home," says, "The question has been put, Does the disembodied soul of the glorified retain something of the form and features of the body in which it once dwelt? Angels have form and feature: souls disembodied must have such attributes: and it may be that it is the features of the soul shining in and through the features of the body, that we behold, when we look into the face of a friend: for, look upon the same countenance after death, and oh, what a change! So changed, to use a mean figure, as the face of the lantern is, when the candle is blown out. Whilst the candle burns within, is it not its form and appearance, and not those of the lantern merely, that you saw when you looked upon it and enjoyed its light?"—*Part* ii., ch, iv. See also "The Spirit Disembodied," by H. Broughton, Edin. 1867, ch. viii.

63. The first printed Hebrew Bible. The Pentateuch, in this Bible, was a reprint of the first edition of the Pentateuch (Bologna, 1482). The editor of both was Abraham Ben Chajim. It should be borne in mind, in connexion with the above, that, in matters of Biblical criticism, Hebrew editions of the fifteenth century are regarded as of equal authority with MSS.

64. S. besonders auch K. v. Raumer's Allgemeine Geogr. 2 Aufl., s. 395–431 und A. Tholuck's vermischte Schriften, Bd. I., s. 177–230.

65. In a note on this passage, the editor of Lactantius, says, "Circumspecte legendum est hoc caput 15, nam nonnullos errores Lactantius implicat. Primus est, Deum ab initio tribuisse diabolo terrae potestatem. Secundus, Angelos non missos ad hominum tutelam, nisi postquam genus humanum coepisset increscere. Tertius, praecepisse Deum bonis angelis, ne terrae contagione macularentur, ne substantiae coelestis amitterent dignitatem. Quartus diabolum paulatim pellexisse bonos angelos ad vitia, et eos mulierum congressibus inquinasse, &c... Sunt omnia ista dogmata absurda, erronea, et à sincera Theologorum doctrina prorsus aliena."—*Lactantii Opera.* (*Librairie Catholique de Perisse Frères.*)—*Paris*, 1845.

66. In the notes on this passage some of the Rabbinical tradition appears—"Angeli delapsi è coelo viderunt filias Cain, quae illo tempore nudae incedebant, oculos stibio pingentes, more meretricum"—*Pirke Eliezer.* Another note says:—"Nominatur in libro *Fuchasin* Machasael ex filiis Dei, qui sub diluvii tempus rem habuerit cum uxore Chami, unde natus sit Sihon. Et relatum in libro pervetusto *Zohar*, angelos quos filios Dei autor libri vocat, consuetudine usos Naamae sororis Thubal-Cain, ex ea genuisse daemones (*vide sup.*, *p.* 187), quos *shedim* appellant, et spiritus malos, qui nunc in mundo."—*Vide Sulpitii Severi Opera. Ed. Horn*, Amst. 1665.